Like Night & Day

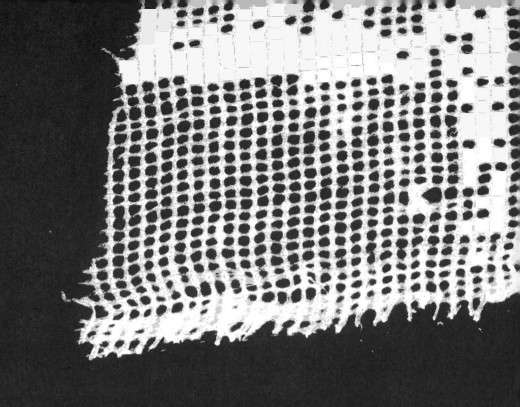

Unionization in a Southern Mill Town

Like Night & Day

Daniel J. Clark

The

University of

North Carolina

Press

Chapel Hill &

London

The paper in this book meets the guidelines for
permanence and durability of the Committee on
Production Guidelines for Book Longevity of the
Council on Library Resources.

Library of Congress
Cataloging-in-Publication Data

Clark, Daniel J.

Like Night and Day : Unionization in a southern
mill town / by Daniel J. Clark.

p.   cm.

Includes bibliographical references and index.

ISBN 0-8078-2306-6 (alk. paper). —
ISBN 0-8078-4617-1 (pbk. : alk. paper)

1. Textile Workers Union of America—History.
2. Trade-unions—Textile workers—North
Carolina—Henderson—History.   3. Strikes and
lockouts—Textile industry—North Carolina—
Henderson—History.   4. Harriet Cotton Mills
(Henderson, N.C.)—History.   5. Henderson
Cotton Mills—History.   6. Textile workers—
North Carolina—Henderson—History.   7. Cotton
textile industry—North Carolina—Henderson—
History.   I. Title.

HD6515.T42T483   1997

331.88'177'009756532—dc20   96-7730

                                    CIP

01   00   99   98   97   5   4   3   2   1

TO CAMERON & DARREN

Contents

Tables

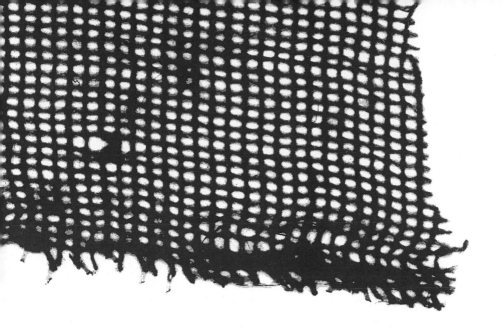

Acknowledgments

I would like to thank William Chafe for suggesting this topic when I was a first-year graduate student, for guiding me through the dissertation stage, and for maintaining his interest in the project. Lawrence Goodwyn convinced me that it was necessary to try, and that it might indeed be possible, to talk to company officials.

This project would never have gotten off the ground without the generosity of the former mill workers in Henderson who allowed me to interview them. And ultimately, Marshall Cooper Sr. made this book possible. I trust that he and his family will respect my right to make my own judgments.

Much of my early research was conducted during intermittent low-budget trips from Michigan to North Carolina. I would like to thank John Carr, Jill Carr, John Selby, Mary Turner, and Joe Sinsheimer for their hospitality on those journeys. I was fortunate to receive financial support from the William F. Sullivan Fund of the Museum of American Textile History in North Andover, Massachusetts, and from Cecil P. and Anna Laura Matthews.

I would also like to thank the School of Textiles at North Carolina State University for allowing me to observe and operate, however ineptly, textile machinery from the 1940s and 1950s.

Most of my research and writing have been completed outside of academia, so I have been grateful for the scholarly connections I was able to make. John Selby has provided me with insights and support for many years. Kevin Boyle offered valuable suggestions and friendship during critical stages of the project. Wes Dick, Mark Walker, and John Shy have been especially supportive, as have the History Departments at Albion College and Oakland University. Keir Jorgensen, research director of the Amalgamated Clothing and Textile Workers Union, AFL-CIO, responded to my inquiries with important documentation. I have benefited from the help of the staffs at the Vance County Public Library, the North Carolina Division of Archives and History, the Southern Labor Archives, the Manuscript Department of the William R. Perkins Library at Duke University, the Duke University Archives, the North Carolina Collection at the University of North Carolina at Chapel Hill, and the North Carolina Textile Manufacturers Association.

I owe an enormous debt to the many people who have provided vital support, friendship, child care, and faith during this roller-coaster process. In particular I want to thank Ami Wilson, Laura Rockafellow, Susan Gray, Kathie Baxter, Cathy Hasty, Kirsten Jensen, Nancy Davis, Ariana Arlen, Sharbyn Pleban, and Mary Meyer. Jim, Marilyn, Lucinda, Tom, and Marilyn Sue Clark have given their all. Jill Van Deusen Clark infused the project with spirit. It will probably be many years before Cameron and Darren Clark realize the extent of their contribution to this book. It has been an amazing journey.

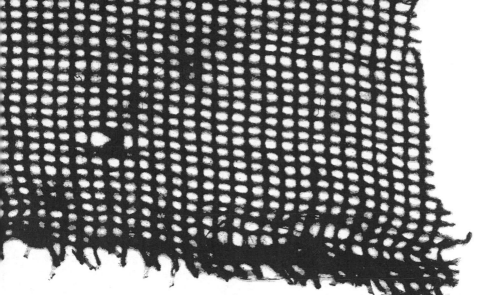

Like Night & Day

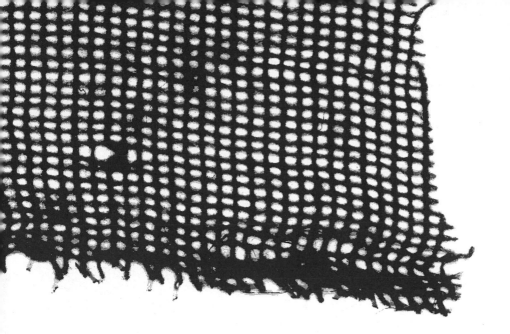

Introduction

In November 1958, over a thousand unionized workers went on strike at the Harriet and Henderson Cotton Mills in Henderson, North Carolina. For these union members, the central issue of the conflict was whether impartial arbitrators or the company president would have the final say in the formal grievance procedure called for in their collective bargaining agreement. That was all I knew, years ago, when I decided that this would be a manageable topic for a research paper in my graduate seminar on oral history techniques. The more I learned about the strike, however, the more compelling the subject became, not only because unionized cotton mill workers were so rare, and vulnerable, in the South. The prevailing interpretation in labor history scholarship held that grievance procedures with arbitration clauses were bureaucratic night-mares, reducing the amount of control workers had over their jobs. Why, then, would a thousand people risk their jobs to defend one? Didn't they know what was best for them? Or was it possible that these workers had experienced grievance procedures differently? Listening to the testimony of former millhands, it became obvious that many of them were far less concerned with the details of the strike, the subject of most of my questions, than with how unionization had affected their lives, which became my new focus.

Oral evidence alone, however, would never have been adequate for this task. However emotionally compelling the oral testimony, it would have been next to impossible to generate from workers' memories the specific, detailed, chronologically precise information about crucial events in their work lives, and in the life of the union, that was necessary to make this project more than just a collection of vague, largely unverifiable recollections. The breakthrough came when I extended my research to include management. Harriet and Henderson officials graciously spent time talking with me and allowed me to burrow in the dank, steamy basement of one of their mills. There I found old boxes of nearly forgotten documents — the records from the union years. Here were verbatim transcripts from union-management meetings in which workers from throughout the mills testified about their grievances, and supervisors and time-study experts rebutted them. The records also contained transcripts and supporting documents from arbitration hearings. This book relies heavily on these unusually rich sources.

What did unionization mean to a specific group of workers and managers during the 1940s and 1950s? What concrete differences did unionization make in their daily lives? Were there changes over time in how workers and managers experienced unionization? No book-length study in the expanding labor history literature either asks or attempts to answer such questions. For years, leading labor historians have taken note of this gap in our understanding.[1] Nevertheless, the reigning interpretive framework for the period has gained great power.

In recent years, most historians who have assessed organized labor in the postwar era have voiced criticism and regret at what they perceive to have been the goals and aspirations of workers and their unions.[2] One central assumption has been that after World War II workers and union leaders became increasingly, almost solely, obsessed with obtaining higher wages and more generous benefit packages, goals that often have been labeled as either "business unionism" or "bread-and-butter union-ism."[3]

These narrow, economic preoccupations are usually contrasted with what are perceived to have been the goals, strategies, ideals, and perhaps even the reality of the labor movement in the prewar era: workers' control over decisions on the shop floor, a willingness to assert and maintain power through strikes or the threat thereof, and a strong voice in national politics promoting European-style social welfare programs. The dominant framework for understanding unions in the postwar era emphasizes a narrowing of focus, a constricting sense of what was possible, and severely limited aspirations.[4]

According to this general interpretation, developments during World War II both solidified the institutional existence of labor unions and seriously constrained organized labor's ability to transform power relations in workplaces. During the war, labor leaders guaranteed their unions' survival by agreeing to outlaw strikes and channel shop-floor discontent into formalized grievance procedures, which usually included some form of binding arbitration in case such measures were necessary to resolve a dispute. In theory, grievance procedures offered the possibility of both justice in the workplace and uninterrupted production. At the time this was explained in terms of the patriotic need to maximize production, without disruptive strikes, to support the troops on the front. Grievance procedures and arbitration clauses became nearly universal in union contracts and remained the norm into the postwar era. They were the cornerstones of what David Brody has labeled "workplace contractualism."[5]

Critics of organized labor in the postwar era—at least those who are essentially proworker—usually lambaste grievance procedures and arbitration, contrasting their bureaucratic rigidity with an open-ended system of shop-floor negotiating characterized by a limited number of set rules and a range of problem-solving methods backed by the threat of direct action. Nelson Lichtenstein, for one, has argued that "the grievance procedure worked to defuse union power and legitimate managerial authority. The system shifted disputes from the shop floor, where the stewards and work groups held the greatest leverage, to the realm of contractual interpretation, where the authority of management and the value of orderly procedure weighed more heavily."[6] Christopher Tomlins has written that "grievance arbitration in the post-war period provided the essential institutional framework for an industrial relations 'system' based on the bureaucratization and routinization of dispute management," which, he argued, was a disastrous accommodation for labor.[7] "Administered by a priestly order of arbitrators, mediators and conciliators," Mike Davis has argued, "collective bargaining constituted a main support of the post-war social order," of which he voiced strong criticism.[8] Elizabeth Faue offers fresh insights into what good and effective union strategy was in the era before grievance procedures, especially the need for women to be very involved in union activities, but she accepts as a given the familiar argument that "bureaucratic, workplace-oriented unionism" was a regrettable step backward, tending "to obscure and suppress, rather than illuminate and express, grass-roots militancy and leadership."[9]

At least initially these critics were responding to an earlier generation of scholars—people who argued that what Brody has called workplace contractualism, with a limited focus on wages and benefits, marked the culmination of the union movement. Irving Bernstein argued in 1970, for example, that American workers were "overwhelmingly committed to business unionism," and that in stable collective bargaining they got what they wanted.[10] For the most part, the disagreements among historians have not been over the content of what happened but over how they interpret the same events, and it has been years since anyone has joined the celebratory side of the scholarly "debate."[11]

Both sets of interpretations, of course, are based on scant research at the local level. This study adds complexity to our understanding of unionization in the 1940s and 1950s by demonstrating how workers could use grievance procedures to gain a relatively enormous amount of control over their lives at work and at home, while at the same time enjoying every wage increase they received and no doubt wishing for even more money. It is not my intention to remain stuck in the same old bipolar scheme by arguing that grievance procedures led workers to the promised land. The documents cannot sustain such a claim. There is ample evidence, however, that union members at the Harriet and Henderson Mills experienced grievance procedures and arbitration as, on balance, positive, liberating forces in their lives.

One simple explanation is that union members at the Harriet and Henderson Mills, like most cotton mill workers in the South and even many northern workers, had no tradition of successful direct action to compare with their experience of using grievance procedures. Having become organized and having signed their first contracts during World War II, when grievance procedures and arbitration were essentially compulsory, Harriet and Henderson workers did not have the option to choose between direct action and bureaucratic grievance procedures as possible methods for resolving disputes. Their choice was between the continued arbitrary authority of their immediate supervisors and higher-level managers and the possibility of challenging that authority with the power and protection of a grievance procedure. Indeed, the extent to which prewar union members used direct action has been implied far more than proved, and those who have looked for concrete evidence of this tradition have often searched in vain.[12] Moreover, there is cautionary evidence that wildcat strikes, the most dramatic form of direct action, could prove to be very divisive among workers, causing many other workers unaffected by the immediate complaint to lose time and money.[13]

There have been challenges to the reigning interpretive framework. Ronald Schatz, for example, has acknowledged the difference grievance procedures made in allowing workers to challenge the arbitrary power of foremen to hire and fire at their whim, calling that change, by itself, "the greatest accomplishment of the union movement of the 1930s and '40s, the achievement which justifies its claim to stand beside abolitionism, civil rights, and women's rights as one of the great movements for freedom and dignity in American history."[14] In his study of the Chrysler Corporation's Dodge Main plant, Steve Jefferys emphasized that we should be wary of the postwar stereotype of passive, money-grubbing workers. He discovered that the frequency of unauthorized wildcat strikes remained high at Chrysler at least until the late 1950s. Many of these strikes, it appears, were efforts by workers to influence their workloads and the pace of the line, to establish what they called a " 'fair' production standard."[15] Union members at the Harriet and Henderson Mills pursued similar ends through their grievance procedure.

Historians often dismiss these kinds of efforts as a limited focus on "working conditions." My research argues that to do so is to declare many of the real experiences of working people irrelevant. It is important to take the concerns of actual workers seriously, even if their ambitions fell way short of workplace control, direct action, and political pressure for social welfare programs. Wherever the aspirations of postwar workers fit on some spectrum of progressivism, it appears that what really happened is more complex than the dominant framework allows.[16]

Despite his criticism of postwar unions, Mike Davis hinted at this complexity, without providing details, noting that in the late 1950s "big manufacturers were bedeviled by the persistence of a regime of 'fractional bargaining' on the shopfloor whereby work-groups, abetted by restrictive work rules, used the grievance process to extract additional, extra-contractual concessions from lower-level management."[17] Going even further, David Brody has boldly suggested that for many postwar union members, workplace contractualism could have been experienced as "the embodiment of industrial justice."[18]

Recent research into biracial CIO unions and the role of women in the labor movement has further challenged our conventional understanding of labor in the postwar years. Judith Stein has discovered that militant unions in the iron and steel industry of Alabama emerged after World War II "through the vehicle of the collective bargaining contract, which proved an instrument of empowerment, not one of constraint and bureaucratization."[19] Nancy Gabin has argued that although the UAW's postwar record in championing women's rights was ambiguous at best, many workers and union officials were addressing, if not resolving, many serious and significant issues in addition to pursuing higher wages and benefits.[20] It would be possible, of course, to categorize women workers' demands for equal access to jobs and equal pay for equal work as a retrograde obsession with wages. But what would be the point of such rigid categorization?

Other long-held assumptions about American labor have been under siege as well. In her study of waitress unionism, Dorothy Cobble has conveyed with great complexity the specific concerns of women who were in a craft union, as opposed to an industrial union. Until recently, Cobble noted, craft unionists have been characterized "as a conservative, apolitical elite who were hopelessly out of touch with the rank and file." This stereotype, however, bears little resemblance to what she discovered. Cobble contends that "any analysis of the AFL or of craft unionism" must consider "its accomplishments in the collective bargaining arena." My research holds that the same is true for CIO unions.[21]

The story of Harriet and Henderson union members is especially remarkable considering the hostile climate in which they struggled. Robert Zieger recently outlined the conventional wisdom about the region's notorious hostility to labor unions:

> The primal question of race, the peculiar circumstances under which large-scale industrial development occurred in the South, and the relative ethnic homogeneity of the region's white working class have led generations of observers to treat the South as a distinctive regional entity insofar as labor is concerned. The textile mill villages, the intense legal and extralegal opposition to union organizing, and the inventiveness of local clergy, law enforcement officers, and business leaders in sustaining a "union-free" environment have been the twentieth-

century equivalent to the nineteenth-century South's "peculiar institution."[22]

Indeed, fewer than 10 percent of southern cotton mills in the postwar decades were unionized. The experiences of Harriet and Henderson workers, then, can be considered a best-case scenario for textile labor in the region.

Southern textile workers have recently been the subjects of a relative avalanche of research, much of which, Zieger noted, has challenged traditional stereotypes about their passivity and intrinsic antiunionism.[23] Few of these studies, however, have paid attention to textile workers in the post–World War II era. Barbara Griffith analyzed various reasons for the failure of unionization during the CIO's postwar Operation Dixie, but she did not examine what existing union locals were doing, or what a successful campaign might have accomplished.[24] Douglas Flamming has studied workers and managers at the Crown Mills in Dalton, Georgia, from the 1880s through the 1960s. Like the Harriet and Henderson Mills, the Crown Mills were unionized during the 1940s and 1950s. This book and Flamming's, however, are far more complementary than overlapping. Although Flamming recognized that the "primary role" of the union "in the lives of most millhands was to settle disputes that arose on the shop floor," he did not address what dispute-settling looked like in practice, what it meant to workers and managers, or how grievance resolution, and the issues being contested, might have changed over time.[25] For all the shop-floor and local studies that have been written, the impact of unionization on workers remains largely unexplored territory in the South and throughout the rest of the country.

Given that in the postwar years roughly half of all cotton mill employees were women, this study also contributes to the gradual expansion of labor history to include all workers.[26] Throughout this book it has been my intention to allow women workers to speak for themselves about their concerns, an approach made easy and self-evidently appropriate by the abundance of direct testimony by women workers in the grievance and arbitration records. My goal has been to emphasize what happened rather than what did not occur, or what might have been. For example, there is no evidence in the records that women union members in Henderson, or TWUA leaders at any level, challenged the inequitable division of household labor. Many women, however, stretched the contract's absenteeism and sick-leave protections to attend to their extensive non-workplace responsibilities.

Equal pay for equal work was not a significant issue for women workers in Henderson. Pay rates had long been assigned to specific jobs, no matter who performed them. Nor was equal access to all jobs in the mills a significant concern for women millhands. Although most positions had a tradition of being reserved either for men or for women, the total number of available jobs for each was roughly the same.[27] Furthermore, although on average men earned more than women, which at the time was generally accepted as fair, some women on women's jobs earned more than some men on men's jobs. There was no clear-cut line of discrimination.

The primary focus of this study is the workplace, which makes it difficult to incorporate race into the main arguments.[28] From the late nineteenth century, when the southern textile industry began to boom, until the civil rights movement of the 1960s, cotton mills were largely white enclaves. In contrast to other southern industries like iron and steel in Alabama and meatpacking in Texas, in textiles it was possible to create an effective union local without building a strong biracial alliance.[29] Most black workers at the Harriet and Henderson Mills belonged to the union, but they represented well under 5 percent of the local membership and were involved directly in only 3 of over 550 formal grievances filed between 1943 and 1958. There is no evidence in Henderson that union members, white or black, fought for job desegregation, and the international TWUA put no pressure on the locals to do so. Race enters this discussion during periods of labor shortage and labor conflict, when Harriet and Henderson management had a clear incentive to consider breaking the informal color barrier by hiring African Americans for production jobs. Throughout, I have focused on what did happen rather than on what did not. Race would be a central theme in any study of struggles for justice in the larger community, but inside the cotton mills race rarely emerged as a significant issue.

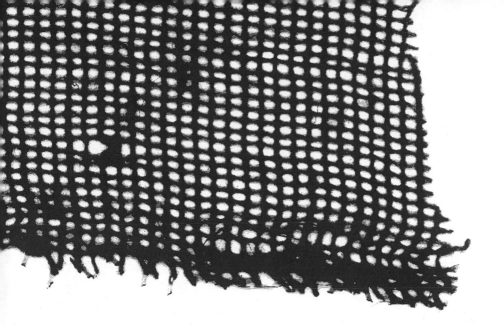

1   Cotton Mill Fever, 1895–1938

Cotton mill fever reached Henderson, North Carolina, in the summer of 1895. The idea had incubated for several years in the mind of David Y. Cooper, a forty-eight-year old native of neighboring Granville County, who had prospered for over twenty years by operating a tobacco warehouse. Located near the Virginia border in Vance County, roughly fifty miles north of Raleigh, Henderson, with nearly four thousand residents, was on the eastern fringes of what had recently become a bright-leaf tobacco belt that straddled the two states for nearly 150 miles.[1] Cooper's first warehouse, which he opened in 1873 shortly after moving to town, served as the major conduit between what was then the main growing region, the coastal plains to the east; manufacturing centers like

Durham and Winston to the south and west; and Richmond, Virginia, to the northeast. Already well-positioned and profitable, Cooper's business flourished even more throughout the 1880s as bright-leaf tobacco production expanded westward. Thousands of farmers shifted to tobacco, often either hesitantly or unwillingly, hoping that a cash crop would be a source of financial independence. Each fall, many of them hauled their crops to Henderson. Cooper's warehouse was by far the town's largest, and Henderson became the main marketing center for tobacco farmers in fifteen surrounding counties.[2]

By the early 1890s, however, Cooper felt threatened by angry, organized tobacco growers. Like many other warehousemen, Cooper purchased tobacco at relatively generous prices, then made his profits by charging large sales commissions and storage fees and advancing costly fertilizer on credit.[3] In the mid-1880s, tobacco growers throughout North Carolina began organizing Farmers' Alliance chapters, in part to counter the power of warehousemen.[4] By October 1888 the Vance County Alliance, its enthusiasm at a white heat, had opened a private warehouse with a 2 percent limit on commissions, compared to the 10 to 50 percent charged by speculators like Cooper.[5] Although few Alliance warehouses thrived—it appears that Vance County's had folded by 1891—the passion behind them pressured the North Carolina General Assembly, in 1895, to place statutory limits on auction fees and sales commissions charged by tobacco warehousemen. While farmers celebrated—prematurely, as it turned out—middlemen like Cooper felt besieged.[6]

Adding further pressure, the American Tobacco Company, organized in 1889 when the Duke family from nearby Durham arranged the merger of five of the nation's largest cigarette manufacturers, threatened to eliminate warehousemen altogether by purchasing tobacco directly from farmers. While the trust's success was still in doubt, American Tobacco Company representatives and warehousemen like David Cooper took turns posing awkwardly as allies of the tobacco farmers, decrying either the evils of monopolies or the wastefulness of middlemen. Eventually securing a stranglehold on the industry, the American Tobacco Company effectively cleared the market of independent warehousemen.[7]

Caught between pincerlike forces, whose interests were strongly opposed to each other as well as his own, Cooper hoped that a cotton mill would be a comparatively safe refuge for his fortunes. Cotton mills appeared to be a profitable alternative, even after the Panic of 1893, when the economy as a whole was mired in depression. It was no coincidence, then, that the southern cotton mill crusade reached its peak in 1895.[8]

David Cooper's brother, John, had observed that even the Dukes considered cotton mills an important part of their investment portfolio.[9] After quickly securing nearly $100,000 in financial commitments from prominent Henderson citizens, who hoped that the mill would boost the town's image and lead to greater economic growth, the Coopers broke ground on a site just north of town; production was scheduled to begin in early 1896.[10]

The venture proved to be a financial success. The mill began production with 132 looms, and another seventy-two were installed within a year. "The Henderson Cotton Mill continues to receive large orders ahead," the *Gold Leaf* boasted in April 1897, "and there is no telling when it will catch up with the heavy run of business on hand." Indeed, cloth production increased from 45,000 pounds per month during the first year to 65,000 pounds per month in 1898, then up to 90,000 in 1899. Profits soared as well. In 1900 alone profits amounted to nearly $83,000, or more than one-third of the company's investment capital at the time.[11] Mill managers planned further expansions, including a second mill on the south side of town. In July 1901 the new Harriet Mill—named for the mother of David Y. and John D.—began spinning coarse yarns to complement the Henderson Mill's bagging, and production could barely keep up with demand.[12] Within a dozen years management added two more mills on the Harriet grounds —called Harriet #2 and Harriet #3—to produce a wider variety of coarse yarns. Growth and expansion had become a habit and an expectation. By the mid-1920s, after converting most of the Henderson Mill's weaving capacity to yarn production, Harriet and Henderson officials claimed that the two complexes together were "the world's largest yarn mill."[13]

As was the case throughout the Piedmont, most of the workers in these mills came directly from the surrounding countryside, escaping the poverty and chronic indebtedness that accompanied tobacco and cotton cultivation.[14] Virtually all mill workers in Henderson were born in North Carolina; the only exceptions were a handful of Virginia natives—4 out of 336, according to the 1900 census—who at some point had moved across the nearby border.[15] Besides its overwhelming population of North Carolina natives, the most significant unifying characteristic of the work force was its whiteness. The Coopers ignored the area's large black population —roughly 60 percent in Henderson Town and throughout Vance County— and hired only white workers for production jobs. Of the 336 Henderson Mill workers identified in the 1900 census—the Harriet Mill was not yet in operation—only 2 were black, and both of them were men classified as general laborers. Job opportunities for blacks in cotton mills remained minimal and severely circumscribed until well into the 1960s.[16] In the wake of the Panic of 1893, the Coopers had little trouble finding enough white workers to begin production at their mill.[17]

There were opportunities in the mill for women, men, and fairly young children. Women operated the spinning and winding frames that produced the yarn and packaged it for shipping, so girls, sometimes as young as nine or ten, usually learned these tasks. Men ran the openers, pickers, and carding machines that broke down the bales and produced the rope-like "roving" that went to the spinners. Men also removed bobbins from the frames—a task called doffing—and hauled roving and yarn from department to department. Boys often began their careers as doffers, then moved on to other jobs reserved for males.[18] It became an expected rite of passage for children in their early teens to take their first positions in the mill. In the 1920s many children worked in the mill from six until eight in the morning, spent the day in school, then worked another two hours before supper. Few of the mill-village children remained in school past the fifth or sixth grade, and many dropped out earlier. Whether they wanted to or not, they ended up working full-time in the mills, establishing another generation of workers.[19]

Although company records contain no lists of employees for any time period, the 1900 U.S. Census provides a snapshot of the Henderson Mill workforce four years after it opened. Working households contained every imaginable combination of residents—nuclear families, extended families, in-laws, widows and widowers with children, step-families, siblings without parents, unrelated boarders—ranging in age from a few children under ten to a grandmother in her eighties. Roughly half were age eighteen or younger (169 out of 336, and 99 of the 169 were girls), over 80 percent were less than thirty years old (275 out of 336), and males comprised about 55 percent of the overall work force (192 out of 336). By 1910 males were two-thirds of a larger workforce (649 out of 972) that also operated Harriet Mills #1 and #2.[20] Males remained a significant, although shifting, majority of mill workers in Henderson until World War II.

Especially in the earliest years, many hands took jobs in the cotton mill without severing all ties with the land, causing seasonal fluctuations in the number of available workers. The Coopers even delayed the initial opening of the Henderson Mill several weeks because the area's farmers had not yet completed their tobacco and cotton harvests. A regional survey conducted in 1906 revealed that whenever prices for tobacco and cotton rose, mill owners reported a scarcity of employees.[21] Henderson Mill managers complained a year later, during planting season, that "production had been necessarily curtailed" because of the "scarcity of labor," causing a "strained condition between ourselves and our customers."[22] Although ties to farms, along with the ready availability of mill jobs elsewhere, clearly gave some workers leverage over their working conditions, the instability of the labor force bedeviled mill managers, who in 1907, for example, contended with an average turnover rate of 176 percent.[23] By the end of World War I, however, as the number of millhands with farm connections dwindled and the supply of available white laborers exceeded demand, only a relatively small number of workers remained in the transient population.[24]

By the late 1910s and early 1920s the workforce at the Harriet and Henderson Mills had stabilized. The Harriet Mill Board of Directors noted the transition in July 1916, reporting that "many of the cottages have flourishing gardens, and pretty flowers around them, changing their appearance to that of houses, and not merely sleeping quarters."[25] For the next four decades, the hands created a lively community in the villages surrounding the mills. "The people around this mill was more or less like a family," recalled Lloyd Wilkins, who grew up in the Henderson Mill village in the 1910s. "They knowed each other's business and what was going on and all." "I could name everybody in the whole neighborhood," Sam Littleton reflected, referring to his Harriet Mill village upbringing in the 1920s. He knew "who was working where, and what their children's names were." "It was just a good place to live," remembered Harriet Mill hand Esther Roberson, who was born in the village in 1910. "People were loving and kind to each other. It was just a good neighborhood."[26]

Memories of the material conditions of life in the villages, however, never measure up to those of the hands' social relations. "It was very pitiful," Edith Adams recalled, describing the Henderson Mill village from the late 1910s through the 1930s, "because all of the houses was owned by the mill company." Unwilling to invest much in the villages, especially when business conditions worsened after World War I, mill managers could not convince many workers to spend their own money and energy to spruce up their rented homes. "The houses was in awful shape," remembered Henderson Mill worker Luther Jackson, who grew up in the 1910s and 1920s. "None of them insulated. None of them were underpinned. None had no bathrooms. You think about getting up at four o'clock in the morning, walking out in the back of the garden and turn your butt up to the moon." Sometimes, however, the rustic conditions contributed to the sociability and sense of community that millhands recall so favorably. For example, although Edith Adams did not care for the appearance of the village, she liked to visit the neighborhood well. "That's where the women would congregate and meet and do a lot of talking," she remembered.[27]

There is evidence, however, that the mill communities were not always as warm and peaceful as much of the oral testimony indicates. Several times during the 1920s, residents of both villages petitioned the company for better police protection in their neighborhoods. Dance halls and honky-tonks attracted a number of the mill villagers and dismayed others. Perhaps some of the hands feared "the bootleggers, rum runners, gamblers, and the roughnecks" that lived on the fringes of the villages.[28] In addition, police protection might have been necessary because millhands and families from the two villages feared and often fought each other. "A long time ago the people from North and South Henderson didn't mix at all," recalled Henderson Mill worker Emma Harris, "didn't get along with each other." Mary Abbott, who grew up in the Harriet Mill village, said she learned as a child that the people in the Henderson village "were mean and rough to get along with." Abbott recalled that when she and her neighbors attended revival meetings in the Henderson Mill village, someone would have to keep watch "and make sure nobody were flattening their tires or stealing something off their cars." Once a year, during the Fourth of July holiday, this intervillage rivalry shifted to the baseball diamond. "Played ball for nine innings," Ralph Harris explained, then "fight for two or three hours." Currents of violence and frustration obviously ran through both communities.[29]

Part of the problem can be traced to the lack of respect millhands received from wealthier citizens. "I reckon they thought they were better than we were," said the Harriet Mill's Esther Roberson. "I wouldn't say that the mill people and the townspeople communicated with each other very much. I know they didn't visit." "The cotton-millers was about the lowest-class people you could get," recalled the Henderson Mill's Joseph Braswell. "The only folks lower than that was the colored folks." Emma Harris remembered that in a city school, where mill-village children went if they continued past the fifth grade, anyone "could have picked out everybody from North and South Henderson easy. They used to tell every one of them, because they didn't have clothes like the other ones." The same was true in town. "All those townspeople dudes was all dressed up," Ralph Harris recalled, "and we were up there with an old T-shirt on, and dungarees." Mill people, Edith Adams recalled, "were not recognized even in the stores. You'd go to buy something in the clothing stores, and they knew those that had money. And they catered to them, and they didn't cater to us."[30]

Indeed, there was a great disparity between living conditions in the mill villages and in the town's wealthier neighborhoods. In contrast with the mill villages' dirt streets and outhouses, by the 1920s the white sections of Henderson Town had twelve miles of paved roads and fifteen miles of concrete sidewalks. Unlike the villages, parts of the town also had running water, a sewer system, electric lights, natural gas and telephone service, three movie theaters, an opera house advertising the "largest stage between Washington, D.C. and Atlanta," and a country club complete with a golf course.[31]

The cotton mills had been the primary industrial generator of the town's prosperity and were by far the area's largest year-round employer. Not surprisingly, then, the Coopers remained the community's most powerful family. Mill founder David Y. Cooper was on the board of directors of several banks across the state, the Durham and Northern Railway, and the Seaboard Air Line Railway. In addition to serving several terms as the town's mayor, mill cofounder John D. Cooper was the chairman of the board at Henderson's Citizens Bank, president of both Carolina Bagging Company and Farmers' Loan and Supply, founder in 1895 of the local telephone company and in 1910 of the Vance Guano Company, and president of the Farmers' and Merchants Bank. After both David Y. and John D. died in 1921, David's son Sidney assumed leadership of the cotton mills, while John D.'s sons, John D. Jr. and Marshall, maintained the family's broader economic influence in the community. After graduating from the University of North Carolina in the mid-1920s, Marshall became a director of Citizens Bank and of Carolina Telephone and Telegraph and served twenty years on the city council. John D. Jr., who graduated from the North Carolina State School of Textiles, quickly became general manager of the cotton mills, in 1925 helped found the local hospital, and in 1923 served as the local country club's first president; eventually he turned that office over to his brother Marshall. Even businessmen who were fairly sympathetic with the mill owners conceded that the Coopers "pretty well ran the city."[32]

The Coopers were not without concerns, however. Profits at their mills were constantly threatened by high rates of absenteeism. As early as 1903 a leading South Carolina mill owner complained that "every cotton mill in this state recognizes that to have a full complement of labor in the mill each morning . . . it is practically necessary to carry a surplusage of 20 to 25 per cent of 'spare help.'"[33] This was particularly true for departments that employed mostly women, who frequently missed work to take care of children, do household chores, or recover from the illness and exhaustion that resulted from their burdens. A federal survey in 1922 concluded that women in southern mills missed 27 percent of available workdays.[34] Harriet and Henderson workers fit the industry profile. Immediately after World War I, when mills adopted a reduced work week of fifty-five hours and wages remained artificially high, David Y. Cooper noted that after a short burst of increased enthusiasm, "their efficiency did not last long, many of our people drifting back to their old habits of idleness." The high pay "enabled them to live without working regularly, which was disastrous to us."[35] Managers at the Harriet and Henderson Mills remained baffled and frustrated by high rates of absenteeism for the next forty years.

Even when sufficient numbers of workers reported, managers frequently complained about "the indifference of the operatives."[36] While the Coopers lamented how difficult it was "to impress upon our people the importance of making hay while the sun shines," many millhands desired instead to maintain a measure of control over when they would work and over the level of emotional commitment they would give while performing their jobs. Although some hands undoubtedly maximized their earnings by attending regularly and working feverishly, most sought a more balanced life. This source of antagonism also persisted for decades.

Until the late 1930s it was possible for many Harriet and Henderson workers to retain their jobs while performing at a pace that was less than full-throttle. Some jobs in the mill had long breaks built into the workday. Doffers worked hard when the spinning or winding frames were full, then rested while the new bobbins were filled. During these years, the most crucial variable for workers' happiness was the personality of their supervisors. Foremen—or "overseers," as they were commonly called—had nearly total control over hiring and firing and could use any style of management they saw fit as long as they kept their departments operating. Esther Roberson recalled that in the 1920s she had one of the more difficult bosses, Bob Gupton. Gupton and his sons, who were related to the Coopers, held many of the supervisory positions in the Harriet Mill. "What the Guptons said, that's what went," Roberson remembered. "When I went to work with him, he treated us like children. If he told you to do something, and you didn't do it, he didn't say, 'I'll whip you!,' but he made you think he would."[37]

Although arbitrary authority was always vested in the foremen and second hands, not every supervisor chose to be a tyrant. Many of these first-level managers had risen from the ranks of workers and still lived alongside, and often were related to, those that they supervised.[38] Some foremen were apparently rather congenial. Lucy Collins recalled that in the 1920s she "had a good boss man. I could go up there and work awhile at a time, and quit whenever I got ready, and go back whenever I got ready. We would work most any sort of way we wanted to. They agreed to let us do that." Some supervisors insisted on enforcing strict rules to keep workers at their jobs and discouraged socializing whenever possible. Most foremen, however, recognized that millhands were going to choose their own schedules whether management liked it or not, especially when workers were scarce. At such times no foremen who wanted to maintain production could risk alienating potential hands.[39]

So although some workers were saddled with ornery supervisors, a number of hands worked when they wanted, stayed home when they desired, and even had time to relax while on the job. In the mill villages they also enjoyed each other's company and support, which compensated for the gap in material wealth between themselves and many white towns-people. The combination of this mill-village spirit and some humane supervision dominates workers' memories of this period, almost to the point of nostalgia. This is significant because with a few brief exceptions, from the early 1920s until the onset of World War II the entire cotton textile industry was in a chronic state of depression, creating economic hardship and turmoil in labor relations at the Harriet and Henderson Mills.

Difficult times in the 1920s followed extraordinarily profitable business conditions during World War I. While the country was at war and the federal government was purchasing enormous amounts of cotton goods, most mills could sell as much as they could produce. As soon as the war ended in November 1918, however, the government left the market, and many textile firms suffered instant depressions. By shrewdly marketing their yarns overseas, the Harriet and Henderson Mills held out against the odds until early 1920, when, according to President Sidney Cooper, "like a clap of thunder from a clear sky the demand for goods ceased." Finished yarn sold for less per pound than the cotton required to produce it, and sales could no longer support the company's payroll. In one year, the company had gone "from the high tide of prosperity to the low water mark of depression."[40] In response, Harriet and Henderson management slashed wages "about 58% from the high mark" and opened a commissary, which sold staple goods at cost. Unlike the exploitative company store depicted in lingering myths, the Harriet and Henderson commissary apparently was greatly appreciated by mill villagers.[41] This act of paternalism helped the Harriet and Henderson Mills avoid the postwar strike wave in southern cotton mills.[42]

Harriet and Henderson officials had used similar tactics before when confronted with the possibility of widespread labor discontent. In 1908, for example, during a brief economic slump that forced the mills to cut the workweek to three and a half days, the minutes of a board of directors meeting revealed that "one half of the houses rent was being given to the operatives in order to keep them satisfied."[43] The Coopers had also made gestures toward their workforce by funding numerous churches in the mill villages, providing rudimentary health care for millhands, offering facilities for hog scalding and canning, distributing candy and fruit at Christmas, and sponsoring baseball teams.[44] The most significant program launched by management was the creation in 1920 of a Sick Benefit Society fund, into which the mills contributed five cents per worker per week. The board of directors noted that "the mill people are very much pleased with this society, and it seems to be a great help to them."[45]

Referring to these kinds of paternalistic actions, many textile executives at the time, as well as the first generation of historians to consider the subject, maintained that mill owners' main motivation for developing the industry had been philanthropic—to provide steady work and additional benefits for suffering citizens, lifting them to a higher stage of civilization.[46] There should be little doubt, however, that the Coopers, like all southern mill owners, cared foremost about the their venture's profitability. Near the end of 1910, when it became evident that the mills would show no profit for that year, David Y. Cooper reported to the board of directors that "our operations at a loss during the year had worked only for the good of humanity and that it looked hardly good business to run at a loss any more for the sake of humanity."[47] Company officials always considered the cost-effectiveness of any plan to spend money to improve the lives of its workforce. In 1910, for example, the board of directors tabled a proposal to install "bath rooms for operatives," deciding instead "to wait till we could have more money to be used for this purpose." At the same meeting the directors authorized spending up to $50,000 for new equipment at the Harriet Mill.[48] Four years later, the company withstood pressure from Henderson chapters of the Women's Christian Temperance Union, the King's Daughters, and the Civic League to engage in "social settlement work." After replying that they "had the matter under consideration," managers chose to go only so far as to announce mill-village "clean-up days," for which they might "offer a few prizes."[49]

Nevertheless, in some mill towns, including Henderson, the absence of public labor conflict indeed lent credence to the notion that the mill owners' fair-mindedness and generosity had created a harmony of interests between workers and managers. As late as 1924, the Henderson Chamber of Commerce encouraged businesses around the country to relocate there with the truthful assurance that in Henderson "there has never been a strike or labor trouble of any kind."[50] A few months after launching this publicity campaign, however, local business leaders were forced to revise their claims.

Labor conflict at the Harriet and Henderson Mills in 1924 resulted from the depression that prevailed in cotton mills across the South, with a few brief exceptions, after 1922. As one student of the textile industry wrote about the 1920s, "Spectacular fluctuations in the price of cotton made the manufacture of cotton products more nearly a gamble than a business."[51] The Harriet and Henderson Mills operated only two or three days a week for most of 1922. When business improved briefly in 1923, managers had difficulty convincing workers, who had learned to compensate for shortened workweeks, to take full advantage of the favorable market conditions. As an incentive for perfect attendance, management offered a bonus of 12.5 percent to any worker who put in a full six-day week.[52] By February 1924, however, with the return of difficult times, managers voted to discontinue the bonus system, which, they claimed, had failed to generate a maximizing spirit anyway. Despite operating only four days a week, two months later the Harriet Mill still had "an inventory of about half a million pounds of yarn on hand, with very few orders on our books." Managers eventually decided to close the mills for a week at the end of August, to start back on a three-day schedule in September, and then to ease up to six-day weeks; at that point, wage scales would be cut another 10 to 15 percent.[53]

When company officials proceeded with these plans, they discovered that it was possible to push Harriet Mill workers too far. On Monday morning, 8 September 1924, supervisors announced to their hands that the wage scale would be cut by 12.5 percent. In response, shortly after their lunch break 250 employees at Harriet Mill #1 walked out.[54]

Remarkably, the local newspaper allowed "a committee representing the workers" of Harriet #1 to explain why they had walked out. The first reason, reflecting the perspective of the striking women, emphasized their patience and understanding while illustrating how for them work was but one of many important responsibilities. "During the summer we only had three days work to the week but we didn't object since it left us two days in which to do our housework," the workers explained. "We also had our gardens." But with gardens fading and the school year beginning, many workers found themselves strapped even before the wage cut. "The laws of this state enforce us to send our children to school," the committee noted, "and how can we with families of six and seven children to feed, clothe, and buy books for with the average man making $9.00 per week with rent, coal, and wood taken out of that?" The company's explanations about market pressures failed to soothe the mill villagers. "Within the last week or two groceries that everybody are compelled to have such as: sugar, flour, meat, coffee and lard, have gone up. The mill company is not giving us our rent, coal or wood," the workers explained. "We are not asking for a raise," the strikers emphasized, although their pay was "little enough as it was." We "only want the same we were getting before and how can men with a spark of humanity refuse."[55] After eight days without production, however, company officials convinced strikers to resume working with the wage cut. In return, the hands said that they had received a commitment from President Sidney Cooper that the company would restore the 12.5 percent as soon as the mills could afford it.[56]

Three years later, when business conditions had clearly improved, Harriet #1 hands asked management to make good on its promise to restore the 12.5 percent cut. When management refused, a group of hands walked out, triggering another episode of public labor conflict. Within a few days, nine hundred workers at the Harriet complex were on strike. The Henderson strike of 1927 grew into the largest and most bitter southern labor struggle since the postwar uprisings, although later, of course, it was overshadowed by the dramatic conflicts of 1929 in Elizabethton, Tennessee, and Gastonia and Marion, North Carolina.[57]

In a statement to the community printed in the *Henderson Daily Dispatch*, the striking workers once again emphasized the severity of their situation: "Most all the family men were not making enough to decently clothe or feed their families. No disrespect is meant to the stockholders or head officials of the mills. But, we the employees of the Harriet cotton mills do honestly think we deserve this raise."[58] At strike meetings, workers complained about company houses with no lights, no hot water, and no toilets. They also resented a new gate policy, which had been designed to keep people at work by making it difficult to leave the mill. Only one gate remained open, and workers were required to have passes signed by their supervisors to go through it. According to one striker, this "worked a hardship on the women in the mill," who had to "hurry home at night to prepare meals for their families." In addition to being inconvenient, the gate policy was demeaning. "We are not a class of people to be locked in," workers protested.[59]

Although somewhat fearful, managers decided in a private meeting that "the best and only thing to do at this time" was to "stand pat."[60] Company officials met with the strikers' committee but made no concrete offers, insisting that "if any employee residing on the Harriet Cotton Mill premises has any personal grievance arising from conditions of premises, if presented to the office of the company, the same will be remedied insofar as the company finds conditions warrant."[61] Management grew more adamant when Alfred Hoffmann, an organizer for the United Textile Workers of the American Federation of Labor, came to Henderson after learning of the strike. Hoffmann told striking workers "to stay out until you get your $12\frac{1}{2}$ per cent raise" and suggested that they should have asked for a 100 percent increase instead. He also promised assistance from organized labor, such as it was, throughout the state.[62] Although several workers apparently signed union cards immediately after Hoffmann's first speech, the strikers' committee kept its distance, perhaps for fear of eliminating any possibility of discussions with management. Indeed, Sidney Cooper did decline an invitation to explain the company's offer at the meeting, arguing that he would not attend any gathering at which a union organizer would be present.[63]

Throughout the strike, Harriet Mill workers tried, with only partial success, to convince Henderson Mill workers to join the walkout. A history of animosity between the villages, a more benevolent superintendent at the Henderson Mill, and different economic conditions at the two complexes separated the groups. The Henderson Mill still produced large amounts of cloth, which was in greater demand than the yarns produced at the Harriet Mills.[64] Despite this limited solidarity, Harriet Mill workers held out, and management's intransigence boosted the standing of the UTW's representative.

Hoffmann, who has been described as "courageous, plainspoken, and sensitive to workers' culture" and as someone who was "all fire in making speeches," seemed eager to lead the strike. According to reporter R. E. Williams, the union organizer "adopted the methods of the local leaders" and remained "in close consultation with them." Hoffmann developed new sources of strike relief and recruited more workers to sign union cards. The union leader arrived at one meeting with $125 that had been donated by labor unions in nearby Durham. However meager compared to the Harriet Mill's $9,000 weekly payroll, this money, according to the *News and Observer*, had a "magnetic effect" on many strikers, convincing them that Hoffmann and the UTW could support their promises. While daily gatherings continued in each village, the UTW also began hosting nightly members-only meetings in the Harriet Mill village, and by the end of the strike's second week Hoffmann claimed to have signed up nearly six hundred hands. The *Henderson Daily Dispatch* warned that it "appeared the strike was slipping into the hands of the union."[65]

The stalemate continued for another two weeks, by which time the trickle of union financial support could not nearly meet the strikers' needs. Sympathetic merchants like William Johnson, who had been extending credit to strikers, faced bankruptcy.[66] Although most hands had concluded that they would have to return to work without winning their 12.5 percent, they still refused to surrender unconditionally. The local strike committee revived itself and compiled a list of conditions that workers wanted the company to meet before they would resume production. Agreeing, deferentially, to "leave the matter of adjustment of wages and living conditions with you honorable gentlemen whom we have known so long," strikers asked "that the conduct of each Overseer be investigated" and made another pitch for eliminating the gate pass system.[67]

Management refused the workers' terms, then took the offensive the following day by issuing eviction orders to nine selected strikers, effective 3 September.[68] Since the strike was obviously fading, the evictions seemed more vengeful than decisive. Impending homelessness, however, certainly made clear the high cost of assertiveness. Although eviction day passed with no effort to remove the targeted employees from their company homes, 75 percent of Harriet Mill hands voted to abandon their demands and return to the mill.[69] By 10 September, with workers having extracted no promises from management, the Harriet Mill was operating at nearly full strength.

The company was not content with victory, however. Management fired "about one hundred" carefully selected employees, after which "Mr. Cooper advised the directors that the labor situation was well under control, and the people were working better than they had ever worked before." To ensure compliant behavior, managers stepped up surveillance tactics. "Some of the Mill Officials made it a point to visit the Mills each night, and at all hours of the night," company directors were informed. As of mid-October, "at no time had they found the employees loafing on the job." Management also instituted "a card index system in order to keep a record of all employees." Identifying targets for retribution would be simpler in the future.[70]

The management's labor strategy also had a conciliatory prong: after the strike, managers offered to purchase schoolbooks for their employees' children for the coming school year at a cost of between $1,000 and $2,000. This expenditure for philanthropy, of course, was far cheaper than granting the workers' demand for a 12.5 percent raise. In addition, the strike probably prompted company officials to hire their first full-time welfare worker to develop programs at both mills.[71]

The clearest lesson learned in 1927 by both millhands and managers was that the company had immense power in episodes of labor conflict. Management could wait until hunger and indebtedness forced workers back. Selected evictions and firings further demonstrated the company's leverage. Throughout the South, workers who struck discovered various manifestations of this imbalance of power. Before the costs of assertiveness became clear to Harriet Mill workers, passionate hope for change had outweighed cold calculations of the probability of success. Failure and retaliation, however, forced workers to rethink.

Perhaps the most revealing example of this powerful lesson in repression came seven years later, when tens of thousands of cotton mill workers throughout the South went out on strike. While details differed in every community, a general sense of the need for struggle "cut through the industry, from the tiniest rural mill to the most imposing corporation," according to recent historians of the period.[72] Yet Harriet and Henderson workers did not stage even a brief walkout. By this time the Harriet and Henderson Mills had also operated without incident during the highly publicized 1929 conflicts in Gastonia, Elizabethton, and Marion, and throughout the early 1930s while numerous other textile communities erupted in less well known struggles.[73]

By no means were Henderson mill workers completely passive in 1934. Several carloads of strikers from other towns passed through the Harriet and Henderson mill villages, and large numbers of workers attended several open-air meetings at which union organizers urged them to "join the union for the government is behind us," a reference to Section 7(a) of the National Industrial Recovery Act, which promoted independent unions.[74] Local officials feared a strike reminiscent of the one in 1927, and Sheriff J. E. Hamlett swore in 150 "special deputies" just in case.[75] Yet production continued at both complexes without interruption.[76] Activism would certainly place one's livelihood in jeopardy.

Addressing the board of directors after the 1934 uprising in other parts of the region, President Sidney Cooper expressed "satisfaction over the manner in which our operatives treated the strike," noting that "they were very loyal at all times" and that he was "deeply appreciative for their loyalty."[77] Workers at Harriet and Henderson remained passive, however, because they justifiably feared the consequences of conflict. Throughout the South, participants in the 1934 General Strike experienced bitter defeat.[78]

The late 1920s and the 1930s were hazardous years for the southern textile industry. Over a year before the stock market crash of 1929, southern cotton mill owners had agreed to take an extended Fourth of July vacation to curtail production and possibly boost prices.[79] Sidney Cooper noted in 1932 that it was still "practically impossible to make a profitable sale of yarns."[80] There was a brief spell of prosperity during the first year of the Roosevelt administration, when it appeared that the National Recovery Administration's textile code, which allowed mill owners to collaborate to establish their own production quotas and wage scales, might restore health to the industry. During the third quarter of 1933, Harriet and Henderson managers reported "exceedingly good" business, nearly "the best in the history of the mills." It appears, however, that the increase in business activity resulted from mill owners and textile purchasers rushing to do business before the NRA code went into effect.[81] These wheelers and dealers proved prescient, because it was impossible for the highly decentralized textile industry to develop enforcement mechanisms for its own regulations. So many companies had violated NRA standards, Sidney Cooper claimed in early 1935, "that the mills who were living up to the code were being penalized severely, not being able to meet the competition." Orders had become so scarce that the Harriet and Henderson Mills' very existence was in jeopardy.[82]

Throughout the 1930s Harriet and Henderson employees were, at best, part-time millhands. There were occasional periods of full-time employment, but short weeks were common, and mill work was undependable. As had been so common since 1921, economic conditions forced Harriet and Henderson workers to blend mill work into their larger survival strategies. Most families depended more than ever on their gardens and hogs. Some of the hands returned to family farms, some left for other mills that were reported to be running full-time, and after 1933 some found jobs with New Deal relief programs. A few foremen organized wood-cutting operations and hired their workers to head for the forest instead of the mill. Some families took in boarders, while others opened little stores. Few people had any cash, however, so store owners usually collected only a stack of IOUs. Henderson Mill hand Lloyd Wilkins recalled fifty years later that he and others had lived off the land. "If it hadn't been for fish and frog legs," he said, "I don't reckon I'd be here now." By providing coal and wood in winter and paying the hands' medical bills, the company tried to keep enough workers in the vicinity to operate whenever possible. "There weren't too much going on somewhere else for you, so you just stayed on," Wilkins summed up the situation. "All you was doing was existing."[83]

By the late 1930s the future of the mills seemed hopeless. Few orders were available for even the offer of a bid, and most of those were awarded to giant firms that had the newest, most efficient machinery. With spinning frames that were, for the most part, original equipment, the Harriet and Henderson Mills could not hope to compete. It appeared to many that Henderson's cotton mill fever had run its course.

2 Modernization and Unionization, 1938–1943

In 1954 the textile industry journal *Whitin Review* hailed the Harriet and Henderson Cotton Mills as an exemplary case study in what could be accomplished by modernizing a plant's production equipment and techniques. "By the mid-thirties the picture was clear, not only in Henderson and Harriet Cotton Mills, but in hundreds of mills in the United States," the trade publication recalled, referring to the bleak context in which the decision to modernize had been made. "The machinery was old —30–40 years; it was expensive to run, inefficient in operation, and represented textile technology of the early twentieth century." Most mill men had simply "tried to hang on, hoping for better days ahead; some were unable to continue." Despite the dire business climate, however, Harriet and Henderson officials had decided aggressively to go further into debt to launch "a long range program, to modernize the plant, the machinery, the auxiliary equipment, the methods, and techniques so that the plants would be really competitive."[1]

Although by 1954 the success of the Harriet and Henderson modernization campaign seemed beyond question, at least to most industry observers, in the midst of the Great Depression top management had not been nearly as decisive as the *Whitin Review* article suggested. There is evidence that modernization plans had been presented to the board of directors as early as April 1936. The proposals languished, however, as the mills earned unexpected profits, marginal as they were, during 1936 and the first three quarters of 1937. Content with these meager earnings, President Sidney A. Cooper had shelved the modernization plans in January 1937. When markets declined in late 1937, this decision proved shortsighted: the company found itself unable to compete with mills that had already invested in long-draft spinning frames.[2]

Resorting to a familiar strategy, President Cooper and the board of directors curtailed operations and waited for better times to come. By April 1938 the options seemed grim. "There would be a loss either way," Sidney Cooper confessed, "with the mills running or standing still." The board of directors "offered no concrete suggestions" on what to do "but seemed to be of the opinion that the management was following the best course in operating only units of the mill necessary to take care of present sales."[3] Harriet and Henderson managers were not unique. Most southern mills were marginally profitable at best in the late 1930s, and few mill owners were willing to risk going into debt to finance new machinery. Only the largest companies had sufficient resources to invest in long-draft spinning.[4]

With the mills facing heavy losses, General Manager John D. Cooper Jr. and his brother, Marshall Y. Cooper, both of whom were sons of mill cofounder John D. Cooper Sr., struggled to convince the board of directors —which included their cousin, President Sidney Cooper—to take some risks. Having spent many years in cotton mills after his formal training at the School of Textiles in Raleigh, John D. Cooper Jr. had the expertise to plan a major restructuring of the mills. Marshall Cooper, who graduated from the first class at the University of North Carolina's School of Business, had firsthand experience running a farm supply business and had connections with several major banks. Referring to a presentation he made to the board of directors in the mid-1930s, Marshall Cooper remembered saying, "I think what we ought to do is either modernize these plants or liquidate them and save what you've got." Despite his arguments for risk-taking, Marshall Cooper recalled, "the particular management was opposed to it."[5]

Whether it was the Cooper brothers' persuasion or the severity of the depression in 1938 that inspired a change of heart, the directors eventually approved a plan to revamp the mills. Early in 1939 the board of directors accepted a bid from Whitin Machine Works, in Massachusetts, for new equipment. Whitin technicians also helped management plan a total restructuring of the mills. Although the directors appear to have been excited about this "initial step in modernizing the mills," surely some must have had concerns, however private, about borrowing $112,000 for new machinery while staring at a profitless future. After factoring in additional costs for modifying existing frames, as recommended by Whitin, the initial outlay for the Harriet Mill alone exceeded $170,000. The planned changes were so extensive that the mills had to be shut down while they were overhauled. According to initial estimates, if everything went well the mills would be idle for nearly a year. Markets for textiles remained weak, which reduced the risk of closing down, but the company would not be able to sell a pound of yarn even if purchasers were to appear.[6] After years of caution and delay, the company had indeed taken an enormous risk.

The company hoped to become competitive by operating with long-draft spinning frames, which in 1951 the *Textile Bulletin* called "the most important progressive step" for cotton mills in the last forty years. Mills that converted to long-draft greatly reduced their costs of production. By 1939, those that had not were considered obsolete.[7] Long-draft spinning allowed finer yarns to be spun from coarser roving (the untwisted, rope-like cotton that entered the spinning frames), eliminating several production processes and much labor. In textiles, the "draft" refers to the thickness of the roving compared to that of the yarn being produced. A short draft, then, meant that roving had to be nearly the same thickness as the yarn it would become. In outdated card rooms, including those at the Harriet and Henderson Mills, it had been necessary to process the cotton three or more times to accommodate old-fashioned spinning frames. In contrast, since long-draft frames could handle relatively coarse cotton roving, the card room only had to process the cotton once or twice at most, creating an enormous savings in time and labor. As an added bonus, mills using long-draft technology could expect "an increase, rather than a decrease, in yarn quality and breaking strength."[8]

Modernization involved more than just machinery, however. Company officials recruited throughout the South and eventually replaced virtually their entire supervisory staff. Unlike their predecessors, most of these new supervisors had received formal training at the North Carolina State School of Textiles or at similar institutions in the South. James Proctor, an experienced superintendent, was hired to oversee the Harriet complex. Company officials lured Joseph Farmer away from the Rockfish Mills, near Fayetteville, North Carolina, to become superintendent of the Henderson Mill. Farmer, in turn, convinced a number of his associates to join him.[9]

By October 1939, well ahead of schedule, the Harriet and Henderson Mills resumed operations, and the modernization plan appeared to be wildly successful. The first postrenovation quarterly report showed a profit, and sales and earnings continued to climb during the next quarter. Productivity also increased. The *Whitin Review* developed a productivity index, called the OMH (output per man hour), which was obtained "by dividing the total production in pounds for a week . . . by the number of man-hours worked in that time." Table 1 reveals the extent of the company's OMH gains. Flush with success, managers immediately committed themselves to an additional $80,000 worth of new equipment.[10]

As it turned out, however, the beginning of World War II allowed even antiquated mills to reap relatively large profits in the early 1940s. While the Harriet and Henderson Mills were being overhauled, Germany invaded Poland, triggering World War II, and the United States government began purchasing large quantities of cotton goods. During the first six months of 1939, North Carolina cotton mills received nearly $1.4 million in government orders. By September 1940 the federal government was purchasing half of the nation's production of cotton goods, including over $1 million in North Carolina textiles every week, and the United States had not yet formally entered the conflict.[11] Throughout the war the modernized Harriet and Henderson Mills could sell virtually everything they produced. The Harriet and Henderson board of directors had timed its risky venture perfectly, if fortuitously, to reap the profits of the wartime boom.[12]

When workers are considered, however, the impact of modernization becomes much more ambiguous. Many problems arose from what the *Whitin Review* called the "utilization of employee skills to achieve maximum efficiency." The long-draft spinning frames operated at a higher speed than the older machinery and therefore produced much more yarn per shift. In order to keep pace, then, the card-room machinery that produced the roving for the spinning frames had to run faster. So did the winding frames that packaged the finished yarn for shipment. Managers

Table 1.

Increases in Output per Man Hour (OMH) after Modernization

Year	OMH	OMH
	Harriet #2	Henderson
1938	100	100
1939	133	133
1942	182	186

Source: "Harriet-Henderson Cotton Mills—And Modernization," *Whitin Review* 21 (September–October 1954): 26. The figures for 1938 represent the premodernization base year.

expected workers in all these departments to operate faster-running machines. To further increase productivity, the company assigned more frames per hand than had been considered normal prior to modernization. Workers called this the "stretch-out system."[13]

The new supervisory staff also alienated many workers. Although foremen and second hands, the first-level supervisors, in theory had always possessed dictatorial power, the new college-trained personnel, who had no roots in the community, seemed more willing to use their authority, whether to demand more effort or to curb what they saw as casual work habits.[14] Tighter supervision began at the top. The new Harriet Mill superintendent, Jim Proctor, was described by one worker as "business, just strictly business. Didn't take no time with nobody." Proctor demanded that lower-level supervisors adhere to his standards. Unlike their predecessors, many of these new second hands had never worked at production jobs and had nothing to do with the hands outside work. Workplace interactions became more rigid and antagonistic. As Esther Roberson recalled, if the new supervisors "didn't see fit to let you off for something very important, they wouldn't. They was real, real strict."[15] Many workers at the Henderson Mill recalled the new supervisors' favoritism. As Joseph Braswell recalled, "You'd go in, they could send you home, let somebody else work in your place. Send you home every day for the week. You didn't get no say about it. Couldn't say, 'I don't want to.' Cause that's it." Lloyd Wilkins spoke from experience. "They'd always have the son of one of the foreman's friends come through," he recalled. "He'd hire him. You'd been on that job all your life and you been working there for years. Take you off and put him on it, tell you to go back and rest a day. It happened to me." Spinner Edith Adams recalled an instance when her husband was the victim of favoritism. "One time the boss man liked another person more so than he did Raymond," she explained. So the boss "told him to let him rest that day, and this other person run his job. There was a lot of unfairness."[16]

The company's disruption of expectations extended to all areas of the workers' lives. Woodrow Johnson of the Harriet Mill recalled an irritating policy initiated by superintendent Proctor. "Anybody that was convicted in city, county or federal court for anything," Johnson remembered, "automatically lost the job. If you got a speeding ticket, you didn't have no job." Proctor kept track of the employees' personal habits and warned them if they appeared to stray too far from the straight and narrow. He cautioned Woodrow Johnson, for example, to stay away from his parents' mill-village store because they sold beer and wine. Management also restricted social life inside the mills. "You stopped at the water fountain to get a drink of water, and anybody that wanted a drink of water, you had to stop about ten paces back," Woodrow Johnson remembered. Proctor "wouldn't have you talk." These new restrictions on personal behavior came abruptly, and according to Johnson they "got worse and worse."[17]

Some of Proctor's new rules, however, appeared to be more directly related to business. The superintendent strictly enforced the requirement that at least two people in every company-owned house work in the mills. "So any time there was two people working for that company," Woodrow Johnson recalled, "if one of them died, the other one had to move." Workers saw this as callous and disloyal.[18]

A similar transition took place at the Henderson Mill when Joe Farmer became superintendent. Farmer replaced Harry Bunn, whom card grinder Lloyd Wilkins described as "a real nice old man" who "was there to help" when they needed him and would "do you a favor anytime." The price for nurturing this type of adulation, however, had been a mill that did not meet the standards of efficiency now demanded by top officials. Bunn died before the renovations, so he was not forced out, but he remained a reference point for workers after the new superintendent was hired.[19] Luther Jackson, who swept floors at the time, remarked that the new management was almost completely unresponsive to the workers' concerns. He recalled a conversation he had with General Manager John D. Cooper Jr. regarding the new supervisory personnel. "'There weren't no need to go to your plant manager,'" Jackson remembered explaining to Cooper. "'The worker was wrong.'" Comparing the mill with a fascist state, Jackson said to Cooper, "'What Hitler was doing over yonder, you were what Hitler was. This company was fast going to that.'"[20]

"The only salvation the people had was to organize," recalled Luther

Jackson, assessing the situation in retrospect. Yet that was by no means an easy or certain course of action. Although unionization had not been warmly embraced by managers or governments in any part of the country, it had encountered especially severe hostility in the South. The wave of post–World War I labor conflict, the massive strikes of the late 1920s, and the General Strike in 1934 had all demonstrated the workers' desire for change, yet each conflict, including the one in Henderson in 1927, had failed to create a union toehold in the region, and striking workers had often suffered immensely. It was not necessarily a logical step in reasoning, then, for southern workers to think that unionization was remotely possible, let alone a positive solution.

Despite past failures, the newly formed Textile Workers Organizing Committee (TWOC) had launched a southern campaign in April 1937. This time organizers could rally around the National Labor Relations Act of 1935, which in theory gave workers the legal right to determine, free from employer interference, whether or not they wished to join a union. At mill after mill throughout the South organizers heard workers complain about the stretch-out. Within a few months, 65,000 mill workers in the Carolinas, Georgia, and Alabama had signed union pledge cards, and the TWOC had secured nine southern contracts covering 5,000 hands. But organizers continued to face harassment, often violent, by local antilabor forces, who could easily kindle many workers' justifiably deep suspicions of what joining a union could do for them. In any event, before the drive could make further headway, the deep recession of 1937 and 1938 greatly reduced the flow of union dues, which came primarily from organized northern mills, forcing severe cutbacks in the southern organizing staff.[21]

Nevertheless, the campaign continued and appeared to score some stunning election victories. In late 1938 and early 1939, workers at Proximity Prints and the Revolution Cotton Mill, both of which were in Greensboro, North Carolina, and belonged to the mammoth Cone Mills chain, voted in favor of the TWOC after surviving organizational strikes. At about the same time, hands at six plants in the Burlington Mills empire voted to organize. The TWOC also won elections at all three sites in the Erwin Cotton Mills chain. Each of these victories might have created beachheads in hostile territory, demonstrating to other workers in the region what a union could accomplish.

In none of these cases, however, was the TWOC able to negotiate contracts with mill managers, who refused to recognize the election results and continued to harass, evict, and discharge union supporters. The southern-based industry publication *Textile Bulletin* encouraged mill owners to resist at this stage. "While mills are required to recognize union organizations as collective bargaining agencies, when employees have so voted," the journal editorialized, "there is no requirement that any contract be signed and we always counsel against signing."[22] Occasionally the NLRB would charge mill owners with unfair labor practices, but enforcement was another matter. In most cases, employer intransigence worked and resulted in no penalties.[23] "Time is always on the side of the employer," a regional NLRB director wrote board members in 1939. "There is really no incentive to the employer to settle when he may avoid his duty under the law for such a long period, for the most part with impunity."[24] Faced with such difficulties, by 1941 the Textile Workers Union of America (the TWUA, which had been formed in May 1939 when the TWOC and a number of United Textile Workers locals merged) had organized only 28,000 employees out of a southern textile workforce of over 400,000. Fewer than 500 out of some 200,000 North Carolina millhands worked in mills with bargaining agreements.[25]

It seemed possible that the peculiar labor market during World War II might help reverse the TWUA's fortunes in the South. Despite heavy demand for textiles and plenty of full-time work, total employment in the southern textile industry steadily dropped after December 1942, and some government war orders went unfilled. With many millhands having entered the armed forces and others having left for jobs in higher-paying defense plants, there was a scarcity of white cotton mill workers for the first time since World War I.[26]

Another factor in the union's favor was that beginning in January 1942, with the creation of the National War Labor Board (NWLB), the federal government expended more energy than usual ensuring fair union elections and promoting authentic collective bargaining. Arguing that what had once been routine, legal challenges to union organizing and negotiations were now a "peacetime luxury which must be sacrificed in the interests of war production," the NWLB, serving as the umpire of last resort, embarked on its mission to expedite the resolution of all disputes through grievance procedures and arbitration. The NWLB had the power to review unsettled grievances and to enforce its decisions directly, bypassing the court system, where the appeals processes were inevitably prolonged. The NWLB could even order managements to sign contracts with specific provisions the businessmen found unpalatable. The National Labor Relations Board did not disappear during the war, but if its functioning, especially in certifying the results of unionization elections, seemed too slow to either party or allowed the disruption of war production, the NWLB could step in and order an immediate resolution.[27] Even given the under-standing that the NWLB was ultimately more interested in strike-free industrial production than in workplace democracy, the TWUA had rea-son to believe that the federal government would be more than mildly on its side in protecting mill workers who attempted to organize themselves and bargain with their employers.

For unions, however, the rewards of more immediate federal interven-tion came with a price. In December 1941 leaders of AFL and CIO unions, including the TWUA, signed a no-strike pledge, eliminating what for many union members had been the most potent tactic for gaining lever-age over employers. Because they disrupted production, strikes would no longer be tolerated. CIO leaders initially took a dim view of compul-sory arbitration, arguing that by abandoning their right to strike, a "key-stone of liberty," workers were heading toward "involuntary servitude."[28] Unions that cooperated with the no-strike pledge, however, benefited from a NWLB-mandated maintenance-of-membership clause, which was intended to guarantee union security by ensuring that new employees who did not renounce union membership would, after fifteen days, remain dues-paying union members for the duration of the existing contract.[29] Undoubtedly, for established union locals with a history of successful work stoppages the no-strike pledge must have looked like a step backward, one that took power out of workers' hands and demanded that they cast their fates with allegedly impartial arbitrators.[30] For unorganized workers, however, which included the vast majority of southern textile workers and a sizable number in the North as well, the very possibility of voting for a union without fear of recrimination, and having any kind of voice in the resolution of grievances, could easily be perceived as extraordinary gains.

At first glance, the TWUA's national success during the war appears to prove that conditions were ripe for union organizing. Whereas in the two years before Pearl Harbor the TWUA organized 47,000 workers, dur-ing the following two years the union gained over 120,000 new members. TWUA membership peaked at 450,000 in 1945. When separated from this impressive picture of overall growth, however, statistics from the South told a different, familiar story. Despite relatively favorable conditions, the TWUA added only 42,450 southern members during the war, making a total of some 70,000 employees under contracts in the region out of a tex-tile workforce of nearly 600,000. Less than 10 percent of North Carolina's 200,000 textile workers were organized by the end of the war.[31]

The lack of southern success can be traced in part to the strategy of top TWUA officials. Efforts in the South prior to the war had been costly and had shown little return. Because the union's financial base rested almost entirely on membership dues, TWUA leaders saw the South as a sinkhole for the money raised primarily by northern locals. The South had long since eclipsed the North as the nation's largest cotton manufacturing region; by 1939 it held three-fourths of the industry's workers.[32] Nevertheless, the TWUA, intent on maintaining solvency during the war, committed twenty-nine organizers to cover Massachusetts, where workers had proven relatively easy to organize, compared to only twenty-four organizers for the area of expanding textile production south of North Carolina—an area that contained some 350,000 largely non-union workers.[33] Moreover, the TWUA leaders' long-term southern strategy did not take into account the most pressing needs of southern millhands. The union's goal was to eliminate the long-standing regional wage differential, in the hopes of preventing industry flight to the South, thus protecting the union's northern base. Therefore, organizers were instructed to convince southern millhands of the technical merits of demanding wage increases that would be sufficient to reduce the differential and protect northern union members. The TWUA officer in charge of southern organizing, George Baldanzi, spent much of the war in the trenches and realized that TWUA officials in the North were out of touch with the southerners they wished to recruit. Baldanzi found that southern millhands were concerned primarily with the stretch-out, yet he faced an uphill battle even within his own organization.[34]

Although the TWUA certainly suffered from strategic shortcomings, successful employer intransigence was still the most significant factor limiting the union's progress. Despite government support for free and fair elections, there was evidence of hard-line employer resistance, including the firing and intimidation of union supporters, in virtually every organizing campaign during the war. Cone Mills officials, for example, resisted elections, refused to recognize results, forced further elections, and dragged out contract negotiations for years—until after the war ended, in some cases. At Cannon Mills, the TWUA squeezed one contract out of mill officials, but only after a direct NWLB order. And Cannon had the final word: it refused to observe the contract. In yet another major example of employer opposition, after a majority of the 12,000 employees at the Riverside and Dan River Mills in Danville, Virginia, voted for the TWUA in June 1942, it took more than a year, even with NWLB intervention, for union negotiators to extract a contract from the company's officials. Taking intransigence to drastic extremes, Burlington Mills managers in North Carolina closed two plants in 1943, in the middle of the wartime boom, rather than obey an NWLB directive to sign contracts.[35]

Employers could risk ignoring NWLB orders because the agency was swamped with more disputes than it could possibly handle—as many as fifteen thousand per month by the winter of 1943. Attempting to expand its problem-solving capability, the NWLB opened regional offices in late 1943, but the flood of unresolved grievances remained a great burden, and long delays were common.[36] A representative of the Fourth Regional War Labor Board in Atlanta noted in August 1944 that in less than a year they had ruled on 19,615 disputes involving wage adjustments alone and still had a backlog of nearly 1,500 cases.[37] All this work was in addition to monitoring basic union elections throughout the Carolinas and Georgia. Because the NWLB's attention was scattered in many directions and its main emphasis was still on maximizing production, most mill managers who strongly resisted unionization were successful.

It was in this context, during the summer of 1942, that a number of workers at the Harriet and Henderson Mills first contemplated organizing a union. Unfortunately, there is no detailed information, or even a comprehensive list, that could tell us more about Harriet and Henderson workers in 1943. Because the military had siphoned off a large number of male employees, it appears that women comprised over 50 percent of the workforce, up from closer to 40 percent shortly before the war. It appears that most were at least in their mid-twenties and married.[38] It appears that the same was true for male workers, although military service created numerous openings for younger and older job-seekers. It seems certain that by 1943, despite the disruptions of war, most mill-village residents were well-rooted in the community and saw their futures linked with the Harriet and Henderson Cotton Mills.

The precise origins of the organizing campaign in Henderson also remain somewhat murky. It seems certain that the effects of modernization provided the most inspiration, yet concrete steps still had to be taken for anything to happen. The TWUA usually started organizing campaigns where workers had already taken some initiative, whether through a letter, a phone call, or a response to a leaflet drop.[39] But there are no documents to tell us which Harriet and Henderson workers first contemplated a union, when the first words were spoken about the possibility, or whether the hands initiated contact with the TWUA. It seems that in terms of numbers the twelve hundred Harriet and Henderson workers should have been an attractive target for the TWUA, but located on the northern fringes of the textile belt, these mills would probably not have served well as "demonstration centers" for the region. As understaffed as they were, union leaders would probably have given priority to larger mills, like those in Greensboro, or further west, like those in Gaston County.

Workers' memories provide clues about the origins of the campaign. Woodrow Johnson, for example, had never thought about the need to alter his relationship with his bosses until the new superintendent, James Proctor, tried to impose restrictions on his personal life. George Nipper, who helped organize the Harriet Mill, insisted that for him, it was the "overseers in there that weren't treating some of the help like they ought to. That's what got me in it." Rachel Jones, who was a teenager at the time, observed that her parents could not rest easily with the changes in the mill. "The people here had just been mistreated, weren't done fair, about the work, the jobs. And the Coopers that owned the mill, they just acted like they owned the people," she recalled. "I mean they brought the union here themselves. They were the cause of it."[40]

It was common for workers to experience the problems of modernization indirectly. Rachel Jones's parents were always treated fairly, she recalled, but "it was a lot of them that they didn't treat right, and Daddy couldn't see nobody harm nobody or do nobody wrong." Woodrow Johnson recalled that although he experienced few problems in his department, many of his fellow card-room hands knew friends and relatives in other departments where conditions were different. "In the spinning room and the winding room," Johnson noted, "them overseers up there, they worked on them women." As a result, some of the most outspoken organizers came from departments with the least objectionable supervisors.[41]

Several workers recalled discussions in the summer of 1942 about the possibility of organizing. Clayborne Blue, for example, recalled that some of the hands had "just started organizing when I went into the Navy in July '42."[42] They determined that it would be too risky to contact other hands while on the job. "You weren't allowed to talk to them in the plant," explained Woodrow Johnson, who was twenty-five at the time. "You had to get on outside." These discussions took place mainly in homes, without the presence of union organizers. It seems that union representatives appeared in the Harriet mill village in November 1942, well after some workers say the organizing began. The professional organizers encouraged private conversations between mill villagers, viewing them as their main recruitment strategy. Roy Faulkner, who was about thirty years old at the time, recalled how one TWUA organizer, Thomas Moore, would rely on the mill workers to get the job done. "He would talk to certain ones that was interested and ask them" if they would help. " 'Well, I'll help you do so much of it,'" somebody would respond. "This one over there, he'll help you so much. That one over there, I'll do so much. And they just said, well, all right, let's see if we can't get organized."[43]

Although it is unclear how many workers participated in the first wave of visits, it would not have taken many to cover the entire workforce. Since almost all of the hands lived close together in the mill village and most had webs of family relationships, by talking only to immediate neighbors and kin a union supporter could reach a significant percentage of potential members. Virtually every department had at least a few people whom workers recognized as strong union advocates. Recalling the early days of the campaign, George Nipper, who was thirty-one years old in 1943, said that he and the others would "get out and talk to people, tell them what good they could get out of the union. Go house to house, sign them up." Esther Roberson, thirty-three at the time, circulated petitions. Harvey Harris, who was twenty-four years old in 1943 and not active in organizing the union, remembered being visited by fellow workers. "The ones that was interested in it, they just talked to you, asked you how you felt about it. 'Would you like to join a union?' They'd try to give you the good points of it."[44]

After several weeks spent testing the waters, Harriet Mill union supporters and the TWUA's Moore decided to host a formal union meeting at a store run by Woodrow Johnson's parents in the mill village. Rachel Jones remembered that her father, although not firmly committed to the union, attended that first meeting. "He was just sort of half going up there, and knowing that that was going to help the people." Roy Faulkner remembered that a friend of his, Roger Norris, convinced him to attend. Norris "got the word around," and they "all went over to the store." Faulkner recalled being "carried away with curiosity." This would have been the first opportunity for many of the workers to see a bona fide TWUA organizer. The meeting itself was rather low-key. "Had some singing, and had a little entertainment," Faulkner remembered. "Then this man he got up, and let it be known what he was after. And they just taken on it from there."[45]

After the first meeting proved successful, the union scheduled more. Music and dancing highlighted the evenings. Woodrow Johnson recalled that they hosted "a dance up there about once a week" featuring local string bands. Amid the festivities, organizers made brief pitches for the TWUA. "More or less, you'd tell them to make up their own minds," Johnson recalled, explaining the union's strategy. "You didn't talk people into it, but when they'd come there, they knew that we was throwing the dance. They knew what we was throwing it for. They knew that to start with. That's what they come there for. They come on their own. And we'd get a few to sign the union cards at the dances."[46]

Almost incredibly, given the history of unionization attempts throughout the South as well as at these mills, Harriet and Henderson management offered only slight resistance to the campaign. Many years later, Marshall Cooper, who in 1943 was both the company's secretary and a member of the board of directors, contemplated the reasons for such weak opposition. "One of the main things," he said, was that "they had a lawyer here on our board, and he just thought that was a thing coming on."[47] Although Cooper declined to discuss the subject further, it appears certain that the lawyer was Bennett Perry; and as the largest stockholder outside of the Cooper family in the privately owned company, Perry had some influence in major decisions.[48] Perry's position on unionization in 1943 can be inferred from the glowing tribute he paid, seven years later, to the state's most prominent liberal public figure, University of North Carolina president Frank Porter Graham. Graham had taken highly controversial public stands as a moderate in race relations and as an advocate for unions that promoted the use of formal grievance procedures to resolve conflicts. He had served on both the National War Labor Board and its predecessor, the National Defense Mediation Board, supporting unions that demonstrated "responsible leadership."[49] At a Graham campaign rally in Henderson, Bennett Perry, who had received both his undergraduate and legal degrees from the University of North Carolina in Chapel Hill, introduced Graham as "the greatest man North Carolina has ever produced." Explaining that "he had never known a man with more courage and determination to fight for the right, for better schools, churches and better living," Perry said that Graham was a "champion of the people" who "overshadows any man who has run for the Senate in my generation."[50] During World War II, Graham promoted collective bargaining as the workable future for labor relations; Perry apparently believed him and advised the Coopers not to resist what he thought was inevitable.

Graham and Perry viewed collective bargaining agreements as a step toward modernized, progressive management. Indeed, collective bargaining had the potential to alleviate several pressing problems. Given the declining attractiveness of cotton mill work, by accepting unionization management stood a better chance of retaining its better employees and perhaps even attracting more capable workers. The labor shortage had forced managers to leave some positions unfilled and to hire a number of people who were not able to meet production standards.[51] Throughout early 1943 it had been impossible for the Harriet and Henderson Mills to maintain peak production. This was a major disappointment, because there was a ready market for every spool of yarn they could ship.[52] In addition, the TWUA's no-strike pledge would in theory assure uninterrupted production, which was essential for procuring the government contracts on which the mills depended so heavily. It also seemed possible that if workers were more contented, having recourse for their grievances, production might become more efficient. Moreover, the Harriet and Henderson Mills would already be fairly well adjusted to collective bargaining by the time competing companies accepted reality and signed union contracts.

Although it might now be difficult to imagine, during the war it really was possible to detect evidence of the inevitability of collective bargaining in the South. Forty miles to the southwest, in Durham, Kemp Lewis of the Erwin Mills had indeed relented under pressure from the National Defense Mediation Board and in 1941 had signed contracts covering some 5,500 workers at the company's three sites. Two years earlier, national officers of the Marshall Field Company had relented under direct orders from the NLRB and signed agreements covering 3,000 workers in five mills about fifty miles west of Henderson.[53] Just across the Virginia border from the Marshall Field plants, over 12,000 employees at the Riverside and Dan River Mills, with the NWLB on their side, endured a year of intense opposition before extracting a contract from mill managers.[54] Even the recalcitrant Cone Mills chain succumbed to government pressure in at least two cases. In January 1943, by the time the organizing campaign had become evident in the Harriet Mill village, the NWLB ordered Cone management to explain its refusal to sign contracts. It appeared certain that the board would order the Cone Mills to sign standard contracts—it did, six months later—and Harriet and Henderson managers were probably taking note. Looking back, historians have found that even after signing contracts, Cone managers bargained as grudgingly as possible and quickly eliminated their unions after the war. In early 1943, however, it appeared just as likely that good-faith collective bargaining would take hold in that chain.[55] Representatives of the NWLB repeatedly warned industrialists that they would have to accept such negotiations as the reality of the future.[56]

It is possible that patriotism also played a role in Harriet and Henderson management's acceptance of union activity. During the war, large convoys of military vehicles routinely stopped civilian traffic on Henderson's main street on their way to Camp Butner, an army base located just over twenty miles west of town. Soldiers from Camp Butner spent much of their free time in Henderson, which made the war effort appear immediate and personal to local residents.[57] Union organizers in Henderson did all they could to link unionization with the war effort. "It is sincerely to be hoped," they stated,

> that all parties, union and non-union, in the interest of the war effort and in consideration of the boys from Henderson who are sacrificing their all on the battle fronts, will join into one big happy family, and will at once enter into an era of complete co-operation to attain the present basic aim of the C.I.O. and of all good Americans—to keep the war materials flowing constantly and [incessantly] toward the battle fronts, so that those boys shall never be in want.[58]

Whatever their precise motivations, Harriet and Henderson managers allowed their workforce the freedom to discuss the merits of unionization without penalty. It is impossible to overestimate the importance of the company's behavior in determining the fate of the campaign. Workers were also emboldened by the fact that the company no longer owned their houses. Although management viewed selling the houses as an economizing measure, it also eliminated a powerful disciplinary weapon. No longer could managers evict assertive workers from their homes as they had threatened to do in 1927.[59]

It is not surprising, however, that the thought of being associated with an organizing effort still frightened many hands. This was, after all, essentially the same top management that had been in charge in 1927, and the news from most organizing campaigns throughout the South ominously resembled the familiar past. Moreover, the company demonstrated just enough interest in the campaign to convince many workers to remain surreptitious. Woodrow Johnson noted that "a company man" could usually be seen outside the building where the union held its weekly dances. Johnson recalled that while local organizers "never paid no attention to it," many others "were scared to go" because the company representative would "check to see who come." This mild intimidation reduced the number of signatures on union cards, which were required to qualify for an election, but those who did not sign were not necessarily opposed to the union. "There was a lot of them that was going to vote for us that wouldn't sign on account of the way their bosses talked to them," Johnson emphasized. "They were scared to sign. Thought they'd lose their jobs." Many of those same people spoke privately with local organizers about how they would vote if an election were held. "I had people to come to my house," Johnson recalled, and they would explain that "they wouldn't put their names on a union card, not before it was organized. But if they ever got it organized, that they would vote for it, and then they would join."[60]

Although management successfully deterred some workers from supporting the union in public, there is no evidence that company officials carried out any of their implied threats. There was never any direct interference with union-related functions, and management never threatened to close the mills or move to another location if their workforce voted to organize. Because of this uncommon restraint, TWUA organizers Thomas Moore and David Moose called the Harriet Mill campaign "the most cooperative contest, on the part of all concerned," that they "had ever witnessed."[61]

When over 50 percent of eligible workers had signed union cards, the TWUA petitioned the National Labor Relations Board, which scheduled an election for 23 March 1943. Although the strongest union supporters anticipated a triumph, many of the other workers on whom they were counting for support must have noticed uncertainty creeping into their thoughts as it came time to vote. "I don't know how to explain it," Roy Faulkner recalled. "When you go in there and vote to organize a union, you don't know whether you're doing the right thing or not. That's exactly the way I felt."[62] A TWUA organizer in the South recalled that it was common for workers to have similar reservations: "Sometimes a person will be for you, and not move because there's a nagging doubt in the back of their mind that maybe they're wrong. I think there's people who believe they're going to vote for the union until they get in the booth. Then they think, 'Am I making the right choice?'"[63]

Despite any ambivalence among workers, though, the local union organizers proved correct. Late in the afternoon on the day of the election, Albert L. Lohm of the NLRB announced that Harriet Mill workers had voted 409–120 in favor of creating TWUA Local 578.[64] TWUA officials on hand immediately called a mass meeting in the South Henderson mill village and cautioned workers to temper their enthusiasm over the election results. After all, many southern millhands who had won election victories had failed to extract contracts. "All of us was tickled to death," Woodrow Johnson recalled, "but we didn't have no celebration."[65]

As TWUA representatives began negotiations for a contract at the Harriet Mill, they also began efforts to organize the Henderson Mill. Although largely uninvolved in the Harriet campaign, Henderson Mill workers were aware of developments in the other village, and a number of them greeted the TWUA organizers at a small store in their mill village. "I reckon there was twenty-five or thirty of us down there," recalled

Luther Jackson, who was about thirty years old at the time. One of the organizers began by noting that Harriet Mill workers had seen fit to vote the union in. Jackson remembered interrupting him, promising that the union "won't have no trouble over here." Next, according to Jackson, one of the organizers asked him,

> "Is anybody up here afraid to sign a union card?" I says, "No sir, I'm not. I just come back from the service, and they learned me not to be scared of nothing." So I signed the first union card. And he said, "Will anybody here take a book?"—you know, a little book like you sign up the membership in—I said, "You give me some." He handed me one. I said, "Give me about twenty-five of them." And he said, "What do you . . . ?" I said, "Because each one of these books is going into one of my friend's hands." Well he came back in about two weeks, said, "How are you doing?" I said, "Pretty good, but I need a few more books."

With such energetic local leadership and a continued lack of company opposition, the Henderson Mill campaign progressed quickly. After thirty days, local organizers had collected over 300 signatures from the 564 eligible workers and were therefore ready for an election. National Labor Relations Board officials returned to Henderson on 28 June 1943, and the results showed 352 workers voting to form TWUA Local 584, and 124 opposed.[66]

Although Jackson and the rest of the organizers had been certain of victory, there was still a fairly large complement of nonsupporters among the workforce. Edith Adams, a twenty-nine-year-old Henderson Mill spinner in 1943 who later became a local union officer, had not been convinced by the arguments in favor of the TWUA. "My husband and I both voted against it," she recalled. "There was just beginning to be right much gossip about their principles and so forth, and we just thought maybe it might not be the best thing. We really didn't know what to do." How could any workers truly have known whether a union would be for the best? Few people working in the mills at the time had any experience with unions, and there were no organized cotton mills in the immediate area to observe for evidence. From much that workers had heard about organized labor, at least from nonunion sources, they could easily have concluded that a vote for the TWUA would mean the end of their careers or the end of their mill. There was plenty of concrete evidence from the region to substantiate that threat. Perhaps Edith and Raymond Adams voted no in order to protect their livelihoods. Edith Adams said of her husband, "He's always been afraid to take a chance, afraid he wouldn't be able to meet his obligations."

She apparently shared many of his reservations on union election day. The fact that there must have been many more workers with similar outlooks makes the overwhelming triumph for the TWUA even more remarkable.[67]

Given the intransigence of so many southern mill owners after elections, it is once again significant that the company signed an agreement with the Harriet Mill's Local 578 on 31 May 1943, just nine weeks after that mill's election and nearly a month before the vote at the Henderson Mill. On 7 July 1943, less than two weeks after their successful election, Henderson Mill Local 584 General Shop Committee members signed an identical contract with the company. Since they confronted the same top-level managers, Locals 578 and 584 agreed to bargain together when the contract came up for renewal or renegotiating. In day-to-day operations, however, the two locals operated independently.

These first contracts established the framework for altering worker-manager relations inside the mills.[68] Immediately after recognizing the union as "the sole and exclusive collective bargaining agency for the employees," each contract created a formal process for resolving disputes. First, in every department workers were to elect a shop steward to represent them in the initial stage of the grievance procedure. Whenever a conflict arose, the aggrieved worker and the shop steward were to attempt to settle matters with the department's foreman. If the parties failed to reach an agreement within two days, the employee and the shop steward were to submit a formal description of the grievance, in writing, to the local union's five-member General Shop Committee, which was elected by a majority vote of the membership. If a majority of the committee felt that the grievance had merit, the dispute would be discussed during regularly scheduled union-management conferences, held twice each month. If the General Shop Committee and company officials failed to reach an agreement, the local union was to request the assistance of a regional TWUA representative, who would negotiate directly with the president of the company. If the conflict remained unresolved after this stage, the union could submit a written demand for arbitration. If the two sides could not agree on an arbitrator, the contract authorized the American Arbitration Association to choose one. Arbitration hearings usually lasted a day or two and were similar to nonjury trials: each side would present evidence and cross-examine the opposing witnesses. The arbitrator's decision was to be "binding on both parties" and "conclusive of the controversy submitted." The cost of hiring an arbitrator, usually $100 per day plus expenses, was to be "borne equally by the Company and the Local Union."

The contract also addressed the primary concern of most millhands—

workloads. While granting management the right to change workloads, the contract specified that the new assignments had to be reasonable and that "in no event" could workers "suffer a reduction in average hourly earnings as a result of any work-load change."

As protection for the most economically vulnerable employees, the contract mandated a "guaranteed minimum hourly rate of pay for piece rate workers on a daily basis." Failure to meet production goals would not necessarily create immediate financial hardship. The agreement also committed the company to pay time-and-a-half "for all work in excess of eight hours in any one day," "time and one-half for work performed on the sixth consecutive day and double time for work performed on the seventh consecutive day." In addition, employees were to receive time-and-a-half for work performed on New Year's Day, the Fourth of July, Labor Day, Easter Monday, Thanksgiving Day, and Christmas Day, and regular full-time hands were to receive a week of paid vacation. As an added economic benefit, any worker who arrived at the mill only to be told to go home, which had been common, humiliating, and unnerving for many hands in the past, was to receive two hours' pay "at their regular rate."

New union members were particularly concerned about the contract's seniority and job security provisions. "Each employee," the contract stated, "shall be permitted to work at his or her job if it runs." This was a major break with the past. In the future, all layoffs and rehiring would be done with respect to seniority, "provided the worker retained or re-turned is qualified to fill the position."

Union negotiators agreed that there would be "no strikes, picketing, nor slow-down of work" for the duration of the contract. Workers who violated this provision, the agreement stated, "shall be discharged." In return for this standard no-strike pledge, the union received the National War Labor Board's plums, a maintenance-of-membership clause and the automatic deduction of union dues from members' paychecks.

These initial contracts in Henderson were at least comparable with, and often stronger than, other union agreements in the industry, in both the North and the South. Near the end of the war the U.S. Department of Labor published the results of a survey that analyzed 45 out of the 140 contracts nationwide in the industry. Over 85 percent of the agreements were with the TWUA-CIO; the others were with the UTW-AFL. About half of the employees covered by the contracts under investigation worked in the North. Every agreement in the study restricted strikes and "established formal grievance machinery" for settling disputes, and "all but one" contained provisions for some kind of arbitration.[69] The Harriet and Henderson contracts were certainly in line with these norms. They were exceptional, however, on several important issues. Only seven of the forty-five contracts surveyed allowed for automatic dues checkoffs, which was guaranteed in Henderson. Twenty-five contracts required individual authorization for deductions. Only "a number" of agreements, presumably very few, protected employees against a reduction in average hourly earnings with new workloads, and only "several agreements" protected temporarily transferred workers from a possible reduction in earnings.[70] The Harriet and Henderson locals were also among the very few, at least in the South, that were able to negotiate a guaranteed minimum wage for piece-rate workers.[71]

Even after these relatively strong contracts were signed, a major problem remained for the new unions. If the sizable minorities in both mills that had either voted against the union or had not participated in the election remained nonmembers, which they were entitled to do, they could seriously undermine the continued bargaining strength of the locals. Luther Jackson helped recruit the uncommitted in the Henderson Mill by pointing out the concrete differences in their working lives. "In sixty days' time I had done signed up them 123," Jackson recalled, referring to those who had voted no. Edith and Raymond Adams were among the late recruits. "We were going to receive the same benefits as those that belonged to the union," Edith Adams recalled. "We certainly didn't want to be a free-rider with anything, so we both joined, and paid our dues." Adams emphasized that she and her husband had made their own decision, based on their sense of honor and responsibility. "I don't think it was anything they said that caused us to join," she explained. "We joined of our own free will because we were receiving the same benefits as the ones that were paying, and we wanted to do our fair share."[72]

Not all skeptics were so easily persuaded, however. "I had one once in awhile that would be kind of hard," Jackson admitted. In such cases union workers did not hesitate to confront or isolate nonmembers. "Some of the shop stewards would put it on them. They just wouldn't have nothing to do with them. Let them know that if you worked in the plant there and you belonged to the union, you went along and paid your share, and everybody was just like one damn big, happy family." A refusal to join could seriously affect one's job performance. "If that [union] man got behind, needed a little help," Jackson explained, "they'd go over there and help him." In contrast, to nonmembers in need, those who had joined would say, " 'Buddy, you're going to have to tote your load by yourself. You ain't helping carry our load, we ain't going to help you carry yours.' " If nonmembers tried to file grievances, which they were technically allowed to do, Jackson recalled saying to them, "'What are you griping about? You ain't supposed to get none of it no way. You ain't paid for none of it. You ain't spent a dime to get this here.' 'Well, I work up here.' 'Well, you ought to help pay for your job then.'" The combination of tactics apparently worked, as both mills consistently had over 90 percent union membership.[73]

Even top managers expressed a certain amount of satisfaction with their decision to participate in collective bargaining. In October 1943, the board of directors noted that "for a long time production had been the chief concern of our mills and that during the past five weeks we had reached the peak, which is most unusual under present war time conditions." Moreover, Harriet and Henderson yarn "was enjoying a splendid reputation and was in much demand."[74] It appeared that unionization had indeed resulted in increased productivity and quality. In the spring of 1944, Bennett Perry traveled to Atlanta to observe the proceedings of the Fourth Regional War Labor Board. He reported back that he "was favorably impressed with the showing" of the Harriet and Henderson Mills "as compared with reports presented on other mills." Perry "was especially impressed with the display of harmony between management and labor in our mill."[75]

Harriet and Henderson's modernization program of the late 1930s and early 1940s reaped both enormous profits and a union. Since the remodeling coincided with the wartime boom, the profits would have been hard to avoid. But the successful unionization campaign was a different story. By doing very little to monitor or resist the organizing campaign, company officials helped create a climate of possibility in which workers voted decisively for collective bargaining, creating what would become two of the strongest TWUA locals in the South.[76]

3   **Initial Conflicts**
Equality, Ambiguity, and
Security of Livelihoods,
1943–1944

In July 1943 it was not clear to what extent the newly signed contracts would alter relations between workers and managers at the Harriet
and Henderson Mills. As it turned out, the first year with a union saw an
avalanche of grievances, which revealed much about the workers' motivations in voting for a union and their hopes for what organization might
mean. Three important themes emerge concerning the immediate impact
of unionization in Henderson. First, workers expected unionization to significantly reduce the distance between themselves and their supervisors
and to be treated as equals worthy of dignity and respect. Second, the
interrelated structure of the textile industry blurred lines of antagonism
and conflict so that many of the first grievances were directed at other

workers. And finally, despite these difficulties, most workers experienced immediate, substantial benefits after unionization, the most crucial of which was securing reliable access to a livelihood.

For years many workers had endured humiliation, abuse, insults, and petty rules because supervisors alone determined who would work each day. After unionization, however, millhands expected their supervisors to treat them quite differently. One example illustrates this clearly. When the Harriet Mill night superintendent, B. D. Redding, saw card-room hand Jessie Reid outside during his shift smoking a cigarette, Redding began "cursing at him and abusing him" for "25 or 30 minutes." Reid filed a grievance, which after several hearings resulted in a formal warning against the superintendent for using foul language. Never before had workers been able to talk back without risk, let alone reverse the traditional disciplinary hierarchy.[1]

A number of supervisors tried to carry on just as they had before. If managers had been able to insult and ignore the newly organized workers with impunity, they could have neutralized the union's influence and demoralized the membership. That was a significant fear for many TWUA officials.[2] In an important early confrontation, Rosa Suggs, a shop steward in the Harriet Mill spinning room, complained that her supervisor, Louis Vick, "refuses to reco[g]nize me as a shop steward." According to Suggs, Vick had been telling workers "that he was boss of that room and I did not have any thing to do with it." Even the foreman, Suggs testified, "told me that I did not have any thing to do with it[,] that Louis was boss just like he had always been and he ment for him to still be boss."[3]

In another early test case, a supervisor used previously uncontested intimidation tactics to try to prevent shop stewards from conducting legitimate union business inside the mill. "I went to the spinning room to see [shop steward] Eva Inscoe on Bussness," explained shop steward Walter Johnson, and "the Boss told me I would have to go back to my room[,] that it was aginst the rules to go out of the room you work in." Aware of his new rights, Johnson challenged his supervisor, Mr. Allen. "I told him that rule was not on the Board" where all work rules were posted, Johnson wrote, but "he said it was. I ask him to read it to me because I did not want to break a rule. But it was not on the Board." Managers could no longer bluff or coerce the hands into submission. Moreover, workers suggested punishments for supervisors who tried to subvert the new system. Johnson argued that "Mr. Allen should be told what the rules are" by top management. Since workers had been long accustomed to criticism and even tirades from their bosses, union members must have derived some satisfaction from seeing those bosses lectured on the correct way to do their job.[4]

Once they discovered that they could indeed speak out, union members challenged numerous arbitrary and demeaning rules that supervisors had once been able to enforce. Ever since the arrival of Superintendent Proctor, for example, plant rules had prohibited employees from talking on the job, even at the drinking fountain. Workers violated this rule, but they were often made to feel like they should try not to get caught. Walter Johnson, who transported bobbins of yarn from one department to another, had always enjoyed conversing with fellow hands along his route. Shortly after unionization, however, Johnson complained that a foreman tried "to stop me from talking to the Boys in the Twisting Room." Johnson argued that the union had not agreed to ban conversation in the mills. "I think this is unfair," Johnson wrote in his grievance, "because it takes all of my Liberty away from me." Johnson won his grievance. Such apparently simple results made an enormous difference to union members, because now workers could act like adults without fear of retribution.[5]

Workers and managers struggled over issues as basic as where employees could eat their lunches. Frank Faucette, who like Walter Johnson hauled bobbins around the mill, preferred for whatever reason to eat lunch in the winding room. Faucette's supervisor, however, ordered him to eat in the spinning room. The spinning-room shop steward argued that Faucette should be able to eat where he wanted, because he "works in one room as much as the other." Union members saw the second hand's stand as a petty exercise of authority—the sort of mistreatment they were no longer obligated to tolerate.[6]

Some workers were so successful at leveling relations with their supervisors that they openly demanded the removal of their boss. Less than a month after the contract was signed, workers in the Harriet Mill spinning room challenged their boss, Louis Vick—who, as mentioned above, had refused to recognize shop stewards—on the principle that work rules should be enforced fairly and equally. Apparently Vick had cracked down on what he considered to be excessive break time taken by certain spinners. He also caught one hand sleeping during her shift. Spinning-room workers argued that Vick was guilty of similar offenses and should be punished accordingly. Union members quietly documented Vick's frequent naps, and the supervisor discovered what it was like to be on the other end of the disciplinary hierarchy. "Some body told him that he had been reported," shop steward Rosa Suggs wrote. "He came to me and said he was not asleep that he just had his head laying down. I told him that his face & eyes were swolen and that any body knew that he had been asleep." Taking their grievance to limits that had formerly been inconceivable, the spinning-room hands called for Vick's removal as second hand, arguing "that he is not a fit man to work for."[7]

It is conceivable that top managers had complaints of their own against Vick; but in any case, the company did replace him. To local union members, this appeared to be a stunning example of how work relationships were changed by unionization. Not only did workers expect to be treated with dignity and respect; they even dared to demand the removal of supervisors who clung stubbornly to the old ways. There is no evidence that many supervisors shared Vick's fate, but a single incident like this certainly must have set an astonishing precedent, affecting worker-manager relations throughout the mills.

Nevertheless, it would be a mistake to assume that the arbitrary power of managers had been the source of all the workers' problems. In many cases, especially during the first months under the contract, workers filed grievances in which the offenders were other union members. It takes some familiarity with the peculiarities of the textile industry to understand how workers who were fresh from a fairly united showing against the company in the union elections could suddenly blame fellow employees for specific problems. Simply put, all jobs in a cotton mill were closely interrelated. The production process was sequential, so a problem in any stage of manufacturing affected every succeeding process. In addition, what was good for one individual was not always beneficial to others. If a worker in one department cut a few corners, even if that person intended only to make a little extra money at the expense of the company, the result was usually a heavier burden for somebody else in another part of the mill. Given this structural source of friction and the long history of suppressed conflict in the mills, it is not surprising that many of the first complaints were directed more at fellow workers than at management.

One of the first grievances to reach the written stage illustrates the complexities of textile production and the interrelatedness of cotton mill workers. The winding department combined bobbins from either the spinning room (single-ply yarns) or the twisting room (multi-ply yarns) into larger packages for shipment. The women (called winder tenders, or winders) who operated the equipment were paid by the amount of yarn they wound each day. The biggest obstacle to their earnings was the time it took to load (creel) their machines, because for that task they had to stop their winding frames. Undersized bobbins ran out sooner and had to be replaced more frequently, which greatly frustrated the winders. Therefore, the winders insisted that they should receive full bobbins of yarn that would run as long as possible, minimizing each winding machine's downtime.

Unfortunately for the winders, however, the workers (doffers) who unloaded (doffed) the bobbins that were sent to the winding room were paid by the doff and could thus make a little extra money if they removed the bobbins before they were full. Shortly after the contract went into effect, the Harriet #1 winders complained "that we have to wind bobbins that is doffed off not full." As a result, they argued, they were unable to earn their negotiated per-hour average.[8]

As it turned out, the small bobbins were not simply the fault of a few spinning-room doffers. Over the years, the entire spinning department, including the supervisors, had worked out a system that allowed for regular "short doffs," which is probably why the winders were so quick to file a grievance. It apparently made more sense, at least to the spinning-room employees and second hands, to allow the doffers to empty some frames early rather than have all the machines idle for creeling at the same time. That way, production in the spinning room could be maximized. Doffing early also allowed everybody in the spinning room to reach a convenient stopping point every eight hours. According to the winders' grievance, the second hand in the spinning room "said they had been doffing them that way and would continue to so the bobbins haulers," who transported the bobbins from spinning to winding, "could lay them up before change of shift." What seemed to be an orderly and sensible procedure for spinning-room bosses and workers brought hardship to the winders.[9]

In this grievance, top-level managers supported the winders. Superintendent Proctor once complained, "The company wants all bobbins run full at top and bottom and to make them as big as possible to maintain good yarn and less amount of waste." The gritty details of the production process, then, could place top managers in opposition to lower-level supervisors, and foreman against foreman, as well as worker against worker.[10]

Similar grievances arose throughout the mills. The Harriet #2 winders complained that "the bobbins we recive from twister room are not full. The supposed to be 8 & 12 oz. bobbins does not have but 6 & 9 oz. on them." The winding-room foreman refused to involve himself further in the case, which before the union era would have ended matters. Now, however, the winders could pursue a just settlement, but their targets were the workers in the twisting room. The twisting-room hands denied responsibility, arguing that many of their frames were simply not able to produce full bobbins. In the end, it did not matter to the winders whether other workers or the machines were at fault. "We the hands have begged & pleaded" for full bobbins, the winders wrote, "but they get worse." [11]

Just as workers in the different departments were interconnected, employees on one shift could affect the performance of their counterparts on another. One such case involved card-room hand Roy Parrish, who ran drawing frames that combined and stretched cotton from the carding machines and prepared it for spinning. Like the winders discussed above, drawing-frame operators were paid according to how much they produced, and their machines had to be stopped for creeling. Parrish contended that the person who ran his machines on the preceding shift was not sharing equally in the unproductive task of creeling the frames. "After being promised a fair deal from the Overseers and second hands I find my job in bad shape every night," he complained in early 1944. When a drawing tender started a shift with empty frames, no production could be made until the machines were creeled. Since the normal run of these machines seldom fit neatly into eight-hour shifts, it was assumed that every worker would occasionally encounter such an unproductive start to a day and that the burden would be shared over time. Therefore, if a worker consistently left "run-out" frames, that hand was probably dumping nonpaying work onto the next person who ran them. Parrish accused the worker on the preceding shift of not carrying his load, but he also blamed the second-shift supervisor for allowing it. "I want Mr. W. A. Bartholomew [second hand] to be made to cooperate and straighten out the job on his shift," he demanded. "I cant live on promises." [12]

There were similar ways to cut corners in the spinning room, and an early grievance about such practices resulted in severe discipline for the offending workers. For a spinning frame to operate efficiently, its rollers, which stretched the cotton until it was the proper thickness, had to be kept free from cotton lint and debris. Felt-tipped boards called "slats" or "clearers" collected much of the loose cotton, and each had to be cleaned, or "picked," regularly. Failure to clean them eventually resulted in clogged rollers and broken yarn. If a spinner neglected her cleaning, however, it was possible that her own production would increase and the impending disaster would affect someone on a later shift. Therefore, the job required a certain amount of cooperation by workers on all shifts. In July 1943 several spinners from Harriet #2 charged that their counterparts on other shifts were not doing their share of the cleaning. When the second hand, Mr. Allen, took action, his solution probably shocked those who filed the grievance, and it undoubtedly created more hard feelings within the department. The company issued formal warnings to the spinners on the other shifts who had neglected their cleaning. Warnings were very serious, because they could result in layoff or discharge, and it was possible that those who were warned were not lazy or inconsiderate but truly had difficulty keeping up with their jobs. So whether or not they had anticipated this result, by demanding clean spinning frames a group of union members had jeopardized the careers of some fellow employees.[13]

Workers continually faced problems that pitted hands against each other, and company officials often acted as referees. Spinning-room shop steward Lucy Collins represented a hand in her department who had what appeared to be a rather trivial complaint: "Charlie Harris complain that the doffer on the first shift puts the bobbins on so tight that he blistered his hands doffing them and has been to Mr. Gupton sevearl times about it." Mr. Gupton, however, did not want to be bothered. The most recent time Harris had complained, Gupton had "told him that if he did not want to doff them to quit." Harris blamed the second hand for allowing the problem in the first place, and then for being indifferent about Harris's hardship. Ultimately, though, the offending doffer bore the brunt of the punishment: he received a formal warning, and superintendent Proctor announced, "If he continues to do this, he will be dismissed."[14]

Millhands could now speak up about what bothered them, but as the previous examples demonstrate, protest could lead down unforeseen, distasteful paths. When the offending doffer mentioned above gave a bobbin that little extra twist, he may very well have been silently taking out his frustrations regarding his job or his supervisor. But the workers who suffered as a result of such actions often had neither the time nor the inclination to figure out the motivations of their fellow hands. The aggrieved workers wanted simply to run their jobs without unnecessary hassles. Ironically, a grievance could result in stricter supervision in other departments and severe penalties for other workers. In the case of the tightened bobbin, unless there was a hidden personal grudge it seems improbable that Charlie Harris would have equated his blistered hands with another person's livelihood. Such ambiguous outcomes solved some problems, but they did little to promote solidarity among the workers involved.

It appears, however, that in some instances particular workers were targeted by grievances because they had either refused to cooperate with fellow union members or failed to join the union. For example, card-room workers and winding-frame fixers had informally agreed to help each other handle increased workloads. On two of the three shifts the cooperative arrangement seemed to work well. A card-room worker would help the fixer keep the winding frames running, and in return the fixer would help in the card room. One winding-frame fixer, however, refused to reciprocate for Sam Johnson's assistance. "Never helps me catch my work up," Johnson complained.[15] Since fixers were near the top of the nonsupervisory hierarchy and were therefore not as likely as production workers to suffer the speedups and other indignities that had inspired the workers to organize, it is possible that the offending frame fixer, B. M. House, had also refused to join the union. Many fixers became union members, but even if House had joined, he was obviously unwilling to cooperate with the union workers who filed the grievance.

Company officials were happy to stand above what they considered to be a squabble among employees. Managers were even more pleased that the workers had taken the initiative to develop new work routines enabling them to handle higher workloads. So in an ironic alliance, the company supported the workers who had filed the grievance and ordered House to cooperate or lose his job. In a sense the card-room hands had won, but friction obviously existed between certain workers, and managers eagerly allowed these conflicts to work to their advantage.[16]

Some conflicts between workers had nothing to do with lack of cooperation or disagreements about the union but were instead the result of widely varying levels of skill in the same department. In the Harriet Mill card room, for example, the few experienced drawing-frame hands who were not in the military felt handicapped by inexperienced wartime replacements. Drawing-frame hands were paid according to the average production of each worker on a particular shift. This "group rate" system was advantageous when all of the workers involved had similar skills; it softened the blow for an individual who had a poor day, which could happen to the best of hands. With the wartime imbalance of experience, however, the senior employees argued that they were consistently subsidizing the others by doing a disproportionate share of the work, so they demanded to be paid on individual piece rates. "I want to be paid for what I produce," explained C. R. Rose, who had run drawing frames at the mill for seventeen years.[17]

It seems ironic that these workers were arguing in favor of individual piece rates. More often, such systems were perceived by workers as a means for the company to increase productivity by setting high quotas, which kept the hands' noses to the grindstone. Although the group rate might appear to be more democratic and cooperative than pay for individual totals, the more productive hands felt that they should be compensated, not penalized, for their skill and experience. Unfortunately for the experienced hands, however, there were no pertinent contract clauses to support them. Until their shiftmates improved, the veterans would continue to resent their low production.[18]

These examples illustrate the complexity of many formal grievances that workers filed after they organized a union. Because of the structure of the work process in the textile industry, many grievances were directed at fellow workers. Although these types of conflicts were common, grievance procedures were designed only to handle complaints against managers, so many disagreements between hands were never resolved through formal channels. When solutions were found, they often divided workers and must have hindered efforts to solidify the gains of unionization.

Despite the number of ambiguous grievances, most workers recognized the enormous benefits of unionization. Perhaps the most significant change involved job security. No longer would millhands work only at the discretion of their supervisors. In interview after interview, former union members emphasized the importance of that difference. "Your job, that was *your* job," explained Joseph Braswell. "If you had a regular job," Edith Adams noted, "and you reported in to work, you could work." Many variables—poor business conditions, machinery breakdowns, injury or illness—still affected the odds on steady, full employment. But with its seniority clause, its protection from unwanted transfers, and its leave-of-absence provision, the union contract offered protection from the arbitrary power that foremen once held.[19]

During the first months after unionization, both workers and managers tested the new job security provisions. Harriet Mill hand David Pulley, for example, refused to work an extra shift when his eight hours were up. (Pulley's supervisor had probably anticipated a shortage of employees for the following shift and asked a few hands to work sixteen hours straight rather than let machines stand idle.) Instead, Pulley went home, and he was fired. Before unionization, foremen could have fired any worker for refusing to "pull a double." As if nothing had changed, Superintendent Proctor argued in favor of dismissal: "This man refused to work. The only excuse (given later) was that his father had a birthday. This man did not give [a] reason when he refused to work." After unionization, however, workers did not require an excuse for refusing an extra eight-hour shift. They had only to report to work for their regular shifts Monday through Friday, and Saturday if the mill ran. Pulley had already worked the first shift, which fulfilled his obligation to the company. He therefore could not be fired for choosing to attend his father's birthday party rather than remain at work. Pulley won his case and returned to his job with no loss of seniority and with $24.70 for his lost time. A few months earlier he would have remained unemployed.[20]

Workers also tested the contract's leave-of-absence provision to see if they could really take time off for what they considered legitimate reasons without losing their jobs. In September 1943, Harriet Mill winder Majesty Johnson faced such a dilemma. She worked full-time, but an uncle who lived out of town was sick, and she wanted to be with family members. When Johnson requested an eight-day leave of absence, her foreman, Gupton, refused. Given the constant pressure from higher management to maintain production and the scarcity of workers during wartime, Gupton could certainly have been reluctant to lose a winder for a week. But despite her supervisor's refusal, Johnson felt that the family emergency left her no choice, so she took the leave anyway. When she returned, however, Gupton penalized her by refusing to let her work for an extra week. Perhaps Gupton had found a replacement for her position, or maybe he opted for punishment over production. Whatever Gupton's reasoning, Johnson successfully challenged her penalty, thereby establishing the right to leave work for compelling reasons and the right to reclaim one's job when willing and able. This case by no means settled the issue, but workers saw that by standing up to their bosses, they could realize the contract's potential for preserving job security.[21]

The union contract also guaranteed job security and seniority protection for women who took maternity leave. In the past, a new mother who was ready and willing to return to work often had to wait several months before a job became available and a foreman chose her to fill it. It was possible that she would be fortunate enough to reclaim a job immediately, but there was no certainty. Lila Mae Ellis recalled that after her first child was born, she was rehired quickly. Another time, however, she waited six months for an opening. The union contract eliminated such uncertainty by providing up to nine months of unpaid maternity leave with no loss of seniority.[22]

The contract also protected workers from arbitrary transfers inside the mill. Before unionization, if labor shortages occurred in any department, supervisors could order workers off their regular jobs to cover for absentees. While management saw this as a necessary prerogative to maintain production, arbitrary transfers could force employees to do jobs that they disliked because the work was difficult, unfamiliar, less well paid, or on a different shift. Also, transfers frequently disrupted carefully planned child-care arrangements. The union contract accommodated management's need to keep the machines running by allowing temporary transfers of up to one week, in case of "emergency," as long as the affected worker did not suffer a reduction in earnings. In any event, after a week she could return to her regular job.[23]

Like every other contract provision, however, the transfer clause had no concrete meaning unless management observed it in practice. The clearest challenge to this provision came barely a month after ratification. Madorline Pendergrass of the Harriet #2 spinning room had filled in on another job at her second hand's request. After several days she told her boss, "I wont able to run these set of sides," and she asked him "to put me back on my job." After a week, Pendergrass pointed to the contract's seven-day limit on temporary transfers. As she wrote at the time, "The answer he gave me [was] if I didn't want them sides it wont any thing for me to do." Take it or leave it: those had been the options before the union, and someone like Pendergrass might have endured the difficult job rather than risk antagonizing her boss and losing everything. By filing a formal grievance, however, Pendergrass successfully reclaimed her regular job.[24]

Workers sought protection from transfers for a variety of reasons, including concerns about health. James Duke had undergone surgery to remove a kidney and had been told by his doctor not to work at jobs as strenuous as doffing. Nevertheless, his supervisor ordered him to doff. Duke refused, and he was disciplined. "I explained to him why," Duke wrote in his grievance. "He incisted that I doff that day anyway." Duke offered to bring a note from his doctor if the company would not trust his word, but after discussing the grievance with the local shop committee, Superintendent Proctor conceded that a person's health, at least in this case, ought to take precedence over complete managerial flexibility. Duke "would not have to doff no more," Proctor said. Small victories like this were extremely important. Prior to unionization, supervisors were not obligated to consider a worker's health when allocating labor.[25]

In addition to gaining protection from undesirable job changes, workers could initiate transfers for positive reasons. In contrast with the pre-union days, when foremen decided who would fill vacant positions, the job bidding procedure contained fairly clear and consistent guidelines. Choices were to be made with strict adherence to seniority and qualifications. Just as before, there were always winners and losers in the competition for certain jobs, but by all appearances, workers never strongly opposed hiring decisions as long as seniority was observed.[26] Personal and family considerations often motivated workers to seek security in a different job. Many parents worked separate shifts to accommodate their children. Some workers opted for jobs that they liked less than others simply to work on a particular shift. "I used to oil [machines] from 2 to 6 o'clock in the morning," explained one worker who transferred to a position that paid less and was more strenuous, "[but] I wanted to get a job on first shift so there would be some one home with my daughter at night."[27]

At first union members closely watched all transfers and job bidding to ensure fair play. Shop steward Walter Johnson, for example, complained that four employees had put in bids for an opening in his department, but when he went to see who would receive the position, the foreman "would not tell me." Since all placements were to be made above the table, Johnson argued that his overseer "broke the agreement that the Company made with the Union." Under pressure, the company agreed that shop stewards should be informed of bidding results within eight hours after job notices were removed from bulletin boards.[28]

Union members in all departments spoke up for what they thought was fair. On behalf of the first-shift yard hands, who were black, Local 584 shop committee members, all of whom were white, once opposed management's plan to have yard workers stay until 4:00 P.M., an hour after their shift officially ended. Besides forcing these particular union members to stay well beyond anyone else on their shift, that schedule would have conflicted with the working hours at a nearby tobacco-stemming plant, where many of the yard hands' wives worked. Arguing that this would create numerous child-care difficulties as well as a violation of agreed-upon first-shift hours, union members persuaded management to give up its plan.[29]

By forcing the company to comply with contract provisions, union members could effect remarkable changes in their lives. Within the first few months after ratifying their contract, fired workers were reclaiming their jobs and even receiving pay for the time that they had lost. Others were successfully resisting temporary transfers that threatened their health, and all of them understood that emergency transfers would last no more than a week. In addition, workers could actively pursue vacant positions with the certainty that the process would be fair and consistent. The transition from arbitrary power had not always been smooth, but there was no mistaking the enormity of the difference.

Yet despite clear, early victories, union members could never take any of the basic contract protections for granted. The threat of arbitrary transfer, layoff, or dismissal never disappeared. In May 1948, for example, Local 584 member Charlie Lowry, who had worked at the Henderson Mill for forty-eight years, lost his job for refusing to perform extra duties demanded of him by his supervisor. Although the contract contained provisions for adjusting workloads, occasionally the company found that process too burdensome. Lowry objected to his boss's request because he felt that his regular assignment was already nearly impossible to complete. His refusal to perform added tasks had not been because of laziness, he argued, or an unwillingness to pitch in and cooperate. "I said, Mr. Keen, I can't do it," Lowry testified. "He said, Oh, yes you will too. I said, Mr. Keen, go get the Shop Steward." In response, according to Lowry, Keen "said he didn't care anything about either the Shop Steward or the Union. He said, I had to do it or quit." Indeed, Lowry was dismissed. Local 584 shop committee member Raymond Wynn noted the danger in Keen's actions. "It seems like to me here that he don't want to go by the Union rules—about anything—he just wants them to do like he wants to do and not have no rules at all."[30]

At stake for both parties were important principles—the same ones that supposedly had been hashed out five years earlier, when the union contract first took effect. Could the company get away with arbitrary assignments by demanding the flexibility to meet immediate needs as they arose? Could workers afford to stand up for themselves when the company violated the union contract, or would the assertion of one's rights result in unemployment? No case could definitively answer any of those questions, but that did not diminish the importance of any individual settlement. As a result of filing a grievance, Lowry reclaimed his job but received no compensation for the several weeks of work he missed before his case was settled. Although he had reestablished his link with his livelihood, Lowry had also suffered much pain. "You all are so chinchy," Lowry lectured company officials. "I don't think it is right for me, a company as strong as this, and as little money as I make[,] to lose that time I been out."[31]

In addition to maintaining protection from arbitrary dismissals, workers also occasionally found it necessary to reassert their rights regarding transfers. Thirteen years after unionization, Harriet Mill winder Venie Gupton, who had recently undergone surgery, refused her second hand's request that she run spinning frames. While she was recovering, Gupton found her regular winding job tolerable, but the motions required to operate spinning frames were different and made her very uncomfortable. "It is harder to spin," she explained. "It hurts my side to pull and lift. . . . You have to reach higher in spinning." When Gupton refused to spin, her supervisor sent her home.[32]

Under heavy pressure to maintain full production, and apparently short on spinners, the supervisor understandably felt frustrated when confronted with what he saw as Gupton's stubborn lack of cooperation. "If she is able to wind, she is able to spin," Superintendent Proctor concluded, defending her suspension. Would managers be allowed, in their quest for maximum yarn production, to assign workers arbitrarily, forcing them to lose either income or their health? Gupton successfully challenged that managerial prerogative and received pay for the time she had been forced to lose. The conditions that gave rise to such arbitrary commands never disappeared, however, so neither did the need for recourse.[33]

One of the most dramatic examples of a worker confronting a boss's arbitrary demand occurred in 1956 and involved another Harriet Mill winder, Esther Roberson. Roberson and a male coworker were "yarn stampers": they identified yarn by size, type, and weight just prior to shipping. Yarn stamping was a strenuous task, often requiring both workers to push crates weighing five hundred pounds or more. In an attempt to cut costs, however, the company made yarn stamping a one-person job. Since she had more seniority than her partner, Esther Roberson had to work solo. The job was more than she could handle alone, and to make matters worse she developed health problems, so she took advantage of an opportunity to bid for a job as a winding-frame tender. Roberson won the bidding, but as was common in these situations, there was not somebody immediately available to run the job she left. Consequently, Roberson's supervisor occasionally insisted that she stamp yarn rather than run her winding frames. As her health worsened, however, Roberson refused to stamp yarn, and for that reason she was indefinitely laid off. Roberson filed a grievance. "I think that I have been treated wrong and I will contend it until I get it right," she told her managers.[34]

The company interpreted Roberson's refusal to be a clear case of insubordination that threatened the production process. Managers claimed that Roberson had no legitimate medical excuse and ought to have been more cooperative.[35] If yarn were not stamped it could not be shipped, and before long there would be no place to store the finished product. President John D. Cooper noted that by refusing to stamp yarn Roberson "could have shut down the whole winding room and could eventually shut the whole mill down."[36] According to the contract, management had the right to make emergency transfers, and the company felt that Roberson had defied that clause.

While arguing her case before the shop committee and company officials, Roberson emphasized the enormity of the impact on a worker when the company decided to pick a fight like this. "Mr. Peck didn't treat me right," Roberson began.

He hasn't got a hand up there that is any [more] regular than I am. My p[er]sonnel will show that. I work regular. I work when I really should be at home. I can't do something that I know I can't. When I get in the bed sick, he is not coming down there and tend to my children and wait on me, and he is not going to pay my doctor's bill. I hope and pray that nobody don't never make it as hard for his wife as he has for me. I hope he has the best of health. He has sure made it hard for me.[37]

After having been out of work nearly four months, Roberson won her case through arbitration. The arbitrator made his decision after visiting with Roberson's doctor, who confirmed that she had suffered a fairly serious internal injury. In return for her perseverance, Roberson received retroactive pay for the entire time she was out, including time-and-a-half for the Saturday work she had missed. Roberson's check totaled $469.55, which to her was an astronomical sum. In contrast, given that throughout this period managers routinely spent hundreds of thousands of dollars on new machinery, the check to Roberson was hardly more than a marginal line on the company's ledger, no matter how much they disliked paying it.[38]

Maintaining job security required constant vigilance and patience. There is no doubt that the grievance procedure was a slow, cumbersome method for resolving conflict. Nevertheless, most union members viewed cases like Roberson's as great triumphs. Roberson recalled a crowd of fellow union members waiting anxiously outside the building where her hearing was held; when she came out, many of them asked her if she thought she would win. To these workers the principle of job security was worth a drawn-out bureaucratic struggle.[39]

There were, however, significant threats to job security over which workers had little control. National economic recessions in 1949, 1954, and 1958 severely affected the southern textile industry and caused temporary layoffs and shortened workweeks. A more frequent threat to job security in the postwar era was the company's constant investment in new machinery. Jobs were lost with virtually every technological modification.[40] As part of the job-reshuffling process, workers with enough seniority in an affected department could "bump" or "pull" less senior workers on other shifts or in other departments who held jobs for which the senior worker was qualified. Therefore, technological progress often meant a painful sequence of layoffs throughout the mills. On several occasions workers who were eligible to bump others could not bring themselves to do so. Perhaps bumping would have meant unemployment for a friend or neighbor. Sometimes it was impossible to switch shifts and still fulfill other responsibilities. For example, Ophelia Short refused the opportunity to pull a worker off night shift because no one would have been available to care for her children.[41] Although many workers were bumped by other hands, there is no evidence of public conflict between workers as a result. The process created hardship, but as long as seniority was strictly observed, workers appear to have accepted it as something over which they had little control.

Fortunately for the workers in these villages, the Harriet and Henderson Mills expanded so much during the 1950s that the total number of available jobs in 1958 was virtually the same as that in 1950—somewhere between 1,000 and 1,200. In the short run workers probably found little consolation in the knowledge that there would probably be jobs available sometime in the future. Despite these harsh realities, though, jobs were far more secure after unionization than they had ever been in the past, and most union members considered that to be a monumental improvement in their lives.

4 A New (Old?) Work Ethic, 1943–1958

Although predictable access to a livelihood was indeed an important change for union members, millhands also wanted to control when they would work and when they would take time off. They developed a work ethic quite different from the nose-to-the-grindstone, overtime-seeking, income-maximizing images one might expect to see among postwar industrial workers. Union members adjusted their work schedules and incomes to accommodate individual and family needs. If necessary, a hand might try to work as much as possible, disregarding sickness, injury, and fatigue while leaving household chores undone. Others determined that they could afford to miss a day now and then. From the workers' perspective, time off was often necessary, whether to recover from an illness, run errands, go fishing, do housework, or just take a break. No matter what their circumstances, however, workers wanted the mill jobs to be there when they needed them. The workers' aspirations had not been dramatically changed by unionization. Before the union contract, however, employees understood that if they missed a day, no matter why, it was possible that they might never reclaim their jobs.

Unionization brought two crucial changes—a formal "utility-hand" system and a contractual procedure for obtaining emergency sick leaves—that protected workers as they fashioned their new work ethic. Basically, a pool of utility hands would be available to fill in for absent workers, and workers had to give their bosses advance notice if they would not be in. Based on these two rather innocuous provisions, union members developed a complex system of work-sharing, covering for absences and allowing themselves both to work as much as they wanted or needed and to have time for other duties and pleasures.

Before unionization, managers had arranged for a pool of "spare hands" to report at the beginning of each shift. After department foremen and second hands determined the number of absentees, substitutes were picked from this group of extra workers. Supervisors selected whomever they pleased and set the terms of employment. Consequently, spare hands could not predict how frequently they would work, and absent regular workers worried, justifiably, that spare hands might permanently replace them. Supervisors often allowed spare hands to stay on well after the absentee had returned to give the extra workers added incentive to report each day. Although it generally succeeded in keeping the machines running, the spare-hand system contributed to the instability and unpredictability of employment that workers feared.[1]

To modify that system, the union negotiated for a formal job category called "utility hand" that would be filled by regular employees with full seniority rights. Like the spare hands, utility workers reported to the mills every day, but available positions were always allocated on the basis of seniority and qualifications, with the most senior hand getting first pick of the openings. Utility hands received the standard pay for the positions they covered, which eliminated the former practice of spare hands underbidding each other for the chance to work, and once on a particular job a replacement was entitled to stay on it until the absent regular worker returned. Unlike before, the full-time hand retained rights to the job. Regular workers could be certain that utility hands were temporary helpers, not rivals.

The two union locals negotiated slightly different utility-hand systems.

At the Harriet Mill, company officials and Local 578 officers agreed to hire a specific number of utility workers for each department, presumably just enough to cover average expected absenteeism. Each of the extra workers, however, was allowed to work a full day no matter how many regular hands were absent. Redundant Harriet Mill utility workers, then, assisted regular employees and performed other tasks at their supervisor's discretion; they were full-time workers without specific jobs. At the Henderson Mill, the shop committee allowed managers to send extra utility hands home if there were insufficient openings. For their trouble, utility workers who were sent home received two hours' "reporting pay." Although the systems were similar, there was added pressure on Harriet Mill managers to minimize the number of utility hands, because an overabundance of labor there cost the company eight hours' pay per person rather than two.

The utility-hand system became an essential part of every worker's life. That is apparent from the extent to which it was used. Daily absenteeism was always well above 10 percent and often reached as high as 40 percent. To put it another way, each day between 100 and 400 of the roughly 1,000 regular hands at the two mills did not report to work. Harriet and Henderson managers seemed to accept, albeit grudgingly, that high absenteeism was almost unavoidable. "As a usual thing we have 20 to 25% of our regular assigned jobs as Utility hands," Superintendent Proctor once remarked. It came as a surprise to management, according to company attorney and major stockholder Bennett Perry, when "a very distinguished" industrial relations scholar visited the mills and remarked that "when absenteeism gets up to 5% it should be investigated and when it gets over 7% it is disturbing. He was dumbfounded," noted Perry, "to find that it ran as high as 25 to 30% here, but it does."[2] In only rare instances, however, did any individual's absenteeism rate approach the plantwide average. Virtually all the hands, it appears, regularly took some time off, which made the average absenteeism percentage quite high.

Women generally had the most pressing reasons to stay home. They worked full-time in the mills and were usually expected to handle the vast majority of household tasks and child care. Women were also more likely than men to miss a day of work to run errands. Few stores remained open into the evening to accommodate women who worked day shifts, so many chores could not be accomplished if one worked five or six days a week. When the burden of all these responsibilities seemed too great, the best alternative was simply to take a day off. "Working 6 days is pretty strenuous on us when we have to keep house, too," Henderson

Mill winder Mae Renn once explained to management. Renn noted that in her department, which employed mostly women, regular employees arranged with the utility workers to spread the jobs around so that each could work fairly regularly and have ample time for home duties. This informal work-sharing system benefited all the women. As Renn explained, "We have quite a few utility hands that don't get a chance to work unless we regular hands lay out a day and give them a chance."[3]

As a result of pressures like these, it was expected that women would have an absenteeism rate at least 10 percent higher than that for men. In 1950 a TWUA representative claimed that in spinning rooms "in most mills around here [North Carolina] you will find very few that average less than 40%" absent daily. Managers had to tolerate higher absenteeism rates in these departments, to some extent, if they wanted to employ women to spin and wind. There is no doubt, however, that the latitude enjoyed by workers relied on broader interpretations of contract protections than management had envisioned. "A lot of times we let people off on account of children," Superintendent Proctor once noted. "There is nothing in the contract about that, but we just try to keep enough utility help to accommodate the people."[4]

Health problems also contributed greatly to high absenteeism rates. There were always a number of hands with temporary illnesses like a cold or the flu, but many times the problem was chronic, like an inflamed muscle, arthritis, headaches, asthma, or fatigue. Although some of these conditions could be completely debilitating, at other times affected hands could make it through a shift if absolutely necessary. "I know some of the employees in [the] mill where doctors told them to stay out until they get well," Local 578 shop committee member Johnnie Carter once testified. "But they still come back to work. They felt like they are obligated." Many could not afford to lose the income. Nevertheless, under similar circumstances virtually everybody would occasionally opt to stay home to rest and recover. The heat, noise, and cotton dust inside a mill, as well as the sheer exertion of working, could be too much to bear. Johnnie Carter noted that often, if regular hands were "feeling bad and don't feel like working, they had rather stay at home than stand a chance of going up there and having to work because they [second hand] did not let the Utility hands run their jobs or would not let them off."[5] When asked if she had ever taken days off when she could possibly have worked, Harriet Mill hand Aliene Roberts admitted, "You know I did. Tell me somebody that worked up there that didn't."[6] Clearly, workers perceived days off for rest and recuperation as essential and unexceptional.

Some absences could be traced directly to injuries suffered while on the job. Although there had been some safety improvements by the 1950s, there were still many ways to injure oneself in a cotton mill. As Harriet Mill winder Lois Wilder once told company officials, "I heard a doctor in this town say that whenever a woman come up there from working in this mill, she didn't have to tell him. Her body was so broke down he could tell where she worked, before he even asked her."[7] Spinners and winders who "wrung off" the last of the roving and yarn bobbins often complained of wrists so sore that they could not continue, and doffers who lifted heavy loads could easily hurt their backs. Card grinders, who sharpened the blades that ripped apart the slightly processed cotton, could expect to lose a finger or two during their careers.[8] With so much whirring machinery in tight quarters, and with so many jobs that required leaning, bending, and quickness, there was always a contingent of employees with bumps, sprains, and bruises.

Whatever their degree of pain and disability, workers relied on the utility system and job security protections to enable themselves to recover while retaining full rights to their jobs. Management usually accommodated workers who had major injuries. Those with less severe symptoms, however, often decided on their own, sometimes against their bosses' wishes, to stay home for a day or two both to recover and to spread the work around.

Some workers were absent more than they might have been because they wanted to avoid unpleasant supervisors. A boss's personality and tactics still greatly affected workers' feelings about their jobs. One of the most annoying supervisory strategies seemed to be constant, critical surveillance of the hands. Lizzie Cleaton once explained to managers that in her department, second hand Bonnie Wagoner often monitored the time workers spent in the rest room. According to Cleaton, "Everytime anybody goes in there, he stands and times them to see how long they stay in there. If they go in to eat, that's about the only place we have to eat, he stands there and eats at the door where he can watch every one of them go in and out." This kept the hands on edge and caused frequent disagreements about the length of breaks. "I don't like for no man to stand around and watch me when I go to the rest room," Cleaton complained. "He got every hand up there hates him. They hate to go in to work. That's why all of them stays out so much."[9]

One could also expect surges of absenteeism immediately after workload increases, which were a constant feature in cotton mills during the postwar years. When workers considered new workloads excessive, they could challenge them through the grievance procedure, but such cases could remain unresolved for a year or more and even then could be decided in favor of the company. Staying home was a different sort of protest—safer than wildcat strikes, which were forbidden by the contract at the risk of immediate discharge—and the extra rest was often necessary to counteract the fatigue caused by the new routines. Some employees who missed shifts after workload changes feared that if they reported for work they would receive job-threatening warnings for failing to meet new production quotas. There were also occasions when technological changes and increased workloads resulted in waves of injuries that forced workers to stay home.[10]

Whether or not workers felt too sick, too tired, or too unmotivated, they often decided to take a day for themselves to do other things. Many women used this time to catch up on housework or run errands. Men who took time off were more likely to get out of the house, often to go fishing. They rarely kept their outings secret. "I've been out I reckon a hundred times to go fishing or something," Eugene Nelson once admitted to company officials.[11] Nearly every worker did it, to varying extents, and accepted it as legitimate. For the most part, second hands made no complaints as long as the machines kept running. Utility hands were generally ready to fill in, and they usually appreciated the opportunity to run full-time jobs.

There was enormous variation among union members in how motivated they were to work regularly. There were countless combinations of family need and personal preferences. Marital status and family size were crucial variables. Some hands seemed especially eager not only to work every day but to stay for a double shift whenever possible. Many union members took pride in their regular work habits and worried more than others about whether or not it was right to be absent when it was not impossible for them to work.[12] In most cases the pressing need to pay bills and put food on the table encouraged steady attendance, although some two-wage families could more readily afford to let one or the other rest a day. Some workers faced both the most urgent need for income and the most pressing reasons to stay home. "My baby has got nobody but me, because my husband is dead," explained one hand. "I try to work when I can, because I know that child is looking to me. I work just as regular as I can, because I feel like I have to."[13] Workers in similar situations experienced awful dilemmas when their children were sick or when their sitting arrangements fell through.

By no means could the contract eliminate every painful choice that jeopardized a family's financial security, but to a large extent workers decided for themselves whether to spend five or six full shifts each week on the job, or whether they might survive just as well, if not better, by taking an extra day or two off to do chores, go fishing, or rest up. Although the work-sharing system was not always popular with management, union members promoted and defended this broad interpretation of absence-related contract language because by so doing they were able to meet many of their needs.

This simple realization forces reconsideration of a basic premise, one that was even held to some extent by top TWUA officials at the time: that workers once had to keep their noses to the grindstone in order to meet the cost of living, and that with the economic boom of the postwar era those same employees chose to work overtime in order to maximize earnings. During World War II the TWUA conducted cost-of-living surveys in several southern communities, including Henderson, intending to demonstrate the dire need for wage increases in order for workers to make ends meet. By calculating the size of paychecks from hourly rates and comparing the totals to the cost of living based on prices in the area, TWUA researchers concluded that millhands worked as much as possible each week and still barely managed to scrape out a living.[14] This examination of actual workers, however, reveals a far more complicated picture. It does not rule out the possibility that many hands desired to consume more, but it also recognizes that many workers, and quite possibly a majority of the most eager consumers, wanted more than simply to work and earn as much as possible. By taking solid control over one of the most crucial conditions of labor—access to a job—Harriet and Henderson workers were doing what they wanted, if not what the experts anticipated they would do.

For the workers' job allocation system to function, union members had to stretch the spirit and bend the letter of the pertinent contract provisions. The crucial clauses involved the mechanisms for excusing oneself from work, announcing one's expected return, and punishing employees who violated plant rules regarding absenteeism. No matter why a worker elected to miss a day, there were only two options from which to choose when offering an official explanation to avoid an unexcused absence. An employee was either absent "by reason of illness" or because of some "other reasonable cause."[15] Since few workers were willing to risk a battle over what constituted a "reasonable cause," the vast majority of absent hands claimed that they were too ill to work. If workers were to fulfill their obligations to the letter of the contract, they had to notify their bosses of impending absences at least eight hours before the beginning of each missed shift. They were also to give eight hours' notice prior to their intended return. According to the contract, exceptions were allowed only "in cases of extreme emergency." In practice, however, decisions about missing work were rarely made eight hours in advance of the start of a shift, so most employees claimed "extreme emergency." Superintendent Proctor once noted that "75% of the notices that come in come in just before the shift changes." Moreover, in most departments nobody bothered to inform supervisors when they would return.[16]

Lower-level supervisors might not have been pleased with this lax observance of contract provisions, but it appears that most of the time they tolerated it. The sheer magnitude of the numbers was enough to force a degree of complicity. Several hundred workers were absent most days, and even the most skeptical supervisors could investigate only a handful of the claims. In addition, such efforts rarely proved worthwhile because so many of those absent were legitimately ill. In practice, therefore, foremen and second hands did not seem to care whether or not workers were really incapacitated as long as the absent employees' positions were filled by utility workers. Harriet Mill hand Aliene Roberts explained that often when workers in her department wanted a day off they would first report to work, then ask "Coy, our boss, second hand, if he had enough help to let us go back, and if [he] didn't have enough help it would be all right." More often than not, Roberts said, "he let us off."[17] Most lower-level supervisors proved accommodating. Henderson Mill employee Eugene Nelson noted that he made little effort to keep his "emergency" fishing expeditions secret, because "when I come in the next day Mr. Brown puts me to work." Another Local 584 member, Mary Kittrell, explained that her immediate supervisors also never punished hands for failing to give eight hours' notice of their intention to return after an excused absence.[18]

Top-level managers knew what was happening. Superintendent Proctor once suggested that the company's acceptance of the workers' habits was an example of management's generosity. "The Company has been very liberal about not raising any issue as to whether an employee is sick or not sick," he once lectured the Local 578 shop committee. "We don't want to operate like that."[19] Henderson Mill superintendent Farmer made similar comments to the Local 584 officers. "Any member of this committee will agree that every time a person gives notice of sickness that he is not sick," he said, "but we don't question that but accept his word for it."[20]

In reality, however, managers acquiesced because they had little choice. After unionization they no longer had unilateral power to inflict punishment on employees who missed work. According to the contract, rules regarding discipline had to "be mutually agreed upon between the Company and the General Shop Committee."[21] Local union officers and company officials, therefore, were forced to establish guidelines that would help them decide both what types of absences would be considered legitimate and how severely an offending worker could be punished. This was very difficult to do. In many cases there were compelling circumstances that did not clearly fit the established guidelines. If they had wanted to enforce the contract more strictly, managers would have had to hire a large number of investigators and health experts, which they were unwilling to do. In most cases, then, ambiguity ruled, which was to the worker's advantage in avoiding harsh discipline.

Managers did have a powerful disciplinary measure at their disposal—the warning. The company had the right to issue a formal warning to workers who had a specified number of unexcused absences in any three-month period. Each warning remained on a hand's record for one year. Upon receiving a third warning during the designated period, usually a calendar year from the date of employment, the offending worker received a mandatory layoff, usually of two to four weeks. A fourth warning brought an automatic discharge.

With few exceptions, every dispute over warnings for excessive absenteeism highlighted the profound difference between the needs of workers and the needs of managers. Managers interpreted such warnings as merely an incentive for the affected employee to work more regularly, something the supervisors assumed could be done. "Just improve on the deal," Superintendent Proctor once told a group of warned workers. On another occasion he said that warnings, "do not amount to much."[22] Workers, however, took warnings very seriously, perceiving them as immediate threats to their livelihoods. Union members made great efforts to have even first and second warnings removed from their records for fear that they would otherwise be dangerously close to unemployment. Local 578 member Margaret Woodlief's challenge of a first warning illustrates the concerns most union members felt when disciplined in this manner. "I would like to know how would either one of you all feel," she asked her supervisors, "if you all's wife was left with a small child like that and that child had nobody to look to, but its mother. How would you all feel, if that boss man come around and warned them?"[23] Not every warned worker could claim such dire circumstances, but almost all had a strong desire to avoid any possibility of a discharge.

The first major effort by company officials to combat absenteeism began in late 1948, apparently in response to the first significant recession after the postwar boom. The union members' work-sharing system had always conflicted with management's ideal of a lean, efficient, dedicated work force. Nevertheless, business had been so good throughout the war and the immediate postwar years that company officials had rarely objected to absenteeism-related inefficiency. The recession, however, forced managers to attack the informal labor system.[24]

To combat absenteeism, management attempted to unilaterally implement a new warnings policy. In the past the company had been able to punish workers only for "unexcused absences." The proposed new policy defined any absence, for whatever reason, as "unexcused." Under these new terms, in any three-month period workers would receive one warning after three absences, a second warning after two more, and a four-week layoff for eight absences, which would have represented roughly 10 percent of available workdays when the mills ran full-time.

It appears that the company carefully selected the first two employees to be disciplined under the new rules. George Owen had missed work 42 percent of the time in 1947, and he had maintained an absenteeism rate of more than 40 percent through September 1948. The company suspended Owen for four weeks. William Mitchell, who had missed one out of three workdays in 1948, was fired. Although most of both men's absences were technically excused, having been for "illness," the company felt that the hands deserved to be disciplined. "I don't like to question sick notices and that is our problem," conceded Henderson Mill superintendent Joe Farmer. But "when you see a man's record like this one," he continued, referring to George Owen, "you have to take steps to do something about it. We feel that if we continue to hire people who are not working regularly and [are] out indefinitely, we will not have a mill that is well run." Attorney Bennett Perry explicitly stated the company's intentions. "If a person is absent continually even if it is for a reason beyond his control, then he is not qualified to work. He ought not to be laid off, he ought to be fired."[25]

The Local 578 shop committee faced a dilemma when called upon to defend Owen and Mitchell. Most union members seemed to recognize that protection from absenteeism should not be unlimited, and for reasons that the documents fail to reveal, these two hands had apparently gone too far. For the most part, however, both had faithfully observed the contract's requirements for notifying supervisors of absences and intended dates of return. Regional TWUA representative R. H. Harris noted that "the larger percentage" of Owen's absences, at least ostensibly, "were because of sickness himself or in the family or death in the family." While not eager to defend either hand strongly, the Local 578 shop committee and Harris argued that absences for those reasons "should not be considered against his record."[26] If the company no longer accepted illness as a legitimate excuse for an absence, then virtually all the hands would eventually receive warnings for what had been accepted practice. Even workers with unexceptional numbers of absences, for reasonable and legitimate reasons, could be disciplined severely.

The company was looking for a way to rein in its workforce without challenging every claim of illness. "Sick notices sent time after time," Farmer lamented. "Sometimes a man sends in a couple notices a week; out 2 or 3 days." While the company felt that it could no longer afford the hands' casual work ethic, both shop committees feared a rash of layoffs and discharges that would severely disrupt, and possibly end, the effective job security and work-sharing system the union members had developed. The bottom line on absenteeism seemed to be, as company attorney Bennett Perry said to the Local 584 shop committee, that "what your idea of reasonable is and what the company's idea of reasonable is may be two different things."[27]

As it became clear that these differing perspectives could not be easily reconciled, management's offensive against absenteeism came to a tentative and ambiguous conclusion. The company was unwilling, in the end, to define exactly what it considered to be an excessive level of absenteeism, and union members refused to concede that absences due to illness should automatically count against a hands' record. In a compromise announced on 20 January 1949, the parties agreed that sickness in the family, personal illness, becoming ill during a shift, and an absence with adequate advance notice would not be counted as unexcused absences. However, the company maintained that it should have some discretion in determining whether sicknesses were legitimate. In addition, the penalty for a third warning was reduced to two weeks' suspension rather than four. To settle the specific cases in question, George Owen and William Mitchell were allowed to retain their regular jobs.[28]

Unsurprisingly, this ambiguous truce failed to inspire union members to change their work habits. The next crisis occurred about a year later, while the mills were still climbing out of the trough of recession. Managers had reverted to tolerating high levels of absenteeism, but they lost patience one day when a number of winding frames at the Henderson Mill sat idle through an entire shift for lack of anybody to run them. Although the company had made allowances for daily absenteeism of over 30 percent—nine utility workers for twenty-nine regular hands—that had not been enough to run the mill.[29] Superintendent Farmer was exasperated.

"I think it will be cheaper to let the frames stand than for us [to] carry enough Utility hands to fill the jobs of all the regular hands that are out when they send notes of extreme emergency at 3:00 o'clock in the afternoon," he complained.[30]

Company officials declared an extreme emergency of their own and bypassed the utility system by hiring temporary workers off the company's recall list. Technically, the recall process was to be reserved for periods of increased production or expansion of the mill, when additional regular employees were needed. Usually those on the list were employees who previously had been displaced by new equipment or who for some other reason had quit regular jobs while in good standing. Many of them were eager to work, even if on a part-time basis. According to the contract, however, the company had to send all recall notices to the appropriate local union president, who would ensure that seniority was observed. This procedure often took two or three days. When machines were idle because of absenteeism, however, managers wanted new workers quickly and were unwilling to accept any delays. During the recession, orders for yarn had been scarce, so when they came in company officials could not tolerate missed opportunities for production. If there were not enough utility hands to maintain operations, Superintendent Farmer argued, "we have to get somebody immediately."[31]

Union members, however, saw the company's attempt to hire unilaterally off the recall list, even if only for temporary work, as a dangerous precedent that threatened their control over their terms of employment. Workers in the Henderson Mill winding room, the department in question, felt that the problem was not excessive absenteeism. "We have been getting complaints from employees that the company doesn't keep enough Utility help to permit people to be off when they have to," TWUA representative Radford Cope told the managers. Cope claimed that a winding department ought to allow for daily absenteeism of 40 percent, which in this case would mean hiring three more utility hands. "Most of the workers are women who have families and they will be out a lot," he explained.[32] The needs of workers and managers were clearly in conflict. "You mean if we have 100 employees we have to have 40 Utility hands and pay them 2 hours reporting time every day," responded an incredulous Farmer. "I don't believe you could operate that way and stay in business."[33] What was fair and sensible from the workers' perspective seemed inefficient and unproductive to managers.

In early 1950 the company also began to discipline workers who failed to abide by the letter of contract provisions regarding absenteeism. On several occasions, for example, workers were laid off a day or more for not giving eight hours' notice before coming back to work after an absence. This sudden clampdown contrasted with the lax enforcement of specific contract language, noted above, that had been normal practice in most departments. Linville Nelson, who had been granted a day's leave to take his wife to the hospital, was not allowed to work the following day because he had not sent adequate notice of his intention to return. "He told him he wanted to be off today to take his wife to the hospital," Local 584 shop committee member Johnnie Carter argued on behalf of Nelson. "He said *today*, and he meant just that one day."[34] Mary Kittrell faced a similar situation after leaving work in the middle of a shift to look for her son, who had disappeared before she reported that day. Despite her anxiety, she worked instead of searching because her department was short on help that day, but after four hours she decided to leave. Kittrell eventually found her son; but she was sent home the next day for failing to give eight hours' notice of her intention to return.[35] Union members were outraged. It seemed that in this case management had taken a firm stand at the expense of common sense.

Managers apparently assumed that absent workers simply lacked discipline and that tough enforcement of the contract would whip them into shape. But even the top officials who called for the new policy usually backed down when confronted with the precise circumstances that had caused the absenteeism. Both Nelson and Kittrell, for example, received retroactive pay for the days that they missed.[36] Workers had diverse, unpredictable, and usually very legitimate needs that were accommodated best by a loose interpretation of contract provisions. Managers never conceded that in principle, but they were often persuaded by workers' direct testimony, which they never heard until they were forced to listen.

Managers, of course, never stopped looking for ways to discourage absenteeism. When company officials once again disciplined certain individuals with high rates of absenteeism in the fall of 1951, their major target was Willie Harper, a shop steward in the Henderson Mill card room who had missed 48 percent of available workdays from June through September that year. The company suspended Harper for sixty days. Although only a few workers had absence rates that the company considered beyond the pale, managers considered each of them a dangerous example. "We have got 5 or 6 more that have bad records," Superintendent Farmer claimed. "If the Union upholds a man whose record has been steadily getting worse, and he is a shop steward setting an example for [the] rest, it is a bad situation." Disciplining people like Harper, managers reasoned, would deter others from even approaching such extraordinary rates of absenteeism. "As long as those people can come and go and work when they get ready, we will never solve the problem," Farmer argued. "We have got to show him that he can't get by with it."[37]

Debates between managers and shop committee members over Harper's fate suggest that most union members, through their elected local officials, had some kind of understanding about what constituted unacceptable absenteeism and what its consequences should be. Missing one day each week might not have been controversial, but depending on the specific circumstances, two or three days off per week might have been enough to cross the unwritten line of propriety. In this case, despite Harper's claim that most of his absences were because of arthritis, the Local 584 shop committee evidently remained unconvinced. Some penalties, the union apparently agreed, were justifiable. Local 584 president Luther Jackson conceded to management that there were "a few people," including Harper, "that we felt were staying out too much and we have talked to them about it."[38]

Although the precise reason for Harper's record remains a mystery, it seems that the quality of his excuses, rather than the actual percentage of days he missed, was the critical factor for the shop committee. During the same meeting in which Willie Harper's punishment was determined, shop committee member Eugene Nelson vigorously defended Ed Peoples, who was also threatened with a long-term suspension for having a work record that was virtually the same as Harper's. Peoples "really is sick," Nelson insisted. "He has varicose veins and had a heart attack." As a result, Peoples was not suspended.[39] The local shop committees clearly played a vital role in determining the limits of justifiable absenteeism and in protecting the rights of members they felt were within those boundaries.

While local union leaders were usually willing to give workers the benefit of the doubt, certain uses of the contract's protections generated little sympathy and at best meek support. Alcohol usually fueled such controversies. Reporting to work while under the influence of alcohol was grounds for immediate dismissal. Eight or nine union members were fired for this reason in the first two years with a contract. In one instance the workers in a department testified against their own shop steward when she reported to work under the influence.[40] The union rarely protested such dismissals, partly because an intoxicated employee endangered the health and safety of other hands and usually did sloppy work that hindered the ability of others to meet production quotas. Missing work on account of alcohol, however, was a more widespread and controversial issue. Taking a day off to go fishing or run errands was one thing, but for many of the hands, to be too hung over to work or to spend a day off drinking was quite another. A number of workers were opposed to alcohol for religious reasons. Others either experienced or observed the horrible consequences, especially for women and children, of excessive drinking, especially by men.[41] From this perspective, it was hard to generate much sympathy for someone who was too drunk to go to work.

Alcohol-related absenteeism put local shop committees in a bind. They were obligated to defend, to some extent, anybody who filed a grievance, yet they also tried to adhere to the general sense of propriety held by the majority of the membership. An indiscretion or two could possibly be overlooked, but according to active union supporter Joseph Braswell, "some people were 'sick' every Monday." Indeed, Henderson Mill superintendent Farmer complained that "Monday sickness is a right common thing."[42] Rachel Jones, former financial secretary of Local 578, recalled that such absences posed difficult problems. Her husband's uncle had been a typical example. According to Jones, the company "knew that he had been out drunk, but still if they said anything to him, he would go to the shop steward and would want them to stick up for him," even if the shop committee knew that the worker was in the wrong. A few people, Jones said, "took advantage" of the contract's protections in this way. And when the local defended any of them, she added, "the union hurt itself."[43]

Management exerted pressure on committee members not to test the company's patience on alcohol-related matters, and local officers exercised their right to defend claims with differing degrees of fervor. Once when arguing in favor of two hands who had been disciplined, Local 584 president Luther Jackson admitted to company officials, "I have got people in the mill that come to me with this type of grievance and I would have hesitated before I would have written it, because I will be honest with you, I wouldn't have believed it." Jackson's counterpart at the Harriet Mill, Sam Littleton, felt the same way. "We have had people that stayed out and I went to them and told them about it, talked to them myself, and they were eventually fired," he explained to managers. "I told them no need [to protest], cause I knew what they were doing."[44]

It is impossible to know precisely how union members felt about their local officers' reluctance to defend workers whose absenteeism appeared to have been alcohol-related. One can assume that workers who were disciplined or discharged were not pleased. Even many generally unsympathetic hands, however, must have felt somewhat ambivalent about harsh discipline, because the affected people would have had the same pressures and needs—illness, child care, housework, recreation—as other workers with high absence rates who successfully challenged their punishments. The boundaries of acceptability were always fuzzy, although on occasion they were apparently crossed.

Whenever alcohol was not the central issue in disputes over absenteeism, workers appeared to be willing, even in marginal cases, to give fellow hands the benefit of the doubt. Time after time the shop committees defended the right of fellow union members to retain access to a livelihood despite erratic attendance. In one 1944 case Harriet Mill hand Thomas West missed several days because he frequently overslept and failed to catch his ride to the mill. After three such absences in the span of a couple of weeks, West received a seven-day layoff. Although they were not eager to reward West for getting his extra rest, union representatives argued that one's access to a livelihood should not be blocked unless the circumstances were more extreme. "It is pretty easy to say we'll take away a week's pay from a man," a regional TWUA official lectured company officials. "This is a pretty lighthearted thing to say. In case you don't know I'll say it from this side of the table, to take away a man's pay is a mighty bad thing." Since arguments had to be based on the contract, union officials claimed that missing a ride to work ought to qualify as an "extreme emergency," which would have excused West's absences. In return, foreman M. C. Mills argued that workers deserved harsh penalties for oversleeping. The layoff stood, but only after the union challenged it all the way to arbitration.[45]

Workers recognized the importance of a job even when supervisors were the ones whose positions were threatened. When Harriet Mill hands successfully ousted second hand Louis Vick, they displayed sensitivity to Vick's need to provide for his family. "We don't want him fired," the workers emphasized, "but we want another man in his place."[46] After Will Bartholomew, another Harriet Mill second hand, reported to work under the influence of alcohol, TWUA representative Toby Mendes claimed that the union was "more or less reluctant to bring up" the case "because it involves a man's livelihood and his living."[47]

Other principles could ultimately prevail, however, as demonstrated by the Bartholomew case, in which workers demanded the equal application of plant rules regarding alcohol. "We feel if it is to be applied to the employees it should be applied to Mr. Bartholomew," argued Local 578 president Albert Burke. In Bartholomew's defense the company offered an argument almost identical to that used by workers in similar cases. "If there is a doubt he is entitled to have it," argued company attorney Bennett Perry. "It is a serious matter. It means his job, his livelihood and his living. He shouldn't be thrown out of his job and given a black name."[48] It appears that when the disciplinary hierarchy was reversed, company officials could see as plainly as workers how severely people were affected by layoffs and discharges.

In granting workers the benefit of the doubt in ambiguous cases, union members were more willing than managers to consider all aspects of a person's life. Lula Betts, a utility hand at the Harriet Mill, had a habit of leaving the mill after two hours whenever she had to wind coarser yarns, which required much more effort than finer yarns. "Every time she gets a job that she can't run she gets off sick," complained Superintendent Proctor, explaining why he had fired her. Shop committee members conceded that Betts was not the most regular or efficient worker, but they argued that she was under enormous pressure as her family's sole means of support. Superintendent Proctor emphasized, however, that the company had "leaned over backwards in trying to help her." The union maintained its objection to Betts's dismissal, arguing that protecting a livelihood for a troubled family ought to be more important than maximizing efficiency. "I know that you feel that now that the war is over that you can get more capable people," pleaded Albert Burke, "but we think that if she can hold down the job, she ought to be kept on the job."[49]

The union held to the principle of job security even under the most unfortunate circumstances. In 1950, the union found itself fighting to retain employment for a member who was arrested for domestic violence. Management fired John Waddell Jr. after the hand failed to report to work because he was in the county jail. Henderson Mill superintendent Farmer had heard that the employee had been jailed for drunkenness, which was grounds for dismissal. It turned out, however, that Waddell had been arrested for assaulting his wife. Mrs. Waddell had apparently asked her brother-in-law to post bond for her husband early the next morning so that he would not lose his job, but the jailed hand's brother failed to appear. The shop committee debated whether or not Mrs. Waddell would have been better off if her husband were both violent and unemployed and the family were to lose his income. The union decided to defend Waddell on a technicality. "I told him that day that if he was guilty of this charge of drunk[en]ness, there is nothing we can do about it," Local 584 president Luther Jackson explained to company officials. However, there was no plant rule about missing work on account of assault charges, Jackson argued, so the company ought to consider "giving him another chance."[50]

Once again, the union's perspective was heavily influenced by the vast, complex range of pressures faced by workers and families. Neither the company nor the union directly addressed the domestic violence that had been uncovered, so no matter what the outcome in the case, serious problems remained unresolved. After considering the potential consequences, the union did opt to try to save the hand's job, even though some members may have questioned whether it was right to defend a drunken wife-beater. The company, however, saw the Waddell case as an opportunity both to enforce plant rules and to make a statement about the danger of absenteeism. Apparently Waddell had missed many days. "He has such a bad record," argued Superintendent Farmer, that "if all our employees worked like he does we would be in such a position that we would not be able to make any definite promise about what we could ship to our customers."[51] Whether or not managers had responded emotionally to the evidence of domestic violence in this case, they had not been immediately willing to jeopardize productivity and efficiency for the sake of a family in trouble. In the end, however, Farmer relented and Waddell retained his job.

Disputes over absenteeism subsided as business improved during the early 1950s. Although the company never condoned absenteeism and there is no evidence that attendance records, on the whole, ever improved, management seemed to tolerate the workers' habits more readily when orders for yarn were plentiful. By March 1954, however, an impending recession spurred managers to enact economizing measures, which included a rash of warnings to discourage absenteeism.[52] This time management was adamant in its insistence that excuses for absences, no matter how reasonable, would no longer be taken into account when company officials considered whether or not an employee would receive a warning.[53] As an alternative to intermittent absences, the company offered employees the option of taking extended, unpaid leaves. "If anybody wants to get off for 9 months, we will be glad to accommodate them," announced Harriet Mill superintendent Proctor, "but [what] we are getting here is a few out 2 days a week."[54]

Although to managers the new policy was a sound business decision, it conflicted squarely with the needs of many workers. If a worker had a heart attack, a broken leg, or major surgery and needed several months to recuperate, an extended leave would make sense. Yet many common health problems, like arthritis, asthma, and hay fever, do not disappear with prolonged rest. Furthermore, although sickness in the family was a major cause of absenteeism, particularly for women, children could hardly be expected to become ill only during a parent's leave of absence. According to the company's new policy, however, all absences, for whatever reason, would be counted against an employee.

Perhaps the most crucial problem with the idea of extended leaves of absence was that a worker's bills would not be suspended during that time. As TWUA representative Julius Fry once noted, referring to medical expenses, "People have to work to pay for doctor's bills when they are sick. They don't have it stacked away."[55] For most mill workers, irregular attendance was the best available solution for the problems they faced. Three or four days per week could allow many families to survive. The same schedules, however, always struck exasperated supervisors as irresponsible. Only when pressured by workers to consider individual circumstances would the company admit that absenteeism was a complex subject. For example, Local 578 president Sam Littleton once pressed company officials to make clear how many missed days would result in a warning. Superintendent Proctor replied, "We are not setting any certain amount. Every case stands on it[s] own. You know that as well as I do." But managers could never reconcile their acknowledgment of ambiguity with their desire for a strict, enforceable absenteeism policy.[56]

Therefore, in late 1954 the company proceeded to discipline workers whom supervisors felt were in violation of the new policy. Seven workers, all of whom were women and all of whom had among the worst attendance records in the mill, protested the warnings they received.[57] Table 2 shows the percentage of days that each had missed. All of these cases involved either a first or second warning, so none resulted in either a layoff or discharge. Nevertheless, the women protested their penalties with intensity. Lillie Lochemy explained to mill officials, "I ain't out on account of myself everytime. I got 4 children and when one of them is sick I have to stay with them." Aliene Roberts complained that on many of the days that were now being counted against her she had received permission from her second hand to go home because there were enough hands present to cover all positions. Bessie Hamm reminded her bosses why she had been out: "You see here," she pointed to her body. "That's where that muscle strained in my back and my nerve kinked." She had undergone surgery for this problem. Margaret Woodlief explained that she had a chronic throat ailment. In case the company doubted her integrity, Woodlief offered a challenge. "You can call Dr. Wester and ask him how much medicine I have took."[58] Nevertheless, each warning stood.

It is impossible to know to what extent, if any, managers might have

Table 2.

Percentage of Workdays Missed by Warned Workers

Worker	1953	1954
Lillie Lochemy	42	35
Agnes Austin	28	19
Aliene Roberts	31	28
Bessie Hamm	21	24
Margaret Woodlief	27	27
Margaret George	15	32
Jessie Johnson	5	26

Source: Typed memo, dated 24 September 1954, listing percentages of absences through 31 August 1954 for those involved with grievances, in Harriet/578 transcripts.

sympathized with the employees who faced disciplinary measures. Superintendent Proctor did recognize, however, what it was like to be the subordinate whose boss would not listen. Although Proctor was near the top of the managerial hierarchy, he still often felt unfairly hassled by higher officials who did not understand the pressures and limits he faced. "Sometimes you all ought to be sitting in a meeting where I am on the other end," Proctor lectured a group of women who were angry about the warnings they had received. Top officials, he said, are "on me every day about the cost [of] utility help." If you could walk a day in my shoes, Proctor seemed to say to the women, you would see that your situation is "not as bad as it sounds." Perhaps the superintendent had to distance himself from the direct testimony he heard so frequently: he was certainly not allowed to talk in those terms when explaining the rising cost of utility help to the company president. In any event, Proctor missed the workers' point. "Go up there tomorrow, those of you [who] want to get off," he instructed the women, "and see your foreman or second hand and say, 'I am not well. I want to be off for 30 days or 45 days, get well and come back to work.'" If those terms were unsatisfactory, Proctor concluded, "then we will hire somebody and put them in there to take your place." [59]

Perhaps another reason why union members had difficulty accepting the company's proposed work ethic was that when market conditions worsened, the company often imposed three- or four-day workweeks on its employees. Short time had been in effect just three months before management's 1954 offensive against absenteeism. [60] It must have seemed incongruous to workers that managers could force many of them to miss 40 percent or 50 percent of what in good times would have been regular workdays, then, a few months later, penalize the same employees for choosing on their own to work a similar schedule. If nothing else, the periodic recessions forced workers to develop alternative survival strategies, many of which were apparently used even after the possibility of full-time work returned.

After the 1954 recession, supervisors began to issue warnings for single instances of missing work. Bertie Gibson was the first target. Her written excuse, delivered to her supervisor by another worker, explained that she had "some business to tend to in town." Vague statements like this, of course, had become accepted practice over the years. "A lot of business you cannot tend to unless on Saturday," Myrtle Peoples argued in Gibson's defense. "Some you have to tend to during [the] week." Gibson was in a state of disbelief as she spoke to managers and local union officials. "I been working off and on now for about 35 years," she said, "and that's the first one that's ever been wrote against me." Local 578 president Charlie Ranes objected to the suddenness of the policy change. "It looks like to me they are just jumping and warning people before they talk to them," he complained. "They are warning people for the least little thing they do, you know that's not fair."[61]

The company, it seems, sought unilateral control over the granting of discretionary absences. According to Myrtle Peoples, who had been present when Gibson was warned, the foreman "said it was his right to write it if [he] wanted to, or he didn't have to write it. He had [the] right either way." Superintendent Proctor explained that absenteeism was getting "so bad, something had to be done about it," so company officials decided they would no longer assume that any excuse had been offered in good faith. "What if everybody wrote in here one morning the same note?" Superintendent Proctor asked the shop committee, referring to Gibson's excuse. "Your job comes first." In the future, Proctor said, if Gibson or any other hand defied a supervisor and missed a day's work, "She would have to take the consequence."[62]

So many workers were willing to take that risk, however, that the company could not strictly enforce its rule. Favorable business conditions relieved some of the pressure on management to limit absenteeism, but in June 1956 company officials lost their patience when not enough employees reported to fill all the jobs in the Harriet Mill. On one shift, twenty-six winding frames stood idle. "We couldn't get the work done," explained another supervisor, Tommy Peck, despite having "a great deal of extra Utility help." Lower-level supervisors were no doubt under extreme pressure from top management to reach production goals, so they insisted that excuses for absences did not matter and issued a number of warnings. From the standpoint of maintaining peak production, foreman B. H. Redding emphasized, "absenteeism is absenteeism."[63]

Despite management's renewed resolve, the basic conflict between production goals and workers' needs had not been resolved. And just as before, this wave of warnings created deeper antagonisms rather than steadier work habits. Harriet Mill spinner Lula Wheeler received a warning for missing work despite having received permission from her supervisor to go home. She had a splinter in a finger that prevented her from performing some of the essential tasks of her job, but under the new policy an injury was no more legitimate an excuse than a hangover was.[64]

Esther Johnson received a warning simply for missing work on account of illness. Unfortunately for Johnson, her department happened to be short on help the day she stayed home. Johnson's foreman was apparently under so much pressure to fill the positions that he personally called on her to beg her to come to work. "He said a lot of them was out sick," Johnson explained to union and company officials.

> Well, I didn't know nobody else was out sick, but myself, and I told him that I wasn't able to come in that night, but I would try to come in Wednesday night, so I did go in Wednesday night. The next morning he gave a warning about it. I couldn't help from being out, because I was sick and I let him know when I was coming back. I did just like I said I was going to do and I didn't think it was fair to warn me.[65]

Ella Adcox had been warned for chronic absenteeism, but she pleaded with management to consider her motivation. "I was sorry that I had been sick," she began, "but Mama was sick and died and if that wasn't reason for being out, I didn't know what was. I stayed up so much night and day with her before she died and it was just impossible for me to work when I was sick, and I lost her on top of it and it was just all I could do."[66]

Although union members successfully challenged some of their warnings and had them removed from their records, the underlying conflict over absenteeism continually provoked new grievances. Antagonisms reached a peak in late 1957 when Fannie Wilson, an employee with fifty years' seniority, was warned for missing nearly half of available workdays in 1957, including the entire month of October. You are out "2 months, then come back and work 3 weeks then out 2 more months," complained Superintendent Proctor. "That is the thing that is getting us." Proctor offered Wilson an extended leave, but Wilson suffered from asthma, which could become quite severe at times, especially inside a cotton mill. "I don't know when I am going to be sick," she explained to company officials. "Of course, if the doctor told me I wasn't going to be able to work for 5 or 6 months, then it would pay me to do that, but how could I do it when I don't know when I am going to be sick."[67]

Hoping to resolve these types of controversies conclusively, both sides decided to take this case before an arbitrator, who ruled in April 1958 that Wilson's warning should be removed from her record. "By no flight of the imagination can I conceive of anyone having asthma of a temporary nature," John D. Cooper fumed to his superintendents. "There must be a change. This I intend to do when the contract is open for negotiation. As I see it, we cannot survive under the interpretation that the arbiter has given to the contract in this grievance."[68]

As always, the differences in perspectives were striking. Workers saw their absences in terms of chronic illnesses, debilitating splinters, work-related injuries, sick children, and dying mothers. To compound these miseries, receiving a warning was a step toward unemployment—a large step, given the capriciousness with which warnings could be issued. On the other hand, supervisors focused on idle spinning frames, unrealized production, and unnecessarily expensive utility-help payrolls. Although conflicts only occasionally reached crisis proportions, these contrasting conceptions of what work should be persisted over the years. Was there any way to develop rigid guidelines regulating absenteeism while still allowing for personal circumstances? Nobody could come up with such a policy in Henderson. As a result, the local union members' system for allocating their labor and fulfilling many of their additional needs and desires remained in constant jeopardy.

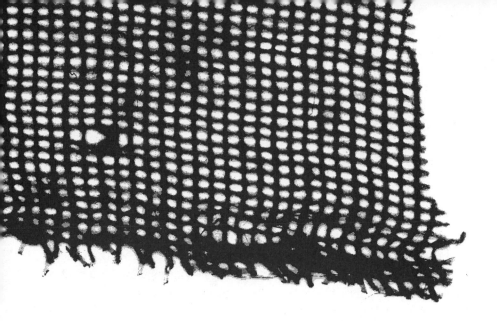

5 The Roots of Workload Conflict

The most frequent and bitter confrontations between unionized workers and managers were conflicts over workloads. Each case represented the intersection of international market pressures and management's productivity goals with the workers' health and endurance. Probably three-fourths of all such disputes were settled between shop stewards and supervisors before formal grievances were written. Nevertheless, hundreds of workload challenges kept shop committee members and managers occupied during the regular biweekly meetings that were held to discuss points of friction.[1] The company's modernization plans provoked the most critical battles. The union members' desire to have some control over their work lives complicated every managerial decision and frustrated the company's most ambitious modernization strategies. As market pressures intensified, particularly after 1949, Harriet and Henderson managers came to see workload challenges as the major obstacle to running their business. Although wild market fluctuations of the competitive, decentralized international textile industry influenced profitability far more than the demands of their employees did, Harriet and Henderson officials could only hope to control local variables like workloads.

Immediately after the union elections, managers acknowledged that workload conflicts would be a standard feature of life with an organized workforce. In July 1943 the company hired its first college-trained time-study engineer specifically "to combat the work-load claims of the Union." There was indeed a minor flood of workload grievances immediately after the contract went into effect. But for a variety of reasons these first-year disputes, as well as those in the early postwar years, lacked the stridency and sense of dire importance that would eventually characterize such conflicts.[2]

Favorable wartime business conditions reduced some of the strongest pressures on management to increase workloads. During the war the federal government controlled what mills could produce, what prices they would receive, what cotton would cost, what wages would be, and what profit levels were allowable. In return the government promised to purchase everything that the mills produced. Therefore, cotton-mill managers were under relatively little pressure to undersell competitors. Management's incentive to economize had not been completely eliminated, of course; managers wanted to ensure that assigned workloads would result in maximum legal profitability. Nevertheless, because the Harriet and Henderson Mills were finally making relatively enormous profits, there appeared to be no need for a widespread campaign to improve efficiency.[3]

In the immediate postwar years the demand for cotton products encouraged sheer output over efficiency even without federal controls. One student of the industry observed that cotton manufacturing, which comprised over 2,000 southern textile mills that together employed well over 600,000 workers, "roared through the first years of the brave, new postwar world as perhaps the most profitable industry in a nation of highly prosperous industries."[4] The domestic market swallowed up virtually everything the mills could produce. John D. Cooper reflected in early 1949 that since the war, "production was the important thing and the cost was secondary."[5] Although there were conflicts over workloads in this period, the company never felt strongly motivated to demand increased efficiency throughout the mills.

Management's greatest concern during the immediate postwar years was to install new machinery and related equipment that had recently been developed. Because the production of new textile machinery had been suspended during the war, Harriet and Henderson's modernization program had been interrupted for four years, and company officials were eager to resume their momentum. Managers predicted that new machinery would be necessary for the company to remain competitive once markets tightened, as they inevitably would. Therefore, months before the war officially ended, management ordered several hundred thousand dollars' worth of new spinning and twisting frames from Whitin Machine Works.[6]

Unfortunately for Harriet and Henderson managers, most cotton-mill executives had similar modernization plans. Whitin already had a large backlog of orders and cautioned that it would be at least two years before any equipment could be shipped to Henderson. As it turned out, three years passed before any new machinery arrived at the Harriet and Henderson Mills. To compound their frustration, company officials learned that the new equipment would cost as much as 40 percent more than originally budgeted.[7] Furthermore, by the time the new frames were finally installed, in the summer of 1948, the nation's economy was headed toward a deep recession. Managers had made what in 1945 appeared to be a shrewd, farsighted investment, but when it came time to reap their rewards, the bottom quickly dropped out of the market for all cotton goods.

The 1949 recession hit the entire textile industry hard. Cannon Mills in Kannapolis, Cone Mills in Greensboro, and Erwin Mills in Durham took the lead by eliminating third shifts. Textile employment in North Carolina dropped from over 230,000 in May 1948 to well under 200,000 by August 1949.[8] In Henderson, Marshall Cooper informed the board of directors in January 1949 that after eight years of unprecedented prosperity the company was "barely breaking even at the [Harriet] No. 1 Mill and showing a slight loss at the [Harriet] No. 2 Mill." Moreover, Cooper warned, the economic forecast "was not favorable." Consequently, the company's workforce experienced layoffs and shortened workweeks for the first time since the beginning of the war.[9]

Each explanation for the severity of the recession had ominous implications for the future. First, it appeared that peacetime consumer demand had its limits. Also, since foreign textile producers had recovered rather quickly from the war, American cotton mills had apparently lost the peculiar competitive advantage they had enjoyed for nearly a decade. "Every nation in the world can manufacture textiles," noted the president of the American Cotton Textile Manufacturers, W. F. Jacobs. "And because of lower standards of living, every nation in the world can produce them cheaper."[10] The president of the Southern Textile Association, Robert Stutts, offered a similar warning. "The low-cost labor of foreign countries may bombard us again," he said, "not with bombs and shrapnel, but with prints, sheets, and denim." To Stutts, the future looked bleak. "I do not share the opinion of those economists who are filled with optimism and believe that our present market condition is only a [momen]tary setback," he confessed, "and that just as soon as inventories are adjusted, Congress adjourns, and the moon changes, that everything will be all right and the buyer will be back on his knees and all of us will be considered smart operators again."[11]

Statistical evidence supported the concerns of these industry leaders. Between 1946 and 1950, American textile companies had prospered by annually exporting an average of $471 million worth of cotton cloth. Foreign demand had declined, however, and at the same time, foreign production had captured an increasing percentage of the remaining market. By 1950 the amount of cloth exported by U.S. textile firms had dropped to only $263 million worth.[12] In addition, although the development had barely begun to be documented, domestic industries were abandoning cotton for plastics and synthetic fabrics. Spurred by wartime needs, industries had consumed 40 percent of the cotton used in the United States in 1946. After 1947, however, average annual industrial consumption of cotton dropped by nearly 50 percent. Paper, plastics, rubber, glass, and synthetic fabrics made enormous inroads in markets traditionally dominated by cotton products.[13]

Harriet and Henderson managers felt especially vexed by the slackening of industrial demand for cotton products. The postwar machinery purchases had been intended to convert part of the Harriet complex to the production of plied yarns, which had been in great demand by the tire industry. Also, some of the new machinery was supposed to allow for an increase in production of coarse cloth at the Henderson Mill. Tire cords and coarse cloth, mainly for bagging, had accounted for 40 percent of industrial use of cotton as late as 1946. Before the new equipment arrived, however, the tire industry began its switch to synthetic fabrics for tire linings. Indeed, tire cords accounted for over three-fourths of the 50 percent drop in industrial cotton consumption after 1947.[14]

Company officials, however, did not stand pat with the onset of adversity. Faced with an urgent need to cut production costs, management initiated its first comprehensive revision of workloads in nearly ten years. As John D. Cooper warned the shop committees, "We cannot meet our competition unless we get this increased work load and cut our costs."[15] Indeed, time-study engineers recommended increases for almost every job. Henderson Mill superintendent Farmer defended the new assignments. "With things as tight as they are in selling our yarn," he argued, "we have to work on getting as well-run [a] plant as we can."[16]

The new workloads had an immediate effect, although not what management intended. Workers throughout both mills filed grievances protesting the increased assignments. Managers warned, in response, that such challenges threatened the future of the mills. Nevertheless, union members pursued their grievances all the way to arbitration and eventually forced the company to concede. Despite their dire pleas, just before the scheduled arbitration hearing company officials rolled back virtually every workload to prerecession levels. For the purposes of this overview of workload conflict, the crucial point is that Harriet and Henderson workers defeated management's first full-scale postwar workload offensive.[17] By 1949, the company's initial postwar modernization program had been effectively undercut by shipment delays, recession, long-term market shifts, and a combative workforce. This became a common pattern.

In the early 1950s the company launched another extensive expansion and renovation program for the two mills. Since markets for cloth and yarn did not necessarily fluctuate together, managers hoped that by not relying too heavily on one or the other, they could maintain overall profitability despite losses on some products. Most of the largest southern textile firms already produced a wide variety of products. Smaller companies like Harriet and Henderson, though, had to expand in order to diversify. In this case, managers decided to double the weaving capacity of the Henderson Mill, mainly to produce coarse cloth for bagging and other industrial uses. Since management did not intend to reduce production of yarns for T-shirts, underwear, and hosiery, the Henderson Mill's carding and spinning capacity had to be greatly increased, and this change required the construction of a second story to the mill as well as massive purchases of new machinery. Managers anticipated that these renovations would cost over $2 million.[18]

Management also had ambitious plans for the Harriet complex. Since the market for coarse plied yarns had all but disappeared, management purchased new equipment and adjusted existing machinery to produce a line of slightly finer plied yarns. Confident that sales of these new yarns would be strong, company officials planned to increase the mill's total production by 10 percent—about ten thousand additional pounds of yarn per week. Although this project alone cost nearly $1 million, company officials expected that the changes would produce from $250,000 to $300,000 per year in additional profits.[19]

The return of booming markets for cotton goods gave mill executives good reason to feel optimistic about their investment strategies. By the middle of 1950 the recession in textiles had ended. "American boys and men apparently cannot get enough polo shirts, T-shirts, lightweight undershirts, basque shirts and other cotton knitted specialties," the *Raleigh News & Observer* announced with satisfaction. The single-ply yarns produced at Harriet and Henderson could be found in all of those products. In addition, conflict between India and Pakistan created a scarcity of jute and burlap, which were in heavy demand as coarse fabrics for bagging. In the absence of these materials, manufacturers shifted to coarse cotton cloth, like that produced at the Henderson Mill. Sales of textile products received another tremendous boost from the threat of war in Korea. Remembering World War II, when the government claimed priority on textile production, wholesale buyers ordered huge inventories in the summer of 1950 to avoid being suddenly cut out of the revived consumer market. Domestic demand had increased to the point where purchasers saw little risk in such moves.[20]

Despite this welcome wave of good news for the cotton industry, company officials must have felt frustrated once again by the length of time it took to complete their projects. Even when things went smoothly it took many months for machinery on order to be delivered, and once the equipment arrived it took at least several weeks to install it. Management was no longer willing to shut down an entire mill during a renovation. Instead, the company maintained as much production capability as possible by replacing one or two pieces of machinery at a time, which prolonged the process. So although the Harriet and Henderson Mills were earning hefty profits in the early 1950s (see Appendix C), managers were not capitalizing on their new investments.

Adding to this frustration, by the time the Henderson Mill weaving addition was completed in early 1953 the market price for coarse cotton cloth had dropped considerably. Superintendent Farmer complained in March 1953 that he "could go out and buy cloth cheaper than we could produce" it. Both domestic industrial consumption of coarse cloth and foreign demand had continued to decline, and foreign producers were beginning to increase their share of what remained of the American market. These negative developments must have been galling to Harriet and Henderson officials. After three years of modernizing, they were finally prepared to turn out twice as much of a product that had become unprofitable.[21]

To make matters worse, from management's perspective, workers once again resisted proposals for higher workloads in every renovated department. Eleven separate workload grievances, involving a large number of Henderson Mill employees, wound their way through the grievance procedure. Company officials encountered similar opposition, particularly from the spinning department, when new workloads were established at the remodeled Harriet #2 mill. Attempting to stop the resistance, Superintendent Farmer pleaded with Henderson Mill hands, "We want to be able to se[l]l this without someone coming along and underselling us. I want all of you to keep that in mind. We know that everybody has got to give a good honest days work." When the shop committee refused to back down, Farmer hinted, as he had in 1949, that the workers' intransigence jeopardized the mill's survival. "If we are out of line we won't get business," he warned.[22]

Farmer's comments underscore a crucial point. Workloads were an integral part of any modernization scheme. Whenever they weighed the potential benefits of any new project, company officials had certain expectations about what work assignments would eventually be. From management's perspective, then, challenges to new workload proposals delayed the completion of already lengthy and expensive programs and threatened to negate anticipated productivity increases. Workers' earnings were protected while their assignments were in dispute, whether or not they met their new production quotas. Therefore, the net effect on production costs of any modernization plan could not be accurately calculated until protesting workers had either been appeased or defeated in arbitration.

No matter who finally won workload disputes, challenges through the grievance procedure always prolonged modernization projects. For example, management had conceived the second major postwar modernization program, described above, in late 1949 or early 1950. It took about three years for the machinery to arrive and be installed. The company first proposed new workloads for the remodeled Henderson Mill in March 1953. The affected workers protested, following the steps in the grievance procedure, until an arbitration hearing in February 1954. Two months later the arbitrator issued his decision. So at the Henderson Mill, the grievance process alone delayed management's modernization plans an additional thirteen months. Similarly, ten months passed between the time the company proposed new workloads at the Harriet #2 mill and final settlements were reached.

Company officials found these delays extremely frustrating, yet they fought tenaciously for the right to set workloads even when the financial stakes, when compared to the capital invested in new technologies, seemed relatively small. In the case involving the Harriet #2 spinners, for example, the arbitrator supported the union members' claim that they had been assigned an excessive workload, and he awarded them retroactive compensation for the several months that they had worked under those conditions. The payment totaled $3,282.34, with individual payoffs ranging from $.14 to $83, depending on how much a particular spinner had worked during that period.[23] It is easy to see why the hands would persist however long it took to resolve a case like this. To a full-time spinner, an $80 check represented a relatively hefty sum, almost two weeks' worth of work, as well as formal recognition that she had been overburdened. In contrast, the company fought long and hard to prevent a payoff of some $3,000 — or about $6,000 per year if the award was made permanent — after having readily invested a million dollars to launch the modernization project. The potential loss of some $6,000 also seems relatively minor when compared to the profits earned at Harriet #2 during the remodeling process. According to Marshall Cooper, Harriet #2 had shown earnings of "approximately $40,000 to $50,000 per quarter over what they would have been" if management had not invested in new machinery.[24] Given the enormous disparity between the figures for investment, earnings, and retroactive payment for excessive work, why did the company fight so hard?[25]

Once again, the undulating business cycle helps explain the decision. Company officials had initiated these new modernization programs in the midst of a recession with the hope of capitalizing on the return of booming markets and reducing the blow of future downturns. But by the time the mechanical changes had been made and workloads had been settled, the country was in the midst of another sharp recession. The importance of labor costs became most apparent in times of economic downturn. For example, in 1954, a very poor year for the mills, the $6,000 judgment awarded to the Harriet #2 spinners was roughly 15 percent of the company's net income for the entire year. The year before, $6,000 would have been barely more than 2 percent (see Appendix C).

Managers must also have been disturbed about the wisdom of their overall strategy. The anticipated benefits of the Harriet #2 modernization plan, for example, had been realized only briefly. According to Marshall Cooper, after a few quarters of increased earnings on finer plied yarns—

the goal of the project—prices for those yarns "deteriorated materially." Plastics had continued to displace cotton plied yarns for industrial use, eliminating many potential customers. Marshall Cooper reported that the Henderson Mill also had "a sad outlook." The new use of rayon for tire linings had undercut the goal of the $2 million modernization program at that plant. Suffering its first quarterly losses since the 1930s, Harriet and Henderson had become, in Marshall Cooper's words, "practically a hand-to-mouth proposition."[26]

The entire textile industry—including nonunion mills—was affected by this business downturn. Intense competition, both domestic and foreign, had drastically reduced prices for virtually all cotton products.[27] Making matters worse for domestic mills, individual producers often defied textbook economic wisdom by increasing output when faced with falling prices. Because the textile industry was highly decentralized, no single firm could hope to boost prices by curtailing production, so many mills produced and disposed of as much as possible before having to sell at a loss.[28] Although on one level this was a sensible, if desperate, way to pay off fixed costs of production, it only intensified the downward spiral in prices. It is not surprising, then, that between 1952 and 1956 seventy-four southern cotton mills went bankrupt. The trend was ominous. After 1950, earnings in cotton textiles had begun to fall below those in other major industries. One researcher concluded that the "normal" condition for most southern mills after 1951 was "no profits."[29]

Powerful market forces obviously bore the main responsibility for the failure of management's second postwar modernization program. With essentially the same wage structure, the company's gross income dropped from $539,271.76 in 1953 to $73,406.70 in 1954. The added labor costs from arbitrations, even including approximately $30,000 in retroactive payments awarded to workers in 1954, was not nearly enough to account for the magnitude of this drop in income. It seems clear, then, that the company's declining profits were caused by the falling prices for yarn and coarse cloth cited by managers in their private meetings and verified by industry analysts.[30]

Harriet and Henderson managers had few options available when deciding how to regain their competitive edge. As noted, it was impossible for any single mill to withhold production from the market in hopes of creating a scarcity that would cause yarn and cloth prices to climb. Textile executives also had little control over the price of cotton, a crucial factor in profitability. According to the North Carolina Textile Manufacturers Association, in 1948 wages accounted for only 35 to 40 percent of production costs, less than cotton's portion, and by 1957 cotton was "by far the largest of all the textile costs, accounting as raw material for 40% to 65% of the textile sales dollar at the mill level."[31] Just as mill owners had little influence on the cost of cotton, the cotton industry could not force rubber company executives to forgo synthetics and continue using cotton sheeting. Threatened by foreign competition, cotton mill owners had begun to lobby for restrictions on textile imports, but it would be two more years before any such limits were set.[32]

Of all the variables in textile production, labor costs were the most obvious target for efficiency-minded managers. In the short run there was not much else they could do, and labor costs were great enough that any savings could prove beneficial.[33] But how could management cut labor costs? The union contract prohibited unilateral wage cutting, and any attempt to violate or rescind that provision would have outraged employees. So the most common managerial strategies for reducing labor costs were to invest in labor-saving machinery and to increase workloads. Since it took months or even years to realize any benefits from new machinery, the only way to make an immediate impact on the cost of production was to increase workloads. As a Harriet and Henderson official once explained, "Somebody has got to take the squeeze."[34] Within this limited spectrum, Harriet and Henderson managers acted aggressively to combat the recession. They ordered the company's Standards Department to make comprehensive studies of workloads with the goal of reducing labor costs by $25,000 per year.[35]

Predictably, during the summer of 1954 workers filed numerous grievances protesting the company's workload increases. Because workers' earnings were protected for at least four weeks after workload changes, management could not expect any immediate savings on labor costs and would realize none at all if the grievances were decided in the union's favor.

Managers had also invested in over $1.5 million worth of new machinery, and they anticipated further workload challenges after the equipment was installed. Significantly, by 1954 top company officials began considering resistance to new workloads when estimating the potential benefits of their investments in equipment. Referring to the company's latest plan to spend $600,000 to renovate parts of the Harriet complex, Marshall Cooper lamented in March 1954 that it would be "practically impossible" to get the equipment in place "before the end of the year," and even then the company would "probably not get any real results profit-wise from them until the first part of next year, as new workloads would have to be established and proposed to the employees." Management should expect at least a three-month battle over workloads, Cooper warned.[36]

Unwilling to allow such delays to become routine, in late 1954 company officials pressed for new contract language that would set clear standards and expectations for workloads.[37] Union members were also anxious to find a better way to determine assignments. They were willing to consider the company's idea of clear standards as long as the workers were involved in the workload-setting process. When management refused to share this power with its employees, union members went on strike. The two sides held firm for six weeks before the company finally relented and agreed to allow union representatives to examine the data used to establish workloads.[38]

Marshall Cooper's private response to the agreement reveals management's profound frustration with workload challenges and the danger that posed for the union locals. Cooper remarked to the board of directors that as long as the company could obtain satisfactory contract concessions, management "preferred to continue with the Union."[39] His comment underscores the vulnerability of southern TWUA locals in the 1950s, scattered and few as they were. In the early to mid-1950s only about 13,000 of North Carolina's more than 220,000 mill workers belonged to unions. Locals 578 and 584 in Henderson represented nearly $\frac{1}{7}$ of the entire TWUA-CIO membership in the state.[40] Regionwide, less than 15 percent of the roughly 600,000 textile workers were organized, and the number of union members was shrinking. Most of the major chains had avoided unionization. Forty-two companies employed nearly half of the South's millhands, and of the 417 mills owned by those firms, only 36 were organized.[41] Against this background Harriet and Henderson managers apparently felt that they had enough leverage to determine whether or not their employees would remain unionized, and workload conflicts had pushed company officials to the limit of their tolerance.

The newly signed contract did little to relieve tensions. As soon as the new equipment that had been ordered in 1954 arrived, Harriet and Henderson management defied the agreement and established work assignments without union participation. Feeling betrayed as well as overworked, union members filed numerous grievances.[42] For the purposes of this overview, it is enough to note that the Henderson Mill spinners, who were greatly affected by the new equipment, eventually won a workload reduction through arbitration. Also, large numbers of Harriet Mill workers pursued their grievances to arbitration and won. Whereas Marshall Cooper had estimated a three-month delay before the Harriet Mill workloads could be finalized, the arbitrator's verdict came nearly a year after much of the machinery had been installed. Once again workers had frustrated management's strategies for recovering from a recession by insisting that there were limits to the amount of work that they could be expected to perform. These challenges prevented managers from obtaining instant labor-cost reductions by "squeezing" more work from employees, and they also forced the company to adjust its expectations about the potential effect of technological innovations on profitability.[43]

Despite these defeats for management, Harriet and Henderson's profits rose significantly during the following year. In October 1956, Harriet #1 was running six days a week and was "still having to turn down business." Marshall Cooper stated in January 1957 that the company's "earnings, based on the dollar volume, would compare favorably with any other company in our particular segment of the industry."[44]

Cooper's observation is very significant. In an industry dominated by nonunion firms, the Harriet and Henderson Mills were doing better than most. During 1956 and 1957, when the Coopers' mills were running full-time, making relatively healthy profits and looking for ways to expand, aggregate cotton-mill production and employment in the South were declining in response to slackening markets. In North Carolina alone a total of fifteen mills went bankrupt in 1956 and 1957. A North Carolina Textile Manufacturers Association speaker, Halbert Jones, declared in May 1957 that "the record of the textile industry during these past years has not been one in which we can take pride." According to Jones, mill owners, nearly 90 percent of whom were not contending with unionized workforces, belonged to "an industry at war," and their "adversaries," who were "every non-textile producer of goods and services," had them "on the run."[45] In contrast, Harriet and Henderson officials anticipated continued profitability by investing another million dollars to increase production at both the Harriet #1 and Henderson Mills.[46]

Relative prosperity, however, brought no end to workload conflicts. Because postwar markets had proven to be so volatile, company officials argued that it was necessary to increase workloads to boost productivity even as sales boomed and profits rose throughout 1956 and into 1957.[47] Given the proliferation of new textile technologies, the continued intense competition, and the frequent deep recessions in the industry, management's claim that the wolf was at the door seemed to have a certain validity. As if to affirm management's warnings, a deep national recession struck again in late 1957 and early 1958. Marshall Cooper complained in March 1958 of the "worst quarterly report" since 1954. Momentarily forgetting the Great Depression, John D. Cooper Jr. called business in early 1958 "worse than it had been since he had been with the company."[48] In addition to the competitive pressures described above, the cotton textile industry in 1958 had been severely affected by developments in markets for raw cotton, the largest single factor in the cost of production. America's domestic cotton production in the 1950s was limited by federal acreage allotments, and the cotton itself was frequently of poor quality. The 1957 crop was particularly small and "inferior in grade."[49] Industry analysts at the time argued that these price supports "held the American mills in a vice of artificial high price, making cotton substantially noncompetitive with foreign-made cotton cloth and synthetic fibers."[50]

Throughout the postwar years, markets for cotton, cloth, and yarn controlled the fortunes of the Harriet and Henderson Mills. When sales had been strong in 1956 the company had ambitiously planned to increase Harriet #1's weekly yarn production from 100,000 to 135,000 pounds. By the time the project was completed, however, markets were glutted and prices were falling. When he launched the expansion program in September 1956, Marshall Cooper had hoped for as much as $175,000 in additional profits each year from the increased output at Harriet #1, but the entire company barely grossed more than $200,000 in the slumping economy of 1958.[51] No matter how hard managers tried to predict market swings, every few years they found themselves either in the midst, or feeling on the verge, of a crisis.

Even though macroeconomic forces bore the primary responsibility for the cotton industry's miseries, at the local level Harriet and Henderson officials could influence their destiny only by improving efficiency with new machinery and demanding greater effort from their employees. Fierce competition and huge, often unpredictable market shifts frequently undercut expensive, long-range modernization strategies. Forced to live with the consequences of unfortunate business decisions made years earlier, managers were under enormous pressure to remain competitive by reducing labor costs inside their mills.

The result was an endless cycle of demands for workload increases followed by protests, which infuriated managers more than any other change brought by unionization. In 1958 Marshall Cooper emphasized to fellow members of the board of directors that workload protests were "the biggest disadvantage of having a Union in your plant."[52] Formal grievances consistently altered management's plans for restructuring the workplace and allowed workers to influence what could be expected of them on the job.

Although union-management relations in Henderson during the postwar years were dominated by workload conflicts, workers and managers continued to care about wages as well. Local union members eagerly accepted the substantial regionwide pay hikes negotiated by the TWUA during these years. The most significant increases came shortly after the war, when the federal government removed wage ceilings. Three raises, in March and August 1946 and February 1947, boosted average hourly wages in the textile industry nearly 40 percent, to $1.19 an hour. While southern textile workers still earned nearly twenty-five cents per hour below the national average manufacturing wage, most considered their new rate a tremendous improvement. In 1948 Harriet and Henderson millhands earned, on average, three times what they had made prior to unionization. Wage increases were relatively infrequent and less dramatic following the 1949 recession. By 1958 four raises, in 1950 (9 cents/hour), 1951 ($2\frac{1}{2}$ cents/hour), 1955 (5 cents/hour), and 1956 (10 cents/hour), boosted the average cotton-mill wage $26\frac{1}{2}$ cents per hour, to $1.45.[53] Undoubtedly, most union members would have preferred to make even more money. On the other hand, managers feared, especially after the 1949 recession brought an end to the postwar boom, that rising wages in their harshly competitive industry would drive the company to bankruptcy. When the TWUA asked for an additional across-the-board raise in 1951, John D. Cooper could not contain himself. "Where is this going to stop?" he snapped. "One increase after another is certainly the way to bring on a depression."[54]

Despite this obvious interest in wage increases, there is no contradiction in arguing that workloads were the primary focus of labor conflict after unionization. Indeed, wages and workloads could not be separated into neat, distinct categories. On piecework jobs they were one and the same. Production quotas, which were another way to describe workloads, determined the wage. If piece-rate workers were to receive the equivalent of a straight wage increase, not based on production, they had to exercise some control over the content of their jobs. Even workers who were paid by the hour closely monitored their workloads, because if they failed to perform their required assignments, they could be warned, laid off, and ultimately dismissed. For that reason alone, union members who were paid by the hour filed nearly as many workload grievances as workers on piece rates.[55] Only a small number of jobs, mainly highly skilled positions like card grinding, were immune from workload increases and production pressures.[56]

Because piece rates directly linked wages with output, they are often thought of as providing incentive for workers to produce as much as possible and thereby maximize individual earnings. That was the philosophy of the most famous American proponent of piecework, Frederick Taylor, who complained early in this century that managers did not allow piece rates to provide a true incentive to produce. Instead, Taylor noted, managers slashed rates whenever possible, forcing workers to produce more and more for the same, or less, money. Writing in the 1950s, Daniel Bell observed that most managers still used piecework as an "output-incentive" plan rather than as a means for workers to earn more money.[57] That was true in southern cotton mills, where managers set and revised piece rates so that roughly half of the hands could meet, or barely exceed, predetermined average hourly wage targets. During World War II the National War Labor Board set and enforced hourly averages for cotton-mill jobs. After the war the private Southern Textile Commission (STC) performed this function, establishing and adjusting what came to be known as "peg points" for each position. These STC peg points became the benchmark for wages throughout the South in both union and nonunion mills.

At Harriet and Henderson, workers and managers alike regarded the STC peg points as almost sacred. A company official once called peg points "the foundation of the house" for determining what wages would be.[58] Union members tended to view each peg point as an inviolable minimum wage. For example, a group of spinners once filed a grievance when their "side-hour" rate—eight sides of frames multiplied by $.1028 per side per hour—allowed them to earn only $.8224 per hour, slightly less than their peg point of $.83. Clearly, their wage demand—for $.0076 per hour—was as much a defense of principle as a desire for more money. On the other hand, managers frequently argued that peg points should also be a maximum wage. In the case just mentioned, company attorney Bennett Perry claimed that if this particular group of spinners succeeded in receiving $.83 per hour, "we would be entitled to reduce the others to 83 cents."[59] When workers on more conventional piecework consistently produced enough to exceed their peg points, managers usually cut the piece rates. Local 584 president Luther Jackson and the company's Carl Page had a revealing exchange on this subject. "Why change the piece rate?" Jackson asked Page. "Earning too much," came the reply. "If they make more money you want to cut them," Jackson complained.[60] Rarely did more than a few of the fastest, most efficient hands in the mills average more than their peg points on a regular basis.

Understanding the relative rigidity of peg points helps clarify the interconnection of workloads and wages. In the wage equation *"piece rate ×*

workload (production quota) = average hourly wage," the average hourly wage at any time was constant. Therefore, any increase in a piece rate was automatically a workload reduction. An employee did not have to produce as much to earn the peg point. Conversely, any reduction in a piece rate was the equivalent of a workload increase.

Influence over workloads was a crucial element in helping all Harriet and Henderson workers fulfill their hopes of earning their wages once they had secured access to livelihoods. Union members hoped that their jobs would provide a predictable, secure income without jeopardizing their health and well-being. Too much work could result in injury, fatigue, chronic ill health, missed days, warnings, and possibly the loss of one's job. On the other hand, a light workload could cause lean paydays and hardship for one's family. Given the frequent recessions and the varying amounts of labor required to produce different types of yarn, there was not always enough work to go around. Under those circumstances, workers with low workloads often demanded more work, hence, more money.[61]

It is important to emphasize what is meant here by the term "workload." In the textile industry, workloads were not merely a matter of the length of the workday or the speed of any particular machine, important as that was. Virtually every conceivable decision regarding the workplace had an influence on job assignments. Workloads were determined by the type of equipment used, the layout of the machinery on the floor, the number of machines and additional duties assigned per person, production goals, estimates of human endurance, the specific yarns to be produced, cleaning and maintenance schedules, quality requirements, and the amount of allowable break time. Union members' concerns about workloads, therefore, intersected directly with what once had been entirely management's domain. Although the public language of workloads —innumerable, arcane piece rates throughout the mills—was money, the negotiations behind each rate involved crucial, specific choices about the utilization of resources, both mechanical and human.

The relationship between wages and workloads complicates efforts to compare postunionization conditions in Henderson with the experience of unorganized workers in southern cotton mills. It would be practically impossible, for example, to compare wages at organized and nonunion mills. Harriet and Henderson officials frequently defended their demands for higher workloads by claiming that their nonunion competitors could undersell them because of their lower labor costs. It is entirely possible that the Harriet and Henderson Mills indeed paid higher average hourly earnings than most of their nonunion competitors. Nevertheless, even if the company had documented its claims by presenting tables of comparative wages, workers would have remained unconvinced. As any winder or doffer knew, average wage figures could be misleading. Workers did not always receive the amount listed for their job classifications. Paychecks depended on production totals, which varied every day. Wage scales, then, were at best theoretical.

An exchange between company Standards Department (Time-Study) chief Carl Page and Local 584 president Luther Jackson illustrates how management's claims about uncompetitive wages failed to persuade workers. "Our wages are higher than 90% of our competitors," Page once complained. "You all always talking about your competitors," Jackson countered. "I try to get to some of your competitors and find out what their production is, what their wage scale is, and sometimes I am amazed at the wage scale," admitted the local union leader. "Sometimes we are probably 3 cents an hour above them on wages. And then lo and behold, we are around 30,000 to 40,000 lbs. in production per week higher than [they] are." Jackson's point, of course, was that wage levels by themselves were meaningless. Moreover, to make persuasive comparisons between mills one would have to know, in addition to total weight of production, precisely what machinery was used and what types of yarn were produced during the period in question. When mills produced finer varieties of yarn, total production by weight was reduced. Those same finer yarns, however, usually commanded higher prices than coarser types, which could mean greater profits despite the superficial appearance of declining productivity.[62]

These variables led toward almost hopeless complexity. While managers could always assert that their union-influenced wage scale was out of line with those of their nonunion competitors, the company could never prove it to the satisfaction of its employees. Harriet and Henderson workers clearly did not destroy the company's ability to compete, because the mills earned profits every year with an organized workforce.[63] The union contract did prevent unilateral downward revisions in peg points. Harriet and Henderson workers also negotiated a minimum-wage structure, guaranteeing employees 90 percent of their peg points on days when their production slipped. Both of those provisions might have resulted in labor costs that were somewhat higher than those at unorganized mills, especially during recessions, when managements not bound by those restrictions could cut piece rates and refuse to pay customary minimum wages in search of a competitive edge. It is difficult to imagine, though, how anyone could document the precise impact of labor costs on the ability of the Harriet and Henderson Mills to market their products. There were, and are, too many significant variables to consider.

Given the absence, then and now, of concrete, objective evidence with which to compare unionized and nonunion mills, it is clear that complaints by Harriet and Henderson management about labor costs were not strictly about wages. Company officials were as aware as anybody else of the complexities involved when attempting such comparisons. However, complaining about high wages was an acceptable, ostensibly authoritative way for managers to vent frustration with the most important impact of unionization: organized workers could vigorously challenge workload increases, while unorganized workers who valued their jobs did not dare.

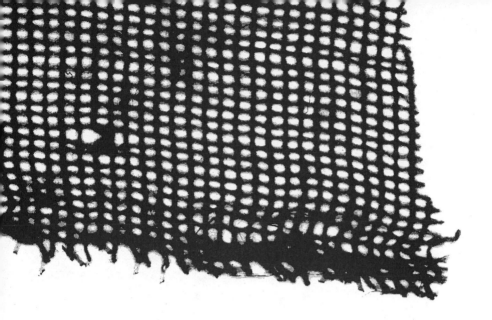

6 The Ambiguous Terms of Workload Conflict

Although specific clauses in the union contract provided for the rational resolution of disputes over work assignments, union members and managers never developed mutually satisfactory language for even discussing workloads. Union members pitted their subjective evidence, based on job experiences, against management's claims, based on scientific time studies, that workloads could be measured objectively. Throughout the postwar years workloads in the mills were debated in terms of aching joints versus slide-rule calculations. Workers and managers often reached such wildly different conclusions that it was difficult to believe they were describing the same job. Tempers flared because the stakes were high for both sides. While managers saw workload challenges as an exasperating obstacle in their quest for lower production costs, workers sought to protect their livelihoods, their health, and their dignity.

The contract allowed managers to take the initiative in revising workloads and piece rates. Company officials had the right to propose workload changes as long as they informed the proper local shop committee of their intentions seven days before the new requirements went into effect. Management was also solely responsible for decisions regarding technological innovations, which always affected workloads. Whenever the company changed workloads, the affected hands were obligated to try the new assignments for four weeks. The contract was unambiguous: "Any employee who refuses to accept such changes shall be discharged." In return for giving any company proposal a try, workers' incomes were guaranteed for the four-week trial. After trial periods, however, workers were guaranteed only 90 percent of their peg points. The hands could not formally challenge new workloads, and managers could not discipline employees who failed to complete revised assignments, until the trial period expired.

During trial periods both sides tried to determine whether or not the new assignments would balance the equation "*piece rate × production quota (workload) = average hourly wage (peg point)*." According to the contract, new workloads that required the same total amount of effort, even if specific tasks had changed, were to provide workers with the same average earnings they had been receiving before the trial period. If a workload were increased, however, average earnings were to be raised proportionally.

There were many reasons why the equation might not balance during a trial period. An occasional day of missed production could easily be attributed to outside factors, but consistent shortages indicated that there were problems. If outside variables seemed not to be at fault, workers were likely to conclude that their inability to reach quotas was proof that the new assignments were excessive. In contrast, company officials were likely to perceive shortfalls as evidence that workers were either unacceptably inefficient or purposefully slowing down on the job. If a worker failed to reach production quotas too frequently after a trial period, without mitigating circumstances, the hand would receive a warning.

The contract limited the specific charges that workers and managers could make with respect to workloads. Management was obligated to set "efficient and reasonable" assignments that provided "adequate" rest, or "fatigue time." When challenging workloads, then, union members had to convince either management or an outside arbitrator that certain workloads were indeed unreasonable. On the other hand, company officials tried to persuade workers, or arbitrators if necessary, that specific assignments were efficient and perfectly reasonable and allowed for adequate break time. The ambiguity in these terms provided the foundation for conflict. How much work was reasonable? How much fatigue time was adequate? The contract offered no firm guidelines.

Although hundreds of workload disputes entered the formal grievance process during the union years, in every case the affected workers' arguments were essentially the same: management expected them to do too much. Testimony from union members in the earliest workload disputes illustrates the variety of ways in which the hands could make their points. In 1943, Harriet #2 drawing-frame tender B. H. Roberson told an arbitrator, "We don't have a minute for nothing. I don't get 5 minutes in every 8 hours." A year later, long-draft spinner Belva Vann assessed her workload by her energy level at the end of her shift. "The main thing is that we get so tired from a day's work," she said. "I think we should get a little bit of relief."[1] Also in 1944, Mattie Fuller, who had been winding and spinning at the Harriet Mill for thirty years, explained the effects of operating long-draft spinning frames, the cornerstone of the initial modernization effort. "It's such a strain on your nerves," she said. "Makes your arms and neck hurt when you go home." More than anything else, the long-draft spinners wanted a reduction in the number of times that they had to "wring off" the last of a roving bobbin. "It's just about the worse job that we have," complained Hattie Pulley. "My arms and wrist give out." Belva Vann added, "This lady had her arm sprained and said it came from wringing off her pieces. There was a blood vessel hurt in her arm. She said the doctor told her that was what it came from and not to wring any more off."[2]

Time and again workers lined up to offer similar assessments of their responsibilities. Fred Boone claimed in 1944 that his card-room job was "about to get the best of me. It was just more work than I could do to run it." Alvin Currin, who ran the same set of frames on a different shift, agreed with Boone. "There isn't anything I can say except that there is more work there than I can do," he testified. "I have run it about 12 months and that's 12 months more than I want it." Dolly Barham offered a graphic illustration of the same workload. "I've worked in mills and on chain gangs," he said, and hauling bobbins was "the hardest thing I've ever run up against." "If you keep up you have to work yourself to death to do it," agreed James Cottingham.[3]

Union members' responses to management's workload crackdown during the 1949 recession followed this pattern. "From what I understand from the employees they have to work at a run at times," TWUA representative R. H. Harris explained to managers. Doffer Henry Stallings, who had lost an assistant in the workload consolidation, complained, "We have to doff all those boxes that they fill on the third shift. Those boxes weigh over 100 lbs. They are too heavy for one man to lift. I have bruises on my legs now from lifting them."[4]

The workload increases in the midst of the 1954 recession were also severe. Mary South, who labeled and hauled roving produced at the Henderson Mill, explained that "they added 12 frames. . . . In other words $\frac{2}{3}$rds of another person's job was added to mine and I was pretty well loaded before." When asked if she took any fatigue time, South replied, "Not at all."[5] Speeder-frame tender Elmore Murphy had a similar problem. "They took two helpers away from me and now I got to do it all by myself and I just can't keep up with it," he said. "We had them two helpers and could get the doff frame started up in 10 minutes and now it takes about 30." After the changes, however, Murphy argued that he could no longer reach production targets. "Can't be at two or three places at one time," he said.[6]

During the same wave of workload revisions, Harriet Mill spinners offered their own definition of what constituted an unreasonable assignment. "Any time I can not run my job I feel I have too much," one said. Mahaley Tharrington agreed that workers should be allowed to determine whether or not a workload was excessive. "They say they have the job set but it is too much work on one spinner and they have to work too fast. It is set wrong." An unidentified spinner pleaded with the managers, "I think we have too much of a job—more than we can keep up. Our job is too heavy. We can not keep it up in the best days. We can not do what Mr. Proctor would like for us to do. Give us what we can do in 8 hours."[7]

In this case, as in most workload challenges that were part of major modernization programs, management remained unconvinced by the spinners' complaints and denied their grievance at the first stage of the procedure. Undeterred, the spinners pleaded with what they felt were more convincing explanations. "With 8 frames like that, you just can't keep up with them," argued Clydie Clopton. "If you had roller skates on, you couldn't keep them up."[8] A spinner identified only as "Wheeler" agreed, testifying, "I checked my watch and I had worked as hard as I could and taken 8 minutes and I didn't set down then, because I had 2 frames ready to doff and when I got back I had 3 frames balled up. I work, nobody can't say I don't. I don't mind giving anybody 8 hours of work a day, but I would like to have 20 minutes personal time. I just got more than I can do. That's all I can say." But she continued anyway. "I want to be honest with the company. I don't mind work, but I don't want to kill myself. I have been out with my feet and the doctor said it was the work I was doing. I have got more than I can do."[9]

These Harriet Mill spinners reached new levels of stridency when the company ordered a trial period with revised assignments that the workers considered to be even worse. Local 578 president Sam Littleton tried to make managers realize how severely these increased workloads had affected the hands. "One lady came out that works on the 3rd shift," he said, and "she was at the point of just screaming, her nerves were all to pieces." "You all just ought to experience some of them jobs you set up there, and then you all would know something about them," one exasperated spinner challenged managers. Upon hearing that the company would consider changes, Minnie Hedgepeth warned, "Be to[o] late to think about it, when we have give out, and you have to get somebody else in there and learn them the job. Just too much excess."[10]

When workers complained about their workloads they often emphasized how their assignments prevented them from fulfilling basic human needs. As long-draft spinner Lissie Harris told an arbitrator in early 1944, "There were some nights last summer that I worked all night long without even getting a drink of water, and I got so hot that my tongue split." Perhaps the workers' most frequent complaint was that they barely had time to eat during a shift. "I have worked in there many nights when I don't have time to eat a bite," spinner Hattie Pulley testified in 1944. "We don't really have time to eat." "I just have to gobble my dinner down in order to get back to get on schedule," explained Mary South. Since the machines never stopped, Harriet Mill spinner Mahaley Tharrington did not waste time with meals. Lunch would be over, she said, "as quick as you can swallow it whole. You don't chew it—you chew it later." Even then, she noted, "when you go back there is ends down," which meant broken yarn and tangled balls of waste clogging her machines. This was a common scenario. "I do go in the rest room just a few minutes and eat," admitted another spinner, Minnie Hedgepeth. But when she returned, she explained, referring to her spinning frames, "Oh my, are they behind. . . . Then you have to work so hard catching them up."[11]

As management became more insistent about enforcing higher workloads, millhands often received criticism for taking any breaks at all. Supervisors were quick to spot pauses in workers' routines and frequently used such evidence to contradict any complaints about excessive workloads. One time-study official disputed Harriet Mill spinners' claims with his observation that "most every time you go through there you see some of them sitting down for a considerable length of time." Another company representative testified that he had asked a spinner if she would be able to complete her assignment, "and she said she didn't think she would ever make it because she didn't have time and later I saw that same girl staring out of the window." [12] According to managers, any time spent taking a glimpse of the outdoors, however brief, was an unnecessary indulgence that compromised the union members' own arguments about their allegedly high workloads.

Harried and unhappy with ever-increasing assignments, union members argued repeatedly that their own experience should be the determining factor in setting workloads. Therefore, when managers refused to concede that particular workloads were too heavy, union members felt that insult had been added to injury. There was no denying, however, that the workers' evidence, which was almost entirely subjective, led to nagging questions. Could workers be trusted to tell the truth about their experiences? Or were union members who challenged workloads really trying to get out of doing a fair day's work? How could any worker's claim be verified? This apparent softness in the hands' testimony provided the company with an opening for counterargument.

Harriet and Henderson managers defended their workload revisions on the basis of science. Their first college-trained "time-study man," William Camp, had studied textile engineering at Alabama Polytechnic in Auburn. Camp's father had developed that textile school as well as a similar program in Lubbock, Texas. After graduating in 1936, William Camp took his first job at a cotton mill in Georgia, where he gained on-the-job experience conducting time studies. By the mid-1940s he was considered well qualified in that field.[13] Time-study engineers carefully observed workers and machines, noted wasted effort, and calculated production quotas for each job. They were the descendants of the "scientific management" movement, the approach to running a business most commonly associated with the work of Frederick Taylor in the late nineteenth and early twentieth centuries. By the 1940s, studying the work process scientifically with the goal of improving efficiency had become a standard management technique. To many managers it had nothing to do with any awareness of theory. It had simply become common sense. Top Harriet and Henderson officials, for example, had apparently never heard of either Frederick Taylor or the term "scientific management," but during the 1940s and 1950s they considered good time-study engineers to be absolutely essential for operating a cotton mill.[14]

The authoritative claims of time studies rested on the premise that in contrast to any subjective claims that workers might make, the content of any job could indeed be measured objectively. William Camp argued that he could calibrate assignments so precisely that all employees who put in "a fair day's work" would earn their hourly peg points.[15] Harriet and Henderson's new engineer was in step with his profession. Numerous time-study consulting firms around the country offered similar promises, and their services, to any interested business. One engineer who headed his own consulting company, and who occasionally served as an arbitrator in textile labor disputes, claimed that a workload was "beyond the realm of conjecture; it is something that is based on facts."[16] Until 1948, even the United States Conciliation Service (USCS), a branch of the federal Department of Labor, had its own corps of time-study technicians to help settle workload disputes.

Collecting time-study data was relatively easy. A textile time studier needed only a stopwatch, a pen, and a piece of paper on a clipboard. Once familiar with a particular job, the engineer or an underling would observe for a specified time and write down everything a worker did and how long each activity took. After reviewing the figures, a time-study expert would calculate how much of the shift the employee in question had actually worked and how much time had been spent resting.

It was not enough, however, for workers to be merely busy. They had to work efficiently. So in addition to calculating raw data on work and rest times, the Standards Department developed a scale, called a "unit" system, for measuring the relative efficiency of employees. Although the tasks in a cotton mill were varied, the engineers determined exactly how much work on each job constituted a unit. Then they measured how many units employees performed each hour. An efficient worker, the company eventually determined, ought to produce at a pace of sixty-eight units per hour.[17]

In most cases, the conclusions the company drew from time studies did not faintly resemble the experience-based claims of the same workers. In one of the first workload grievances, for example, drawing-frame hand B. H. Roberson argued that he had less than five minutes of fatigue time in an eight-hour shift. The Standards Department, however, concluded that Roberson and his coworkers enjoyed at least "69 53/100" minutes of rest each day, well above the one hour that the company considered adequate.[18] In another early case, a spinning-room section man complained that he had a full load keeping forty-eight spinning frames in running order. In contrast, the Standards Department argued that an average section man ought to be able to service seventy frames.[19]

Time studies also contradicted the early claims of the long-draft spinners, who complained about sore arms and wrists from wringing off roving. The Standards Department insisted that the difficulties were the result of the spinners' own inefficiency. If the employees had performed their tasks correctly, the company argued, they would each have had "about two hours' rest" per shift.[20] To the spinners' dismay, even an outside engineer, James Bradbury of the A. M. Pullen Company, concluded that the women "could perform a larger number of sides than they were then doing." Bradbury collected time-study data on Belva Vann, who testified about how tired she was at the end of each shift and how hard her supervisor drove the spinners. Contradicting Vann's account of her own experience, Bradbury argued that she could not possibly have exhausted herself on the job because she had enjoyed 109 44/100 minutes of rest per shift. "I think the little girl was offering some pretty good ones there," Bradbury said. Unable to counter the objective data presented against them, the spinners lost their grievance in arbitration.[21]

Compounding such early setbacks, union members learned that even time-study data that was initially in their favor could be manipulated to their disadvantage. In 1947, Henderson Mill winder tenders protested that their wage increases had been unfairly accompanied by increases in their production requirements, making their workloads excessive. Skeptical of the company's calculations, the union requested that USCS engineers be summoned to provide independent time-study data. The government engineers produced a document that listed, among other things, the number of minutes of work required to wind one hundred pounds of each type of yarn then being produced. Using those figures, the union calculated how much fatigue time a winder tender could expect to receive during a shift if she met her production quota. In one representative example, the TWUA's Toby Mendes concluded that a winder processing a particular type of yarn would receive only sixteen minutes of fatigue time, well below the company's recommendation of sixty minutes per shift.[22] Although it seemed clear to the winders that the Conciliation Service's time studies proved their case, William Camp argued that the government figures could not be taken at face value. The USCS engineers, he explained, had measured in actual minutes of work, a "60-unit-hour" pace, which was well below the 68 units per hour the company demanded of its employees. Therefore, the Standards Department adjusted all USCS figures by a 60/68 ratio. In one representative example, whereas the USCS calculated that a winder would need 107.81 minutes to produce one hundred pounds of one type of yarn, the Standards Department figured that only 95.13 minutes were necessary.[23] Using the same objective data, management calculated workloads over 13 percent higher than the union's figures.

All time-study data was subject to this type of recalculation, a procedure that the company called "speed rating." Adjustments were made because Standards Department engineers assumed, for good reason, that workers intentionally slowed down during time studies. As Henderson Mill doffer Joseph Braswell recalled, "When that man from the Standards Department checked the job that was to be changed, the workers had a tendency to stay busy all day long, but not at a fast rate."[24] Most union members felt that a pace less than full throttle could still be considered reasonable. What union members considered a fair rate of speed, however, could be seen by managers as an unacceptable slowdown. On one rare occasion when a TWUA technician was allowed to study workloads in the mills, his data conflicted with that generated by the Standards Department. Company officials criticized the union representative, Toby Mendes, for not using a speed rating. "You didn't notice when they were slowing down?" asked the Standards Department's Carl Page. "They didn't slow down," Mendes answered. Different assumptions obviously produced markedly different results.[25]

The speed-rating system repeatedly transformed apparent defeat for the company into the potential for victory. In one of the first workload grievances, William Camp observed that Alvin Currin, who operated superdraft frames in the Harriet Mill card room, worked 456.13 minutes per shift, "which only gave him 5% rest for the 8 hours." Since the company considered 12.5 percent to be adequate fatigue time, Camp's data appeared to bolster the frame hand's argument that his workload was unreasonable. Camp calculated, however, that Currin had "worked at an over all speed rating of 55," well below what the company expected. If Currin had worked efficiently, Camp figured, "he would have had 28% rest," over double what was considered adequate. The company concluded that instead of complaining about his workload, slow-working Currin should have been grateful even to have a job.[26]

In another typical example, when spinners at the Harriet Mill protested against new workloads in 1954, time-study figures seemed to substantiate their claim. According to Camp, on the day he studied Ethel Allen she had received 42.31 minutes of fatigue time, which amounted to an inadequate 8.8 percent of her shift. Camp determined, however, that Allen's "overall speed rating on the study was a 50." If she had worked at a pace of sixty-eight units per hour, he argued, she would have had nearly two hours and forty minutes of rest during an eight-hour shift. Trying to be fair, Camp factored in the time it would have taken Allen to perform cleaning duties that she had not completed that day. "Had she done that cleaning at a fair rate of speed," Camp claimed, it "would have taken her 39.93 minutes," which "would give a total adjusted minutes of work of 357.72." Altogether, then, the speed rating had turned 42.31 minutes of break time into 122.28, or 25.5 percent of Allen's shift.[27]

The Harriet and Henderson Standards Department was in step with current practices in the time-study field. A textile industry expert claimed in 1954 that speed rating "is the most practical method yet developed to adjust the actual times obtained on a time study, and is used by almost 90 percent of the time study departments of the country."[28] Millhands throughout the South, then, were frustrated by similar calculations.

Harriet and Henderson workers viewed speed ratings as a subjective fudge factor that allowed the company to conclude whatever it wanted from time studies. A 1953 exchange between Henderson Mill superintendent Joe Farmer and shop committee member and winder tender Mae Renn illustrates the union members' resentment. After warning the committee that "we will all be happier if we meet competition" and that he wanted the union "to keep that in mind," Farmer suggested to Renn that management's proposed work assignments would be all right "if you would do them like Mr. Camp sets them up." Unwilling to defer to science, Renn snapped back, "He has got [the] ability to pick out a work load. I have a job and a half."[29] A member of the international TWUA's research department supported Harriet and Henderson workers by noting that speed ratings were so subjective, a worker "has no assurance that one engineer's concept of a 68 [unit-hour] performance will not be called 60, for example, by another engineer, or 92 by still another."[30] Union members had reasons of their own to believe that the Standards Department made its conclusions in advance and adjusted data accordingly, but internal company records verify the workers' suspicions. During the 1954 recession, for example, top management ordered the Standards Department to conduct studies not in the quest of impartial truth but rather with the specific goal of cutting $25,000 from labor costs.[31]

When union members questioned the validity of time-study data and speed ratings, they were not necessarily accusing any particular observer of acting in bad faith. Millhands understood that accurately measuring work and determining the reasons for low production was a formidable task. As a rule, a cotton mill's output fluctuated so wildly, for reasons beyond any worker's control, that if time studies were to be scientific the company would have required a Standards Department staff virtually as large as its production workforce. It was difficult to conclude, after the fact, precisely which variables caused low production on any particular day. Investigators had to be on the scene. Therefore, each job would have had to be studied every day, defeating the purpose of time studies by significantly increasing payrolls. Moreover, a large staff still would not have ensured indisputable results. Cotton-mill workloads defied quantification.

The quality of the cotton entering the manufacturing process greatly influenced production totals. Although company cotton purchasers and receivers did their best to select only acceptable bales, they processed several hundred thousand pounds of cotton each week, so it was always possible for some low-quality raw material to slip through. Once inside the system, poor cotton affected each stage of the production process. When it reached the spinning frames, for example, it increased the frequency of yarn breaks, which meant machines sat idle, awaiting a busy spinner's attention. If a spinner did not quickly discover and repair "broken ends," the damaged yarn streamed through the frames, wrapping around the rollers and causing "ball-ups" that took much longer to untangle. If the yarn entering the mill contained too much waste and debris from the cotton field, the carding equipment could not extract it all and the specks of foreign material created "slubs" in the yarn. Slubs lowered production totals by causing additional snags and tears. To consider all relevant variables when evaluating jobs, time-study engineers would have had to monitor the quality of every bale of cotton unloaded at the mills.[32]

Even a good bale of cotton, however, could create problems if the weather failed to cooperate. As Harriet Mill card-room foreman Carson Mills once remarked, humidity "has more to do with cotton work than anything else." High humidity, which was constant during a North Carolina summer, profoundly affected production. "July and August are the worst running months in the year," confirmed Harriet Mill superintendent Proctor.[33] Accurate time studies, then, required a daily record of humidity levels inside the mills.

Comprehensive time studies also had to verify that problems stemming from practices in one department had not negatively affected workloads and production totals for workers further along in the process. It was to the spinning-room doffers' advantage, for example, to remove bobbins before they were completely full to increase the number of doffs they performed each shift. Undersized bobbins, however, forced the winder tenders to creel their frames more frequently. Since machines sat idle during creeling, small bobbins both reduced production and made the winder tenders' work harder than usual. On the other hand, oversized bobbins often became tangled, halting production while the winders unclogged their frames.

Although the company claimed that its engineers took bobbin size into account when measuring work and that winders were paid by the hour to process those that were too large or small, there were often strong disagreements between workers and supervisors about the definition of an inferior bobbin. When confronting her foreman, Henderson Mill shop steward Mae Renn once complained, "Any number of times I have brought you around and shown you the oversized bobbins. So often when they [the supervisors] checked on them they wouldn't consider it an oversized bobbin."[34] On another occasion, despite claiming that her bobbins had been "too small all that week," Harriet Mill winder Esther Roberson received a warning for low production. Roberson had counted 236 small bobbins in two boxes from the spinning room. "I know you will sometimes find 10 or 12 too small," she said. "That's understandable. I don't grumble over that." But this batch, she argued, had given her headaches. Roberson asked her second hand to measure the width of the bobbins. "Finally he found one that fitted the ring," she testified in her defense. "He said, 'Esther, you see here, this bobbin fits.' I said, 'That one is right, James, but the rest of them are too small.' He said, 'Oh well, if one bobbin fits out of the whole box, the box will be counted big enough.' I said, 'Well, the horse won't pull two ways. If one bobbin is big enough to make the whole box big enough, one bobbin too little will make the box too little.'"[35]

Bobbin size obviously made a difference in the difficulty of the winders' workload, but to account scientifically for this variable, supervisors would have had to measure the countless numbers of bobbins flowing from the spinning room and to compile detailed records. After all, time-study technicians could not measure bobbins after they had been emptied of their contents.

Measuring workloads and rating the effort of each worker required the accurate assessment of each job's idiosyncrasies. A spinner's production, for example, depended on how well she and the women who operated the same job on the other two shifts cleaned their frames. Lint-filled machines caused yarn to break and wrap around rollers rather than bobbins. If a spinner had a bad shift because of dirty frames, however, it was not necessarily the other worker's fault. Since lower-level managers were also under severe pressure to maximize production, they often encouraged spinners on their shifts to skip cleaning and to fix broken ends instead. When the gamble succeeded, the second hand and workers on another shift suffered the consequences. For the Standards Department to establish, beyond doubt, who was at fault, somebody would have had to observe the spinners on every shift.[36]

There was also controversy over how long an engineer should observe a job before assigning a workload or calculating a speed rating. Could a time studier extrapolate from a short observation period to determine, with any degree of certainty, what a particular job would be like later in that shift, or the next day? On any job, tasks that went smoothly early in the shift could later become nightmarish. Conditions could be optimum for a week, then turn sour for two more. This problem arose in one of the first workload disputes, when the company argued that based on a ninety-minute study of card-room jobs, the hands should have enjoyed over an hour of rest per shift. The TWUA's Red Lisk, however, asked whether or not an engineer, through such a brief study, "could determine how much fatigue time the men had?" Local 584 president Luther Jackson, who, like all local officials, held a full-time job, directly challenged the results of such short studies. "I saw you in there a couple of days and the longest you stayed was 15 minutes," he said to the time-study engineer. "You checked me in 6 minutes. You never even saw me with a brush in my hand." How, then, Jackson implied, could the company have any idea how long it really took to clean the frames?[37]

There were no simple solutions. If the observer had watched Jackson for eight hours, the results of that study would not necessarily have been valid for others who ran similar jobs that day. Other pertinent questions had to be answered: were all the frames equally dirty? Did the frames producing fine yarn require more cleaning than those running coarser varieties? If so, how much more? Given that there were over one thousand production jobs between the two mills, the Standards Department, which had at most a dozen employees, could not possibly make regular eight-hour studies of every position. Therefore, the company deployed its resources selectively, usually wherever there was a workload change in progress or a formal grievance to be resolved. Even then, the observers could rarely devote a full eight hours to any one job. Nevertheless, all of these questions, and more, had to be answered to make indisputable, scientific calculations of proper work assignments.

In practice, however, managers and workers could not even agree on the distinction between work and rest. That was a major reason why workers' claims and management's figures often differed so greatly. The union argued that "fatigue time" should be defined as periods when workers could sit down and relax away from the job. The company disagreed. One basic point of contention was whether time spent walking should be counted as work or as leisure. In one early case an engineer calculated that a protesting employee had adequate fatigue time "if you figured the time he spent in walking through the room and up and down the frames." TWUA representative Red Lisk argued, however, that when workers walked up and down the aisles they were observing spindles, looking for problems. "The time that he spends up and down the frames is patrolling time and is counted as occupied time, not unoccupied time," Lisk insisted. Thirteen years later, this ambiguous source of contention had still not been resolved. Instead, it had increased in importance, because with each mechanical change the company assigned more frames to each worker. "You all take in a lot of things for fatigue time that we don't recognize as fatigue time," snapped Luther Jackson in a 1957 workload dispute.[38]

To union members, the Standards Department's distinctions between work and rest often appeared ludicrous, most notably when applied to the meeting of basic human needs. Regional TWUA representative Julius Fry once goaded William Camp on the engineer's methods and assumptions. "Now let me ask you if a person was walking up the back alley on a job and stopped at the window a moment and took in a breath of fresh air and then continued on. Is that counted?" Fry asked Camp. "I don't hardly think we could pull it [the stopwatch] out that quick," Camp replied. "I don't think that would be counted." Fry pressed further. "I was just wondering how fast reaction time was," he said. "If he used 1/10th of a minute and took a real long breath that would be fatigue time, wouldn't it?" "Yes," answered the engineer. "I had a man not long ago," Camp continued, "didn't make any difference where he was going, if he passed the water cooler, he was going to get a swig of water. He wouldn't do anything but turn it on and get a mouth full and go on, but he was going to get it." "So you charged it against him." "Yes Sir. It's not work time, is it? We don't require him to drink water."[39]

Although this may seem like a minor quibble, the union was exposing fundamental flaws in the science of time studies. Machinery in a cotton mill had regular maintenance schedules, including required oiling and repairs, that were considered necessary for maintaining maximum production. Oiling machines was work time. Management did not require its employees to drink water, however, and did not post bodily maintenance on the bulletin board as part of any job specification, although during these years before air conditioning, the humans were greatly affected by the overwhelming heat inside cotton mills, especially in summer. Workers argued that high temperatures reduced their stamina, hence their production. As spinner Minnie Hedgepeth emphasized, "It's so hot up there you see, that's got a whole lot to do with it. You can't work rushed, it's so hot in there you can't hardly stand it."[40] Workers resented the idea that a quick drink or a breath of fresh air counted against them.

Even if the two sides had agreed on definitions of work and rest, there would still have been many thorny problems with measuring workloads. Throughout the postwar years, skill and experience made an enormous difference on nearly every job in a cotton mill. While mill owners and union leaders debated whether the employees or the machines set the pace in mill work, nobody disputed that some workers produced far more than others. "There are some speed kings and some low ones found on most all operations," Standards Department head Carl Page once remarked.[41] William Camp also noted a great disparity in skill among different hands who worked on the same machines. "Find as high as 40% variation," he said.[42]

Workers carefully noted whom the company chose to study in a particular department. Although the engineers, with their limited resources, could rarely study each employee, everyone on a particular job was affected by the data collected on those who were observed. Union members claimed that because the company usually studied only the fastest workers, production quotas tended to be unattainable for the average hand. Instead, the union argued, only the slowest workers should be studied, so that everybody could earn the peg point. Under this proposed system, faster workers would probably earn well above their hourly wage target, so the company refused to consider it. Indeed, when Harriet Mill winders asked that they all be able to earn their peg point, William Camp responded that to do so would be fiscal insanity. "You would have everybody in the mill wanting the winder job and making from 1.25 to 1.30 an hour," which was well above their peg point.[43] Camp's fears demonstrate that perfectly normal variations in ability undercut his allegedly fine-tuned piece rates. Although the Standards Department insisted that job assignments required only a fair day's effort from an average worker, it was possible that there were only a handful of "average" employees in a department. Even then, their "average" production would have depended on many outside variables and would have fluctuated considerably.

The company's inability to study everybody created additional problems. Because it was rare that two jobs were perfectly identical, time-study data from the observation of one job in a department was often of limited use when applied to another similar position. Work assignments in a cotton mill were directly related to the type of yarn being produced, to the particular machines in use, and to the exact layout of the machines, which affected walking distances, proximity to elevators, and ease of bobbin supply. During the postwar years the company was always making mechanical changes somewhere in at least one of the mills. Often the change was not a wholesale replacement but rather a modification of an existing frame. As a result, each mill was filled with a hodgepodge of equipment specially adapted to meet the company's needs at a particular time.

When presenting its time-study data, management frequently argued that slightly different mill jobs were similar enough for the purpose of setting workloads.[44] To concede otherwise would have implied that many more studies were necessary. But when union members tried to compare jobs to gain an advantage, company officials emphatically rejected their claims, often citing subtle differences in machinery specifications. When interdraft tenders in the Harriet #1 card room argued that their piece rate should have been equal to that of interdraft tenders at Harriet #2, Superintendent Proctor argued that the room layouts and machinery in the two card rooms were significantly different. Harriet #1, Proctor said, had Woonsocket frames with a balanced carriage, while #2 had Whitin frames with a dual carriage. Since the #2 spinning room had older frames, the #2 card room had to produce smaller bobbins than those made in #1.[45] Because textile mills were so idiosyncratic, the union could never successfully argue that jobs in different mills were identical and should therefore have the same piece rates. That same conclusion, however, implied that to obtain scientific data rather than approximations that were crude at best, the Standards Department would have to study, every day, virtually every job in the mills.

The accuracy of time studies could also be affected by the condition of the machinery on any job. Workers often charged that just before a time study the company repaired and maintained all equipment, ensuring that the cotton stock coming through was first-rate, and saw that all bobbins were the right size. In other words, workers claimed that management made studies under extraordinary circumstances that resulted in artificially high production totals. To be completely accurate, the Standards Department would presumably have had to conduct studies during all phases of the regular maintenance cycle to determine whether there should be variations in production expectations. Although the company denied arbitrarily influencing time studies in this way, union members were always suspicious. In one instance the company replaced a twist gear on a card-room frame for one observed shift and refused to allow the shop steward to see what they were doing. Whether or not the company had acted in good faith, the incident revealed the union's distrust of the process. "You make those two frames run good that they were checking so the Standards Dept. . . . would have a better check on them than what the rest of them ran," charged Local 584 shop committee member Raymond Wynn. "This has brought them to a point that they lose confidence in the studies," said TWUA representative R. H. Harris. "They are looking for flaws in time study."[46]

The accuracy of time-study data also depended to an extent on the attentiveness of the observer. Lapses were possible, especially during an eight-hour study. In addition, when time-study technicians succumbed to their own needs they could hinder the performance of the employee under observation. At one hearing, Nannie Hughes, a spinner with thirty years' experience, testified that she had been "checked three times" by the company, and on those days she "had to send in the rest room for my checker to come on, I was behind."[47] Once when TWUA representative Toby Mendes was allowed in the mill to conduct time studies, the company assigned one of its observers to study Mendes. The Standards Department's time study of the union's observer revealed that Mendes occasionally let down his guard. From "8:15 to 8:25 he left the operator, Sue Manning, punching rollers and talked to a yarn-sizer in another alley," reported the company's Douglas Allison. "Mendes again left the operator from 7:55 to $7:56\frac{1}{2}$ to talk to a girl mopping under-rockers two frames away."[48] Who knew what workers did when the time-study technician's eyes wandered? Were Standards Department personnel always completely vigilant? If not, what effect did that have on their data, especially when work and rest time were presented as accurate to the hundredth of a minute?

Even if time-study observers could remain alert for an entire shift, it was possible that none of them would be available when their services were needed most. Depending on what orders they received, company officials might switch production to a new type of yarn every few days or every couple of weeks. Given the peculiarities of yarn orders, each change often required slightly different machine specifications, hence revised workloads. Although workers could file grievances if they felt their new short-term workloads were excessive, there was no guarantee that their jobs would be studied before the company made its next change. "Our orders are what regulate the yarn numbers," explained Superintendent Farmer in one such case. "We can't do anything about that."[49] But managers could hardly expect that their own shrugged shoulders would convince affected employees that the interim work assignments had been reasonable.

Local union members and TWUA representatives constantly argued that objective time studies were unattainable. As Henderson Mill winder Mae Renn once explained, "Any winder will tell you you can't make the same production each week or year. You never know how the work will run."[50] TWUA representative Wayne Dernoncourt argued similarly that "conditions will vary even on the same yarn number, some days they have good runs and the next day she may have poor runs. The conditions are not the same."[51]

Some arbitrators also understood that tremendous variability was to be expected. "The same person working at the same speed and efficiency may have 2 hours' rest on one day and not be able to complete the work schedule the next day even though no time is taken to eat," explained Richard Lester, from Duke University, when assessing spinners' work assignments. "It is quite clear that the work-load is excessive on such 'bad' days, and is too low on certain 'good' days."[52]

Even Harriet and Henderson managers agreed that there were countless variables to consider. Company attorney Bennett Perry once played down the need to explain a period of excessive yarn breaks by arguing that there "is always a fluctuation in the running of the machines. Some times they run better; and some days they run worse."[53] Likewise, William Camp once testified that "spinning frames do not run the same from day to day" because of "the weather, way the spinner feels that [day], the humidity in the room and humidity outside." A time-study engineer, he said, could "check them one day and get one answer and another day and get another answer."[54] Certainly, then, low production could not automatically be attributed to slothful workers. Nevertheless, Camp felt confident that his scientific method could account for "all of the miscellaneous factors." The safeguard, he said, was "to check them a good many days and average them up."[55]

But how many studies would be sufficient? One textile industry analyst called Camp's strategy "impractical and indeed often impossible," because "the time and expense involved in such an analysis would be prohibitive."[56] Formal workload grievances alone often overloaded the Standards Department's resources. As Superintendent Proctor once told a group of protesting hands, "We can not bring Willie [Camp] in everytime."[57] Therefore, on many occasions management told workers to be patient and trust their supervisors, assuring the hands that time-study personnel would get to them, if necessary, as soon as possible.

To union members, time studies and speed ratings were parts of a technical-sounding scheme by which managers hoped to command the obedience of their workforce. The difference between the hands' workload-measuring system and the managers' is encapsulated in an exchange between Harriet Mill winder Lois Wilder and Superintendent Proctor. Wilder claimed that her workload was "too heavy and hard for a woman to do it every other day." Proctor replied that time studies contradicted her experience. "Well, Lois, where did you get that information that it is too heavy for a lady to do it every day?" he asked. "I got it right here in my hand," she replied. Although the numbers came up short, Wilder could feel the excessive work in her body.[58] The stage was constantly set for fierce battles over workloads.

7   Taking the Offensive
Seeking Greater Control over Workloads, 1948–1958

Throughout the union years, Harriet and Henderson management clung to the fiction that time studies accurately gauged the content of jobs and the pace at which work should be performed. While union members protested in heartfelt terms, their odds of success depended almost entirely on whether or not individual arbitrators accepted experience-based evidence as legitimate. After numerous early setbacks, union officials altered their strategy. They exploited the ambiguity inherent in time studies to seek joint control over the setting of workloads. This approach resulted in several major arbitration victories, and by early 1955, after a six-week strike over workloads, it appeared that the union would be allowed to review time-study evidence and raise challenges before management officially established job requirements. Compared to their counterparts in most southern textile mills, Harriet and Henderson workers had their managers on the ropes. Company officials, however, defied arbitration verdicts, keeping labor-management relations in a constant state of crisis.

The fate of nearly every major workload case depended to a great extent on the perspectives of individual arbitrators. Throughout the 1940s and 1950s, most potential arbitrators had entered that profession working for the National War Labor Board during World War II. Indeed, the federal government's wartime emphasis on strike-free dispute resolution virtually created the professional arbitrator, while giving practitioners the experience and reputations to dominate the field in the future. According to a 1952 survey, arbitrators averaged eleven years of experience, with "only a handful" having entered the field since 1947. The majority of arbitrators were either lawyers or college professors who settled labor disputes on a part-time basis.[1]

Even though their profession was in its infancy during the immediate postwar years, many arbitrators were optimistic about their potential peacetime role in national affairs. Maxwell Copelof, a leader in the field who presided over a 1947 dispute in Henderson, had great faith in the attractiveness of arbitration for both management and labor. "Why should we let a rank outsider tell us what to do? What does a college professor know about our business?" he wrote in 1948, paraphrasing the concerns of many managers. "Ask the people who have tried arbitration. If there ever was an instance where a company and a union had once agreed upon arbitration as the terminal point in their grievance procedure, and then abandoned it, this fact has been carefully concealed from students of American labor history."[2]

During this period experienced labor arbitrators took steps to formalize their profession and enhance its prestige. In 1947, forty-three professionals, convinced that "the arbitration process could be preserved only if it were kept in professional hands and away from both the amateurs and the shysters," created the National Academy of Arbitrators. While the American Arbitration Association helped parties in disputes choose arbitrators, the National Academy of Arbitrators saw its role as ensuring that there would be an adequate supply of qualified arbitrators from which to choose. The academy's membership, which rose to 105 in the organization's first year and to 250 by 1957, established criteria for admission to the profession and collaborated in 1948 with both the American Arbitration Association and the Federal Mediation and Conciliation Service to produce a

"Joint Code of Ethics" for the arbitration process. Prior to this, arbitrators had complained of feeling "adrift on an uncharted sea," unable to find out how their colleagues handled the tense environment at arbitration hearings, and largely ignorant of how other cases had been decided. Because publication of an arbitrator's decision required the consent of both parties to the conflict, only a tiny percentage of case reports ever became available for review. To eliminate their feelings of isolation, then, NAA members scheduled regional meetings to discuss their various experiences, to critique each other's performances, and to better prepare themselves for future cases. Since over 90 percent of collective bargaining agreements in the United States provided for some form of arbitration, NAA members could expect plenty of opportunities to benefit from their new insights.[3]

Throughout the 1940s and 1950s, however, a number of NAA members were troubled by their organization's inability to pinpoint exactly what kind of education, training, and experience were necessary to prepare one to become an arbitrator. To be invited to join the academy, prospective arbitrators were to be "of good moral character" and to have "substantial and current experience as an impartial arbitrator" or to "have attained general recognition through scholarly publication or other activities." Since it was increasingly difficult, especially after the creation of the NAA, for a novice to be chosen as an arbitrator and thereby to acquire the expertise necessary to gain a scholarly reputation, aspiring arbitrators were effectively locked out of the profession. By the mid-1950s some colleges offered courses related to arbitration, but few of those already in the profession believed that classroom lessons could adequately prepare candidates for what they would face. Indeed, no matter how impressive an arbitrator's credentials, a promising career could end abruptly by acquiring a reputation, justified or not, for being partial to either management or labor. While arbitrators complained that critical evaluation of their performances was "based on gossip," union representatives, textile manufacturers' organizations, and antilabor law firms compiled lists of acceptable and blacklisted candidates.[4]

Thus, while some arbitrators were enthusiastic, others felt troubled by the ambiguity inherent in their profession. Gabriel Alexander, for example, frustrated some colleagues at a 1957 NAA convention by lamenting that the organization "gives no hint as to what studies a man ought to pursue to achieve competence as an arbitrator; or what personality traits he ought to develop or avoid; or what experience he should try to establish." In the end, Alexander conceded, there were also no objective guidelines for deciding cases. The evidence that arbitrators evaluated, he said, "is almost always contradictory and unresolvable except by the uncertain process of credulity and belief." The arguments made by unions and managements, Alexander continued, "seldom emanate from any generally accepted set of principles, and on occasion are so diverse in their basic premises that they defy analysis within existing laws, contracts, and customs."[5]

During the mid-1940s, however, arbitrators who were called upon to resolve workload disputes in Henderson did not seem fazed by the contradictory evidence before them. Each expert accepted management's time-study data at face value. In an early 1944 case involving the Henderson Mill long-draft spinners, for example, union members had complained of the breakneck pace and injuries to arms and wrists caused by wringing off the ends of roving bobbins. Nevertheless, the arbitrator, Raymond Jenkins of Catawba College in Salisbury, North Carolina, concluded that "no evidence was provided by the Union to indicate that the present workload is too onerous for workers having normal health."[6] Spinners, of course, had argued that the amount and nature of their work prevented "normal health." In another 1944 decision, W. L. Wilhite, dean of Catawba College, concluded that "the Union did not show that the figures presented by the Company as to the amount of rest time allowed was not correct but simply stated that the work load was too heavy."[7] Once again, workers' subjective evidence counted for little against time-study calculations.

Even when arbitrators did not accept the Standards Department's testimony uncritically, a victory for workers was not guaranteed. After listening to time-study evidence and union members' contradictory claims in 1946, James Ward of Clemson College in South Carolina concluded that "obviously something is wrong." Nevertheless, he decided against the workers.[8] Likewise, after reading transcripts of hours of conflicting testimony from a 1948 case, exasperated New Jersey lawyer David Cole bemoaned that since he had no "convincing or satisfactory evidence of what the facts truly are," he could not "conscientiously make a definite award which would close the matter." Instead, he returned the case to the company and the union.[9]

For the first seven years with a contract, workers who claimed to have excessive assignments never persuaded arbitrators with their experiential evidence. There had been roughly fifty opportunities for arbitrators to decide workload cases at nineteen hearings between 1943 and 1950. (Several grievances were often presented at a single arbitration hearing.) One decision, the case heard by David Cole, had been inconclusive. The company had also withdrawn its challenges to several grievances, usually just before the scheduled arbitration hearings. No decision by an arbitrator, however, ratified workers' claims that their workloads were excessive. At this point union members must have felt ambivalent about their contract's power to affect their job assignments.[10]

Searching for new strategies in workload cases, especially as the economy tightened in 1949, TWUA representatives focused on exposing flaws in time-study data. If time studies and speed ratings were based on concrete, objective information obtained through scientific methods, the TWUA argued, then company officials should have no reservations about sharing their results with workers. Most TWUA officials and virtually every local union member believed that in truth the company's data would be so full of discrepancies and false assumptions that its credibility could be easily refuted. By casting doubt on the company's numbers, union leaders hoped they could convince arbitrators to take the workers' subjective testimony more seriously.

It appears that Harriet and Henderson officials inadvertently contributed to the germination of the union's strategy for opposing time studies. On several occasions during the war, management allowed TWUA time-study technicians to study disputed workloads, and when one of those conflicts reached arbitration, managers demanded that the union share its data. If the union would not provide the numbers, the company pleaded, then its time-study evidence should be stricken from the record. Perhaps that is what the union representative intended, because he immediately responded, "Have we the right to ask you for the worksheets and data that you presented?" This foreshadowed what would eventually become a standard union argument.[11]

International union leaders tried to convince managers that even though sharing time-study data might cause short-term delays, the long-term benefits would more than compensate for the hassles. The most important fact for mill owners to bear in mind, TWUA Director of Research Solomon Barkin stated, was that "the collective bargaining process in the textile industry has in no way interfered with the introduction of new technical changes, manufacturing procedures or operations, nor in the routine adjustment of plant operations to market needs." Having read the *Whitin Review* article praising Harriet and Henderson's modernization efforts, top TWUA officials identified those mills as prime examples of the union's willingness to accommodate the technological changes necessary for cotton mills to remain competitive. Without citing specific examples, Barkin claimed that managers who allowed workers to participate in setting workloads had modernized "with considerable success" by moderating "the tremendous human and social costs resulting from these changes. While the individual innovation may have been made at a somewhat slower pace, the process of collective bargaining has promoted greater understanding and thereby assured more progress in the long run." Linking the emerging union goal with basic American values—a difficult task in the postwar years, especially following the Taft-Hartley Act—Barkin argued that when managements unilaterally imposed technological innovations and workload assignments, they "violated the basic democratic principle that workers should participate in the determination of their own conditions of employment."[12]

The TWUA's strategy took some time to evolve. It appears that in the mid-1940s top TWUA officials disagreed about whether or not time studies could indeed provide objective data. TWUA representatives who spent most of their time discussing grievances with workers insisted that experience was always the best measure of a job. On the other hand, the TWUA had its own Research Department, which often confronted textile managers with time-study data it claimed was more accurate than any management-sponsored study could produce.[13] It is possible that some TWUA officials believed a workable time-study system could be developed. At this point the union's position seemed unclear, and for the next few years the union did not aggressively pursue access to time-study information. It is possible that the goal did not seem as urgent to workers until the company ordered severe workload increases during the recession of 1949. It is also possible that some TWUA officials believed local members could win workload cases if the time-study data were collected by an impartial third party. On several occasions during this period, TWUA representatives and the company allowed studies by either private companies or the U.S. Conciliation Service, with the understanding that the independent results would be considered final and binding.[14] Unfortunately for the union, however, impartial time-study engineers rarely collected evidence that substantiated the workers' claims. These frustrations, along with workload increases, apparently prompted the union to challenge the validity of all time studies.[15]

As a first step, before a 1948 arbitration hearing TWUA officials arranged to have local union members conduct time studies on themselves. Their presentation was a parody of the company's usual testimony. Workers held and consulted their own time-study sheets, stating exactly how many minutes they had taken to eat, use the bathroom, and rest. All union members testified that their daily fatigue time had been less than the sixty minutes the company considered adequate for most jobs.

The company fell into the union's trap. William Camp argued that the Standards Department's data contradicted the workers' conclusions. "Mrs. Hughes testified that she had approximately 45 minutes fatigue time on June 4, 1948 and we say she had 90 minutes," he testified, dismissing one worker's evidence. After the arbitrator, David Cole, remarked that he was "looking for some explanation of this discrepancy," TWUA representative Dan Finkle drove home the point of the exercise. "We still can't compare anything with the company," he complained, because the union did not have "full information" concerning the "results of time studies." Without access to the company's data, Finkle argued, workers "cannot accept results determined in this manner as a reliable estimate of the time required to perform the job."[16] Although the arbitrator sympathized with the union's argument, the question of access to information had not been part of the formal grievance, so he was only able to make nonbinding recommendations on that issue. He suggested that future time studies "should be made jointly by the Company and the union on an eight-hour basis to ascertain what the facts are and to avoid unnecessary disputes over facts."[17] Management ignored this recommendation.

Encouraged but not yet victorious, the union made access to information its primary goal in the next major workload arbitration. When the company revised workloads during the recession of 1949, union members filed a grievance demanding "that the Company furnish full job specifications."[18] The union demanded access to:

1. All mechanical machinery and room conditions information.
2. Job descriptions—detailed descriptions of the elements indicating starting point and break point.
3. Normal minutes per element per occurrence.
4. Standard frequencies.
5. Fatigue and personal time allowances.
6. Mathematical calculations.
7. Other allowances.
8. Records of performances, including efficiency, earnings, frequency checks, weights, etc., all day.

Apparently frightened, shortly before the scheduled arbitration hearing the managers agreed to settle all of the workload complaints on the workers' terms if the union would drop its demand for data.[19] Previously company officials had argued that their revised workloads had been both reasonable and essential to meet competition; by backing down they seemed to confirm that their secret figures were arbitrary. The union, however, accepted management's offer to cancel the workload increases and dropped its demand that the company share information either in this case or in the future.

Since many additional workloads grievances were filed during the 1949–50 recession, it is unclear why the union did not include a demand for time-study information in every case. Perhaps union officials did not want to risk a defeat on this issue in arbitration, which could have set a fatal precedent. It is also likely, however, that the union was willing to see whether the company would decide, on its own, to share information. There seemed to be reason for optimism. When another major workload case appeared destined for arbitration in early 1950, managers agreed to meet with TWUA representative R. H. Harris to discuss exactly what information the union desired from them. Harris argued that because two other companies—the giant Dan River Mills in Danville, Virginia, and a smaller mill near Goldsboro, North Carolina—had decided to share time-study figures, Harriet and Henderson should as well. Company officials, however, made no firm commitment. "We would like to find out what other companies are giving first and sort of keep in line," explained the company's Carl Page.[20] To deny access to information was definitely to keep "in line" with the policies of most southern mill owners. As the TWUA's Solomon Barkin noted in 1953, "Most mills will not have or will not furnish complete specifications. The union must continually strive to obtain such specifications from management."[21] Harriet and Henderson management never offered any time-study data for the jobs in question.

Unwilling to rely anymore on management's goodwill, by the early 1950s the TWUA demanded that arbitrators treat time-study figures as subjective evidence.[22] In Henderson, this strategy had its most significant impact when union members challenged workload revisions during the recession of 1954. At an arbitration hearing for Henderson Mill grievances, TWUA representative Sumner Shapiro argued that if the company's data were not shared, then time studies ought to be considered "merely the personal opinion of a member of management's staff." Shapiro reminded the arbitrator of the scientific method. "It would seem reasonable to conclude that a scientific union review of its raw data sheets would reinforce management's conclusions," he claimed. "Peculiarly enough, management never sought to exploit this golden opportunity."[23]

Despite their refusal to share their data, Standards Department staff members insisted that their scientific method was preferable to the subjective claims of union members. "The only evidence submitted by the Union was the personal opinion of a few employees that they would like to have the workload reduced and the pay increased," management argued in a posthearing brief. "This testimony did not even pretend to be objective, scientific, or based on anything but personal ideas and preference." The union's evidence, the company claimed, "gives a distorted picture of conditions and cannot be the reasonable basis of any sort of evaluation of work or jobs."[24]

In effect, both workers and managers challenged the arbitrator, Adam Abruzzi of the Stevens Institute in New Jersey, to determine which type of evidence was most credible. Although Abruzzi focused only on the specific case before him, his decision proved that the union's arguments against time studies were gaining force. He argued that the company's "time study results can be considered only as informed opinion, and not as factual material carrying decisive weight in adjudicating specific issues." By no means, however, did union members score an unqualified victory. Abruzzi dismissed the majority of union testimony for the same reason the company did, because it was "largely verbal and based on opinion rather than fact."[25] Nevertheless, the overall effect of the decision marked significant progress for union members.

Even though Abruzzi had officially discredited the standard evidence used by both the company and the union, his investigation into one crucial grievance lent credence to the union's claim that experience was the better measure of a job. In the case with the largest potential monetary settlement at stake, Abruzzi decided for the union on the basis of his own personal observations of the jobs in question. The dispute involved superdraft and speeder tenders who had been expected to increase the card room's production with no new equipment and two fewer hands per shift. Luther Jackson recalled feeling elated when the arbitrator announced that he wanted to see the jobs firsthand. In the eleven years that the company had had a union, no arbitrator had personally observed a disputed job assignment, and never had a group of workers felt as vindicated as they did now. Eighteen card-room hands split roughly $28,000, the largest retroactive payment ever at these mills, as compensation for being overworked for nearly a year. In addition, Abruzzi ordered the reinstatement of one worker per shift.[26]

Several months later, Harriet #2 spinners experienced a similar victory. In this case the arbitrator, John Abersold from Philadelphia, lacked Abruzzi's investigative initiative, but he nonetheless supported the union's assault on time-study evidence. In the written explanation of his verdict, Abersold complained that he had "been forced to spend many unnecessary hours going over and over the testimony and studying and restudying the various exhibits in an effort to make some sense out of an almost hopeless array of evidence." From this confusion Abersold determined that the company's changes had resulted "in an unreasonable work load" but that "no evidence was presented by either party which could reasonably be said to measure the amount of the work load which could be deemed unreasonable." Despite his uncertainty, Abersold ordered the company to add one employee per shift and to divide over $3,000 among the spinners for the time they had worked without the services of this helper.[27]

These 1954 decisions show that union representatives had cast enough doubt on the legitimacy of time studies that they were able to win significant victories. The company actually won more individual grievances than it lost in the major 1954 arbitrations, and management remained far ahead of union members in the number of workload cases won since 1943. Nevertheless, company officials were infuriated by the decisions that had gone against them. Arbitrators were now making judgments, unabashedly, on the basis of informal observation and guesswork, defying management's claim that workloads had been measured objectively.

There is no evidence that company officials, in response to their 1954 defeats, ever considered sharing information or reforming their time-study technique. Instead, management assigned new workloads that were more strenuous, according to the affected workers, than what had just been ruled unreasonable in arbitration. Shortly after winning their 1954 arbitration case, for example, Harriet #2 spinners were "at the point of just screaming" over their supposedly reduced workloads.[28] Company officials refused to negotiate adjustments to these new assignments. "You all won't bargain on one thing with us," Luther Jackson complained.[29] Union members soon discovered that company officials had decided to reassert their control over workloads by demanding specific changes in the contract when it came up for renewal in November 1954.

While local union members voted to renew the existing agreement, company officials, hoping to restore the authority of their time studies, demanded a contractual provision making sixty-nine units of work per hour the required pace for all jobs in the mills. Seizing the opportunity, union negotiators agreed to accept the sixty-nine-unit-hour if the Standards Department were required to share its time-study data.[30] Shortly before the agreement expired, with no breakthroughs in negotiations in sight, Locals 578 and 584 voted to strike rather than work without their contract.[31]

Both the union and the company held firm for over a month. It appears that managers might have welcomed a short strike because during that year's recession they had accumulated and stored a substantial amount of yarn. The work stoppage allowed them to sell some of this excess inventory. For its part, the TWUA prepared for the possibility of a lengthy walkout by funding commissaries to provide strikers with food.[32] Significantly, management made no effort to reopen the mills, and after seven weeks both sides appeared anxious for a settlement. Privately, the company claimed that it lost $75,000 at the Henderson Mill and $66,000 at the Harriet complex during the strike. Furthermore, the strike delayed completion of major modernization programs at both mills. Negotiators for both sides intended to stay until they reached an agreement, and at 3:00 A.M. on New Year's Eve the company finally conceded, agreeing to a contract clause permitting the union to review time-study information. As it had promised, the union agreed in return that the Standards Department could set sixty-nine-unit-hour workloads throughout the mills.[33]

While company officials claimed victory, calling this contract "the best one they had ever had with the Union," union members also felt like winners. Aware of the difficulties inherent in measuring workloads, the hands were confident that by securing access to time-study data they had triumphed over their managers. Indeed, union shop stewards noted a surge of enthusiasm among workers during the first week after the settlement.[34]

The good feelings that emerged from the settlement soon vanished, however. The company continued as if nothing had changed, revising numerous workloads without offering the union any time-study data. In addition, supervisors threatened to issue warnings when employees failed to reach revised production quotas during trial periods, before workers were allowed to file formal grievances. In apparent violation of the new contract, managers demanded that employees accept the Standards Department's job proposals as the final word in workload disputes. "We will have to go by what these gentlemen tell us," Superintendent Farmer told a group of protesting workers, pointing to the company's time-study engineers. "They have got a good measuring stick." Many lower-level supervisors, however, did not even pretend to rely on time studies when pressuring workers to do more. TWUA representative Julius Fry complained that some bosses "have gotten on the people and said you got to do so and so, you are not doing a 69 and [workers] would say what is a 69 and they would say I don't know, but you are not doing it." As it turned out, not even foremen had access to the information used to calculate workloads.[35]

Workers were outraged by this breach of faith. Management had failed to provide any time-study information since the strike ended, and union members pressured TWUA representative Fry and the local shop committees to force the company to comply. As Fry told company officials, "That was the basis for the settlement of the strike, and the committees and officers are catching 'H.'"[36] It appears, however, that workers felt most bitter toward managers. Addressing a group of angry spinners, Standards Department head Carl Page said, "The company is as interested in this as you all." "No you are not," snapped spinner Gladys Branch, "because if you had been, you would have done something about it a long time ago." "We think we understand what you want," Page insisted. "Think?" Branch responded. "I want you to know, not think. If you would come thru that mill sometimes you would see something you all don't know, sitting up there in that office."[37]

Union officials tried reasoning with the company. "If it is possible for you to figure it out enough to where you just slam the work on them," Julius Fry argued, "it is possible for you to give us the figures you use to give us a chance to see whether they are right." The company, however, was far more interested in completing major renovations in the mills, including the installation of over $600,000 worth of new equipment in the Harriet complex. "We are trying to give you the best we can," claimed John D. Cooper. "We don't want to shut the plant down."[38]

Union leaders suspected that the company's strategy had been developed with the guidance of one of the region's most notorious antilabor attorneys, Frank Constangy. In fact, Constangy, based in Atlanta, had been advising Harriet and Henderson officials about potential arbitrators, specific arguments to use in arbitration hearings, and the implications of arbitration awards, since the late 1940s.[39] Top TWUA officials had long viewed Constangy as a formidable and brash adversary. CIO organizer William Shiflett recalled a time when Constangy "reared back in his chair and said that he and the company insisted that they should have the right to discharge a man if they didn't like the way that he parted his hair." After Constangy boasted that he could keep any formal union legal challenge tied up in court at least five years, TWUA general president Emil Rieve admitted that the antilabor attorney had "understated his own talents."[40]

No matter who was aligned against them, however, members of Locals 578 and 584 were unwilling to give up their quest for more control over workloads. Displaying considerable patience, workers filed several grievances at each mill, charging that the company had breached the contract by refusing to share time-study data when changing job assignments. Although it seemed impossible to them that they could lose, union officials took nothing for granted in this case, because its outcome would determine whether or not workers could ever expect to gain access to time-study data. Indirectly, larger questions would also be addressed. Could management ignore negotiated agreements at its discretion? If so, what was the purpose of the union?

For the Henderson Mill, union officials chose spinning-room grievances for their test case. The spinning-room workloads were the culmination of an extensive modernization project begun before the 1954 strike. Management's goal had been to improve productivity by keeping the spinning frames cleaner, reducing both the frequency of slubs (yarn imperfections caused by debris) and the number of times the yarn broke in the machines. Fewer breaks meant less downtime, hence more production. The plan involved two key technological additions: overhead blowers and Pneumafil. The new blowers sat on top of the frames and kept the roving bobbins free from cotton dust and other contaminants. Pneumafil, a series of suction tubes on spinning frames, was designed to prevent messy, production-reducing "ball-ups" when yarn broke. It was supposed to capture loose ends and direct the waste into special containers.

Having spent over $1 million for this state-of-the-art equipment, mill officials expected significant benefits. William Camp remarked that he had observed the overhead blowers at a recent textile machinery exposition and was "very impressed with them." Superintendent Farmer called Pneumafil "the greatest improvement put on a spinning frame in my life time." According to Carl Page, if all went as planned the spinners would spend less time cleaning the frames and removing balled-up yarn, enabling them "to attend more sides [of frames] with the same amount of expended effort."[41]

Unfortunately for managers, however, these dreams failed to materialize on the spinning-room floor. The changes required a number of rearrangements that had unanticipated consequences. The most severe adjustment involved the delivery of the roving bobbins. Before the addition of overhead blowers, bobbin haulers placed fresh roving bobbins on top of the spinning frames. A spinner relied on having new bobbins close at hand to replace any that had run out. Now that blowers sat on top of the frames, however, roving bobbins had to go elsewhere. To solve this problem, the company gave the spinners wheeled carts that held nearly two hundred pounds of roving when full. Workers were to push these carts as they patrolled their frames.

The spinners considered this change disastrous and immediately filed a grievance focusing on the new roving boxes. "I'll tell you when I took the box, it liked to killed me," complained Lissie Harris, who had spun at the Henderson Mill for thirty-nine years. "I had a box that was easy to turn over and the roving bobbins was on crates and it was very easy to turn, especially when it was pulled, and it turned over with me in the cross alley one day where I was changing bobbins." Blanche Lewis complained that she was "suffering from painful bruises" after being hit by a roving box. "It hurt to push it," Thelma Clopton explained. "I had a few bruises on my legs from pushing it where the floor was unlevel. Sometimes it would roll back and hit me on the leg when I would leave it setting in a stick of roving. Sometimes I would get in a hurry, I would be behind, and I would push it up side the frame and it would fall back and hit me again."[42]

Blanche Lewis argued that the spinners' increased frame assignments had also contributed to their injuries. "We had so much work that we [were] trying to go at a high rate of speed to keep it up," she explained, "and we just couldn't take time to watch where we were going and we tried to get around our work and that's why we were getting over the box." The spinners had failed to reach production goals even when given assistance, which to them proved that their assignments were excessive. "Not a shift up there that hasn't had help," Luther Jackson informed company officials. "The other day my wife run them and her hands were blistered. I know she got help, too." Melvin Renn noted that his sister "worked all the time and didn't sit down any and she is losing as much as 1 to 2 pounds [of production] a week." When a company representative expressed doubt about Renn's report, Renn responded, "My sister is a Christian woman and she don't lie."[43]

The installation of Pneumafil caused further difficulties. Before the changes, spinners had been able to see ball-ups from the end of an aisle. They would walk down aisles only when necessary to repair broken yarn. Pneumafil, however, prevented most ball-ups, so spinners had to be directly in front of broken ends to see them. Therefore, with the new technology spinners had to make regular patrols through each alley to locate problems. Since there could be empty roving bobbins anywhere on their circuits, spinners had to keep their carts close at hand or risk having to waste time walking long distances for replacements. TWUA representative Sumner Shapiro attempted to describe the spinners' new routine to the satisfaction of Superintendent Farmer: "All she has to do then is push this heavy truck around, at the same time, watch out she doesn't run into anything, so she won't fall into the truck, push it with her hands, of course, and with her eyes she has to be looking at the spinning frame and she has to be looking very closely to be sure she finds the broken ends." "That's correct," Farmer replied.[44]

To make matters worse, Pneumafil did not always work. When the company installed the new suction-tube technology at the Harriet Mill just before the 1954 strike, the affected spinners were unimpressed. "Get the Pneumafil man down here," pleaded one spinner. "Maybe he can tell you what is wrong." Minnie Hedgepeth told her supervisors that yarn breaks often escaped capture and instead wrapped tightly around the rollers. "Some days it was half, half of them rollers choked instead of going through that hole," she said. "Then you have to reach over and lift that heavy eye, what it is, and take off and then have to wring and wring and then you just kill yourself and that's every [broken] end just about." Hedgepeth recognized the potential of the technology. "If it would just go through that little hole," she said. "It wouldn't be so bad[;] it's just something wrong about this." [45]

Spinners had another gripe about Pneumafil. The tube that sucked away the spoiled yarn deposited the waste in a box at the end of each frame. Since spinners were supposed to locate and repair broken ends promptly, management felt that the amount of waste in the box at the end of a shift served as a reliable measure of their performance each day. The more waste, according to the company, the lazier the employee. Spinners, however, argued that excessive waste could just as easily be caused by external variables like cotton quality, humidity, and card-room performance. Local 578 president Sam Littleton also suggested that waste totals were bound to increase whenever yarn broke while a spinner was pushing her box somewhere else in her "half acre" of frames. "I didn't stop for nothing except to eat and go to the rest room," remarked Lula Wheeler, "and I made 14 lbs." of waste. Nevertheless, supervisors issued warnings if Pneumafil boxes contained what the Standards Department determined to be excessive waste.[46]

Spinners responded to this upheaval in a variety of ways. Some had little choice but to endure. "I couldn't stand to work," explained Blanche Lewis. "I cried awhil[e] and hurt awhile, but I kept on working. . . . I felt that I had to work because my husband was out sick." Several others quit rather than wait for their grievance to be settled.[47] Some workers stayed home more often, risking warnings for absenteeism. Shortly after the changes, Helen Multon, who normally cleaned rollers, noted that "lately I have been used as a spinner, because we have had so much absenteeism."[48] Others, like Lissie Harris, missed days because of injuries suffered from the roving boxes.

Those who reported to work faced job-threatening pressure from supervisors to fulfill their new assignments. Lissie Harris, who had never been reprimanded for poor work in her thirty-nine years at the Henderson Mill, recalled that during this trial period, "I did not work but a day and a piece before Mr. Byrum sent for me to come in the office and when I got in there, he said that I was just not trying." Harris testified that her supervisor said "if I didn't get it done, they were going to disqualify me." Before she quit, Lizzie Medlin had also been under pressure to complete all of her assigned tasks: "Mr. Byrum come in there one morning and I had worked all night and hadn't even been to get a drink of water, coca cola or been to the bath room or nothing," she explained. "He said, 'Mrs. Medlin, are you doing all you can do to keep up these sides.' I said, 'Yes, Mr. Byrum, I am doing everything I can do. I don't leave it to get a drink a water or nothing else.' He said, 'Well, I just don't agree.'"[49]

Company officials defended their new equipment and work assignments. Superintendent Farmer argued that "in order to keep our mill competitive," managers had "to make certain changes" and union members had to allow them "to get something modern." Suggesting that Pneumafil, overhead blowers, and roving boxes had an unambiguous track record, Farmer said that the company would not "pay a million dollars for something that hadn't been approved by other mills. . . . We feel like that when a third or half [of an] industry has done something, we can certainly do the same thing."[50] Mill officials also claimed that the spinners were to blame for their injuries because they had not been pushing the roving boxes correctly. Although William Camp admitted that "the floor in some cases is not perfectly level and they may turn the box loose and it floats down there for a few feet without them pushing it," the company felt the spinners should be able to control the carts.[51]

The lines of argument were clear and familiar. According to the spinners, the new workloads were excessive and dangerous; according to the company, the Standards Department had calculated reasonable assignments, and anything less jeopardized the existence of the mills. Specifically, management argued that because the contested workloads were less than the sixty-nine units per hour allowed under the contract, instead of grumbling about their current responsibilities the spinners ought to be doing more.[52] Workers, however, refused to accept Farmer's numbers: as Jackson explained, the company "was to give us a complete study of the job before and after the change, and they haven't lived up to it. We ain't got nothing." Indeed, in April 1955, two months after the changes were completed, Carl Page told Jackson that the Standards Department had not yet finished compiling time-study data for the revised jobs and that the information would not be available for another six weeks. "You won't have it to me before this contract goes out, at the rate you are going," Jackson responded.[53]

At the arbitration hearing that September, the union exploited a crucial inconsistency in the company's reasoning. TWUA representative Sumner Shapiro asked William Camp on what basis the Standards Department could claim both that it did not yet have time-study information to share with the union and that the jobs in question required less than sixty-nine units per hour. "On my estimate," Camp responded. "Scientific estimate, if I may call it that." When Shapiro pressed Camp for details, the engineer admitted that "to be perfectly frank with you, I reached up in the air and got some of it, particularly that concerning the [roving] truck." "Just how do you scientifically reach up into the air?" Shapiro wondered. "How does that differ from just ordinary reaching up in the air?" "I've been in time study work for a good many years," Camp responded, "and I think I can hit a job very close by estimating it."[54] Despite the engineer's confidence, however, up to that point no company officials had made such a damaging confession in public.

Management's scientific claims appeared even more dubious after Camp accounted for ambiguous and contradictory evidence. During a study of one spinner's job, for example, Camp had estimated that there should have been 665 broken ends. Instead, he had counted 1,258, "a whale of a difference" that greatly increased that spinner's workload. Although Camp acknowledged that there were "a lot of technicalities" in determining the causes of end breaks, he blamed the spinners. "Somebody definitely broke them," he charged. According to Camp, sabotage was easy and virtually impossible to detect. "Anybody can do it if they want to," he claimed. Spinners could neglect "to twist the roving as much as necessary when they creel that bobbin," or they could "twist it just a little bit too much." Also, he added, "you can be walking down the alley and you can rub up against the side of an end or two and knock them down."[55]

Whether or not Camp's accusation was true, his conclusions had nothing to do with science. Managers felt sabotaged when their dreams failed to materialize. On the other hand, workers suffered bruises, humiliation, and knots the size of fists in their legs. Those were the concerns behind the sparring over unit-hours and numbers of end breaks.

In a brief filed after the hearing, mill officials abandoned time-study jargon to clarify the basic issue: workload challenges had cut to the core of managerial authority. "The installation of, or methods of using equipment are solely within the discretion of the company and are not subject to arbitration," the company argued. "The Union has no right either under the contract provision or without the contract provision to question the rights of management."[56] Nearly thirty years later, Marshall Cooper recalled his anger and frustration with the union's challenge in this particular case. "All the while you were losing production. You had all this equipment you done bought and you weren't getting all the best results out of it. That's where the damn union comes in."[57]

The arbitrator, Adam Abruzzi once again, ruled in December 1955, almost a year after the strike-ending agreement, that the company had violated the contract by not sharing complete time-study information with its employees. There was more for union members to celebrate when Abruzzi, in his verdict regarding the specific grievances from the Henderson Mill spinning room, concluded without the benefit of additional time studies that the new workloads exceeded sixty-nine units per hour. Abruzzi rejected the Standards Department's research on the basis of the workers' testimony, which he called "qualitative, to be sure, but evidence nonetheless." Even though Abruzzi had no idea what the spinners' workload was, in terms of units per hour, he reinstated one hand on each shift. He also awarded the spinners, as a group, roughly eighteen cents per hour in retroactive pay—about $1,700 in all—for the excess work they had performed during the previous forty-four weeks.

By no means had the arbitration been a total rout. Considering the stridency of the spinners' complaints, the amount of compensation appears rather small. Moreover, concerning the roving trucks, a matter of utmost concern to the spinners, Abruzzi ruled that the use of any particular piece of equipment was management's prerogative and could not be challenged.[58] It was obvious to all, however, that managers had been humiliated on the most crucial issues. After reviewing a transcript of the arbitration hearing and a copy of Abruzzi's award, Frank Constangy chastised the company's efforts. "Our impressions over-all," he wrote, "are that you did not devote as much time to the preparation of a completely rounded case from an engineering standpoint as you could have done." Consequently, he concluded, the award contained several "dangerous implications," most notably "that time studies should be submitted."[59]

It was still possible, although increasingly unlikely, that a different arbitrator might have been more sympathetic toward time studies and the Standards Department. According to sociologist Daniel Bell, Adam Abruzzi was one of the first experts to publicly break ranks with those who believed in the objectivity of scientific time studies. While Abruzzi remained hopeful that a truly objective work-measuring system could be developed, he recognized that in practice, every time-measuring system he had observed, not only those employed in the textile industry, had failed to persuade him of its accuracy: "It should be clearly understood that such procedures are scientific in no sense; they are and should be labeled as components of the bargaining process between management and labor."[60] Based on his own experiences, Peter Seitz delivered a satirical address at a National Academy of Arbitrators convention suggesting that all arbitrators, overwhelmed by the contradictory evidence presented to them, decided grievances by "black magic."[61] Indeed, there was no better explanation for Abruzzi's "precise" determination of the amount of excess work the Henderson Mill spinners had performed. For years the company had won cases with appeals to reason based on allegedly scientific data, but by the end of 1955 that era was a dim memory, and there was little prospect that arbitrators would ever again be easily persuaded by management's evidence.

Although the company had been ordered to include its employees in the workload-setting process, no arbitration decision could either eliminate the underlying economic pressures that motivated management to seek increased efficiency or somehow enable the Standards Department to make timely, convincing studies. Fearful of constantly fluctuating business conditions and the consequences of union involvement in setting workloads, managers ignored Abruzzi's decision and continued to revise assignments unilaterally, further antagonizing their wary and increasingly hostile workforce.[62]

Upon discovering that the company was not going to comply, union members, convinced that they were on the moral high ground, refused to take seriously any managers who claimed authority to determine a sixty-nine-unit-hour pace. In early 1956 Local 578 president Charlie Ranes told members of the Standards Department that for spinning-room doffers, "36 doffed frames and 6 full frames is a 69 unit hour. You can count it up anyway you want to." "Who told you that?" responded Carl Page. "Somebody else can figure these as good as you all can," answered Ranes. When Page told Luther Jackson that the Henderson Mill spinners' new workload was "a long ways from a 69, way below," the local's president dismissed the calculation. "You all figure 69 one way and we figure 69 another way," Jackson said.[63]

Union members grew even more furious, and desperate, when management issued warnings to several Harriet Mill winders who missed production quotas on a single shift. The winders claimed that they had been plagued by small bobbins; if their claim was true, the low production totals would not necessarily have been their fault. Privately, managers conceded that the workers were right. Second hand James Wheeler informed his superiors that the department had suffered small bobbins "practically the whole week." Nevertheless, the company preferred not to remove the warnings, which had apparently been only a scare tactic. "We had no intention of firing them," William Camp insisted to fellow managers. "We want them all to do the work. That's what we want them to do."[64]

It was more likely, however, that arbitrary punishment would have the opposite effect. As Harriet Mill winding-room shop steward Mattie Roberson explained to a group of supervisors, "It tears up the whole room when anybody gets a warning."[65] The winders who received the warnings filed a grievance and pursued it until they won in arbitration in early 1958. Although the judgment involved no money—it only removed the warnings from the hands' records—top managers were agitated beyond hope of consolation. Looking to the future, John D. Cooper threatened "that the contract should be changed so we can live with it, and I intend to propose such a change."[66]

Since neither time studies nor warnings had forced workers to submit to management's revised workloads, company officials, with Frank Constangy's guidance, explored other provocative strategies for lowering labor costs. At the Harriet Mill, the company assigned utility hands to full-time jobs while classifying them as "helpers" and paying them the plant's minimum wage. Full-time workers argued that their need for assistance proved that their assignments were excessive. Company officials replied that only lazy workers required help. "We are not working anybody to death," William Camp said to Local 578 president Charlie Ranes. Carl Page agreed, noting that "studies don't indicate—" "Studies could be wrong, you know," Ranes interrupted. Union members no longer had patience for such time-worn claims.[67]

Managers also attempted to undercut the clause protecting workers' earnings during trial periods. Because many of the company's modernization programs took months or even years to complete, keeping workloads in a long-term state of flux, the company had agreed in 1955 to guarantee employees their previous earnings for up to nine months after the end of any four-week trial period.[68] Frank Constangy had warned that with guaranteed earnings, "there would be no incentive system and the right of the company to make changes would be inoperative."[69] Following Constangy's advice, company officials set workloads that union members considered excessive, then supplemented workers' pay for the mandatory nine months while refusing to discuss possible revisions. Managers frankly admitted their motives. In April 1956 Carl Page reminded the union officers that in three more months "that guarantee goes off." "And you can cut wages," Julius Fry responded, acknowledging what would happen without supplemental pay. "They will be on their own," confirmed John D. Cooper. "You know in that 9 months they ain't going to make as much effort." "Mr. Cooper, don't do us that way. You got more integrity than that and I respect you more than that," Fry pleaded. "If I were to do you that way, you ought to slit my throat."[70]

Although workers successfully opposed most of these aggressive strategies, union members were angry that they always had to work under unnecessarily harsh conditions for many months before arbitrators ruled in their favor. In August 1958, a group of workers expressed their frustration by bypassing the formal grievance process and launching a wildcat strike, the first at these mills in thirteen years. During the only other documented wildcat, the company immediately discharged the participants, and union officials went to great lengths to get the hands reinstated by agreeing not to protest the firing of any future wildcat striker. It would probably have been suicidal in the South for a marginal union like the TWUA, which hoped to make future inroads in the region, to condone acts that clearly violated a contract. Any decision to engage in a wildcat strike, then, involved great risk both for individuals and for the union itself. Management triggered the wildcat strike in 1958 by warning several spinning-room doffers for low production during a trial period with a new workload. The doffers argued that management had no right to issue warnings during a trial period. When the company refused to remove the warnings from their records, the doffers went home.

Although union officers resolved this wildcat strike after sixteen hours —second-shift doffers also refused to work—they clearly sympathized with the hands. "I had [to] spend some hours over here the other day doing some things that are very distasteful for me to do," Fry told managers, referring to his efforts to end the strike. "If you don't believe it, check around and see." Shop steward and shop committee member Johnnie Martin explained that when his fellow doffers decided to walk out, "they called me over there right in front of the pepsi cola machine and asked me and I told them it was in violation of contract, and then they went on down there and done it." Martin had been careful to fulfill his contractual obligation by not authorizing the wildcat strike, but he did not share management's anger that the workers had ignored him.[71] "What can we do?" Superintendent Proctor asked the shop committee. "Can you all control them, or are we going to have to come up there and control them?"[72]

This wildcat strike was the last straw for Harriet and Henderson managers. Business conditions had been poor. Time studies no longer carried any weight with arbitrators, and workers considered them a joke. More expensive renovations were under way, and managers foresaw, at best, endless rounds of workload negotiations that would stall and possibly prevent their desired gains in efficiency. It should be emphasized that in practice, the union's influence over workloads was largely defensive. Workers had no role in selecting new machinery, they were not allowed to file protests until four weeks after management changed a job, and then the formal grievance procedure could drag on for months. Nevertheless, union members had hoped for more and, in arbitration, had argued successfully for an earlier, more substantial role in decisions involving work assignments. Within the framework of formalized conflict resolution, workers had scored significant victories against traditional managerial prerogatives. Reeling from these defeats, company officials refused to accept any level of worker involvement in running the mills and ignored each apparent union triumph.

Indeed, rather than subject themselves to further humiliation in arbitrations, in the fall of 1958 exasperated Harriet and Henderson officials sought to dismantle the grievance procedure. Working closely with Frank Constangy, managers decided privately that when the contract came up for renewal in November, they would demand that no grievance could go to arbitration without the consent of both sides. In effect, then, the grievance procedure would end with company president John D. Cooper. "If we succeed in getting what we want," President Cooper told the board of directors a month before the contract expired, "we may possibly have a strike, but it would be worth it."[73] Management wanted nothing less than the elimination of the union's power, whether or not the union locals survived.

As part of their provocative strategy, managers announced in early September their intention to make changes but waited until 29 October, just twelve days before the contract expired, to reveal their specific proposals, which also included eliminating both the automatic checkoff of union dues and pay guarantees during workload trial periods. Increasing the likelihood of a strike, company officials refused to begin negotiations until the day the agreement ended.[74] Upon receiving the company's demands in late October, union leaders offered to work under the existing contract until a new settlement could be reached. John D. Cooper declared, however, that after 15 November the old contract provisions would no longer be in force.[75]

Although it is clear why managers felt antagonized by recent developments in arbitration (one should remember that the company had also consistently lost crucial verdicts regarding absenteeism), it is less certain why management offered its workforce the right to strike over unresolved grievances whenever the company refused to arbitrate. After all, by accepting arbitration both the company and its workforce had surrendered the right to self-help during the life of the contract, which ensured that production would not stop when conflicts arose. Since the company had consistently refused to abide by arbitration rulings, it was possible that some union leaders or local members might also have welcomed the abandonment of the grievance procedure for the right to use contract-sanctioned strikes as a means for settling disputes. Given the recognized ability of any department within a mill to disrupt the entire production process, it seemed possible that direct action could give workers great power and could result in much quicker resolution of disagreements. Why would managers want to take such risks? Yet facing this opportunity in Henderson, TWUA officials, led by regional representative Julius Fry, complained that arbitration by mutual consent only would leave workers "in the unhappy condition of having no alternative except to strike to gain redress of grievances."[76] Perhaps higher-level union representatives feared for the future of their institution in the South if it were perceived as backtracking on its long-time insistence on the superiority of formalized grievance procedures over production-disrupting strikes. But what about local members?

Ironically, the fact that any small group of upset workers could fairly quickly shut down an entire mill both supplied the union with potential power and made such strikes potentially very divisive, thus undercutting its virtue as a tactic. The wildcat strike that triggered the company's contract demands revealed much, from the workers' perspective, about the pitfalls of direct action. Within an hour or two after the handful of doffers walked out, the disruption in supplies forced the entire mill to close for the day. Although one might think that this would inspire production-conscious managers to settle quickly at the first hint of discontent, it is important to realize that workers' livelihoods were also directly related to production, and few could afford frequent, unplanned interruptions. After this particular wildcat strike, for example, hundreds of nonstriking workers who had been forced to go home demanded two hours' reporting pay from the company. "It is not the hands' fault," Roy Faulkner explained. "They didn't know anything about it."[77] Such strikes would have been especially upsetting to hands who only worked three or four days a week and therefore counted on making full production on those shifts. Moreover, workers did not automatically assume that every grievance was just, and it was difficult for people to quickly become informed about the concrete issues in other departments. Knowing each other as well as they did, mill villagers understood the wide range of temperaments and tolerances among those who might refuse to work. Participants in direct action, then, would have to convince fellow union members that their decision was justified. By allowing strikes to disrupt production, managers could ensure that many other workers would be inconvenienced, possibly to the point of being quite angry at fellow union members. If nothing else, management had seen how hundreds of local union members did not willingly accept the consequences of the wildcat strikers' behavior.

There is no evidence that any local union member in Henderson welcomed the opportunity to abandon the grievance procedure and gain the right to strike during the life of a contract. In a letter to the editor of the local paper, Lloyd Wilkins, who had thirty-seven years' seniority in the Henderson Mill card room, stated the position of most local union members: "I don't see how we can be expected to work under a contract with no rights of arbitration." "A contract with no arbitration is no contract," said Local 584 member Joseph Braswell, recalling his reaction at the time. "The company could do anything it wanted to."[78] From the workers' perspective, arbitration represented the heart of the contract and had to be defended.

Negotiation sessions with the company underscored the importance of arbitration and made a strike appear certain. After union representatives insisted "that arbitration provisions of the old contract be carried over into the new contract," John D. Cooper replied that he had given the union's position "careful study and consideration" and found "that it is not acceptable to the compan[y]." As the 15 November deadline approached, each negotiating session produced the same result: the union demanded the old arbitration clause and the company refused to consider it.[79] Because union members had been so successful making their cases in arbitration, they faced the possible loss of the fruits of their struggle—their ability to influence their working lives.

8   **Beyond the Mills**
Local and Regional Contexts

Now that a strike had become seemingly inevitable, TWUA officials and local union members contemplated what unionization in Henderson had meant to them and assessed their prospects for success. Workers
perceived that enormous changes had taken place in their lives since
1943, both inside the mills and in their standing within the community.
They felt confident that they were necessary for the future profitability
of both the mills and the city of Henderson. Whether or not many local
union members realized it, however, the outcome of any strike depended
to a great extent on local and regional economic developments and the
links between political power at the state and local levels, particularly
regarding agendas designed to address the serious problems caused by

the long-term economic changes. If workers struck, why might they feel they had a chance to win? Why would they risk a defeat? What kinds of coalitions could they foresee arrayed with them? Who was likely to be against them? Over what economic and political factors could union members hope to exert any influence? Which were beyond their control? Was anybody really making such calculations?

On the union side, regional and international TWUA officials were in the best position to consider the larger contexts that affected the outcome of any strike, and to them, the company's tactics resembled those used in virtually every campaign to destroy existing union locals. Eight years earlier, TWUA general president Emil Rieve had identified the general pattern. Managements on the offensive, he testified before a U.S. Senate Committee, "will agree to almost nothing proposed by the union. In turn, they make demands which they know the union cannot accept. They refuse to meet more often than every week or two." In most cases, Rieve noted, antilabor attorneys worked closely with mill executives. The goal in each case, Rieve explained, "is to provoke a strike, then break the strike and the local union." This strategy had been very effective in combating existing and newly formed TWUA locals in the late 1940s.[1]

Although managerial offensives had been far less frequent in the 1950s —according to TWUA records, between 1950 and 1958 no existing union locals were liquidated as a result of lost strikes—there was still no reason for union leaders to celebrate. Mill-owner opposition to unionization had been so successful that there were very few union locals left in southern textile mills, and they posed no significant threat to the industry as a whole.[2] The late 1950s had proved even more grim for unionized textile workers. Between 1956 and 1958, six organized mills, employing a total of 1,675 TWUA-CIO members, shut down in North Carolina, victims of the economic crisis in textiles.[3] Therefore, from the perspective of TWUA leadership the stakes involved in any potential strike were very high. If the union were ever to make headway in the South, it could not afford to lose either of the Henderson locals.

Although TWUA officials often charged, and feared, that southern mill owners conspired to destroy functioning union locals, there is little evidence to suggest that Harriet and Henderson managers were acting in conjunction with any other textile executives.[4] Mill owners detested unions, of course, but most managers did not have to deal with organized workers; they no longer felt threatened by the possibility of unionization, and in a volatile market for textiles, they had other more pressing concerns. Virtually every mill executive in North Carolina, including the Coopers, belonged to the North Carolina Textile Manufacturers Association, which met annually to discuss the state of the industry. At these meetings, and in formal association correspondence, mill executives voiced great concern about cotton quality and cost, the cost of electric power, the burden of state and local taxation, and the potential consequences of pending legislation regarding stream pollution, workers' compensation, and unemployment insurance. There were numerous speeches about the general business climate for textiles, especially the threat of foreign competition. Nowhere in the organization's records, however, is mention made either of a perceived threat from organized labor or of any desire to confront unionization efforts or existing unions. Some speakers voiced generalized complaints about rising wages and relatively unproductive employees, but these characteristics were never linked directly with unionized workers. Every mill owner, it seemed, had similar concerns.[5] It appears unlikely, then, that the aggressive negotiating position taken by Harriet and Henderson managers was anything more than their own reaction to developments over time within those specific mills, even if they could be fairly certain of receiving moral support from their colleagues. Strident antiunionism did not necessarily translate into a willingness to bear any share of the burden in ridding the region of organized labor.

At the local union level, the stakes were obviously high for workers, who viewed the impending conflict as a referendum on whether or not they were willing to return to the preunion order. Significantly, a large number of the 1,050 local union members in 1958 had worked in the mills prior to 1943 and had experienced firsthand the difference that unionization had made in their lives. "It was a whole lot of our members that was in the strike could remember working" before the union, recalled Local 578 recording secretary Esther Roberson. "There weren't very many younger people. Most of them were the people that did know." And to them, Lloyd Wilkins recalled, the difference was "like night and day."[6] "We didn't have too many young people," agreed Local 584 financial secretary Edith Adams, "because the young people at the time that this happened, they had other places of employment, and they were in school and so forth, and weren't many of them choosing the cotton mill for their vocation." Indeed, mill-village children were much more likely than ever before to graduate from high school, and a few had even gone on to college. Their parents, however, did not perceive that they had options in their lives. Most intended to hold jobs in the mills for the rest of their working lives.[7]

When these union members reflected on the years since their first contract, in addition to altered relations with managers, they recalled great changes in their villages—some of which, in reality, had little to do with unionization. In the late 1940s, for example, the county blacktopped the villages' roads, and by 1958 most union members took great pride in owning their homes. The blacktopping was part of a statewide improvement effort under the administration of Governor Kerr Scott, who became known as the governor "who got the state out of the mud."[8] The possibility of home ownership for Harriet and Henderson mill villagers arose prior to unionization when the financially strapped company no longer wanted to pay to maintain the houses. In 1958, however, most workers associated these developments with unionization.[9]

Workers also associated higher incomes with the union. Although the TWUA had certainly pushed for raises, the increased pay scales were primarily due to peculiar conditions caused by the war and the subsequent boom years. When southern mill owners finally chose in 1951 to take a stand against a TWUA demand for wage increases, the union proved unable to exert enough pressure to force concessions. Nevertheless, for Harriet and Henderson workers, the timing of the largest wage increases coincided with the early years of unionization, and that created the perception of a causal relationship.[10]

Regardless of causation, the benefits of home ownership, improved roads, and higher wages dramatically altered the quality of life in the mill villages. Luther Jackson recalled some of the modifications the new home owners made: "They had them painted good. They had pretty flowers in the yard, nice curtains up." "It was the biggest difference in the world," Joseph Braswell remembered. Over time most workers also acquired more material possessions and enjoyed the comfort of many modern amenities. During the 1950s many union members installed indoor plumbing and bathrooms. Many could afford to purchase radios, better clothing, and new furniture. Eventually a fairly large number were able to afford refrigerators and televisions. Joseph Braswell bought his first electric refrigerator in 1948. Braswell was also one of the first in the Henderson mill village to buy a television. "I know in the early fifties, didn't many people have televisions," he recalled.[11]

Quite a few mill workers in 1958, however, still could not afford basic modern appliances like refrigerators. Many shopped for perishables on a daily basis, so small, easily accessible, family-owned grocery stores were crucial for mill villagers. In addition, as late as 1958 very few millhands owned automobiles. Even Joseph Braswell, who was among the first to purchase major appliances, did not own a car until the 1960s. Shopping in town, then, was usually a once-a-week event. "We got paid on Friday back then," Braswell recalled, "and on Saturday morning a whole lot of women, you'd see them walking, and men, too, but I mean they was walking to town to do the shopping, to go to the store."[12] Yet even though they were not enjoying a lavish 1950s suburban lifestyle, most mill workers experienced a material existence worlds beyond anything that they had previously imagined.

In addition to changes in their economic well-being, mill workers became more active in politics in the 1950s. The TWUA encouraged local union officers to attend regional workshops that emphasized voter registration. "When I went in that local union as president I bet you that I didn't have 10 percent of my members that was registered to vote," estimated Luther Jackson, who attended TWUA classes for Local 584. Shortly after he took office, however, Jackson recalled that "every member in that local union and everyone in their family was registered to vote." A similar effort took place in the Harriet mill village. "That's one thing we encouraged," recalled former Local 578 president Sam Littleton. "Everybody to register, everybody to vote."[13]

Although the local unions involved themselves in politics, the direct impact of their efforts was slight, limited mainly to influencing the character of county offices like sheriff or clerk of the court. Since mill villagers lived outside the city limits, they had no voice in mayoral campaigns, and their numbers were too small to affect statewide campaigns even in combination with union members throughout North Carolina. Moreover, local voting records reveal little about issues or candidates that might have inspired union members, and they cast doubt on workers' memories of immediate politicization after unionization. Although it may be true that voter registration increased considerably after the organizing campaign, the actual numbers of voters in the two districts most heavily populated by mill workers do not reveal the immediate difference one would expect from oral testimony.[14] For example, in the 1940 primary election for governor, three years before unionization, 566 residents of North Henderson cast ballots. In the 1942 primary for sheriff, there were 577 total votes. In the 1944 primary for governor, one year after unionization, 561 voted. The South Henderson evidence is also murky. In that district, 385 voted for governor in the 1940 primary, and 333 voted for sheriff in the 1942 primary. After unionization only 255 voted for governor in the 1944 primary, and 406 for sheriff in the 1946 primary. At best, it seems likely that voter participation, and probably registration, increased somewhat after the war ended and veterans returned.[15]

Beyond sheer numbers of voters, however, it is difficult to discover any particular candidate or issue that mill workers backed during these early years of unionization. It appears that candidates received support out of habit, statewide reputation, and name recognition as much as anything else. Whereas U.S. Representative Harold Cooley received solid majorities of mill-village votes throughout the postwar years, as he had since the 1930s, the congressman's majorities were equally impressive in every other Henderson voting district. In the 1944 U.S. Senate primary, both mill villages, as well as the rest of Henderson, strongly backed former governor Clyde Hoey, who had made his reputation prosecuting striking textile workers in Gastonia in 1929.[16] The one gubernatorial candidate in the immediate postwar years who was considered not rabidly antiunion, Kerr Scott, failed to receive even a plurality of votes in the mill villages in the first 1948 primary. Indeed, in 1948 Scott received more votes in the wealthy west end of town.[17]

Likewise, local races seemed to turn on personality and neighborhood familiarity rather than any political programs supported by union members. In the 1946 and 1950 primaries for sheriff, different candidates finished first in the two mill villages. By 1954, both mill villages supported E. A. Cottrell, who had been the sheriff for twelve years, but so did every other voting district in Henderson. The mill villages also gave majorities to different candidates for Recorders Court judge in 1946, for Superior Court judge in 1948, and again in the first primary for Recorders Court in 1956.[18] These were the types of races in which one could possibly expect the union voting bloc to make some kind of difference in local politics, yet no clear pattern emerges.

The one statewide race in the postwar era that mobilized mill village voters more than any other was the 1950 Senate contest between the relatively liberal University of North Carolina president Frank Porter Graham, who had recently been appointed to the Senate by Governor Kerr Scott upon the death of the incumbent, and the antiunion, overtly segregationist corporate attorney Willis Smith, who had served as president of the American Bar Association and chaired the board of trustees at Duke University. Graham, of course, was sympathetic with organized labor and had served on President Truman's Committee on Civil Rights, which recommended "the elimination of segregation based on race, color, creed, or national origin, from American life." Although he opposed any legal remedy to end discrimination—he preferred instead to rely on education and persuasion—Graham was clearly on the progressive end of the North Carolina political spectrum.[19] This high-profile campaign, coupled with a countywide voter registration renewal, boosted voter participation throughout Vance County, as it did across the entire state. Whereas 723 North Henderson residents voted in the 1948 U.S. Senate primary, 1,128 participated in 1950. In South Henderson, the difference was more dramatic: the turnout jumped from 314 in 1948 to 1,209 in 1950. Graham won a narrow plurality over Smith in North Henderson (490–430, with 200 votes for Robert Reynolds) and a narrow majority in South Henderson (624–404, with 165 for Reynolds).[20] Statewide, Graham won a plurality but not a majority, forcing a second primary.

In the second race, emboldened by the announcement of U.S. Supreme Court decisions outlawing segregation on Pullman dining cars and ordering state universities in Texas and Oklahoma to admit blacks, Smith ran an aggressive red- and race-baiting campaign against Graham. Despite the formal endorsement of Graham by both Locals 578 and 584, Smith's tactics appear to have had an effect, especially in the North Henderson mill village. Smith won the second primary in that district, 625–516, on his way to statewide victory. However, Graham still won a majority, albeit narrower than in the first primary, in the South Henderson village, 591–476.[21] It is probably significant that in 1950 there were nearly 200 blacks registered to vote in the district that contained the Henderson mill village, compared to only 28 registered blacks in the South Henderson voting district.[22] Local union members were not likely ever to see a candidate more sympathetic with organized labor than Frank Graham. Nevertheless, it appears that Graham's vulnerability on the charge of being soft on segregation, and possibly that of being soft on communism, persuaded many mill villagers to ignore the endorsement of their local unions and vote for a staunchly antiunion candidate.[23]

The 1950 election, however, also included a local contest that proved to be heartening for many mill villagers. Longtime county commissioner Henry Hight, who grew up near the North Henderson mill village, ran a successful campaign to become Vance County's clerk of the court. Referring to Hight, former Local 578 president Sam Littleton recalled, "If you had a problem with anything, and if anybody had to go to court, he'd treat them like a human being. . . . He had a feeling for the people, I mean poor people." Hight received the equivalent of his countywide margin of victory in North Henderson, which supported him 771–456. Significantly, nearly 100 more North Henderson voters cast ballots in the first primary for clerk of the court than for all candidates in the controversial U.S. Senate race.[24] It should be noted, however, that the wealthiest section of town, West Henderson, also gave Hight a solid majority, 760–567, with 142 more votes cast for the local office than for the Senate race.

Although union members recall their postwar political organizing with pride, their efforts, in the end, were mostly an exercising of citizenship rights rather than any kind of political movement. The local unions were superb at transporting people to the polls, monitoring who had voted, and emphasizing the importance of casting ballots. The election of Henry Hight, however, was the only discernible highlight during the 1950s, and he was nearly as popular among the town's elite. The importance mill villagers attached to their political participation, however, should not be discounted by those looking for a coherent ideological purpose in such activities. For the first time, millhands perceived themselves as full-fledged citizens, exercising their constitutional rights, and they were proud of it. Most mill workers apparently believed that the union had been responsible for the increase in the political involvement of the local membership. This connection contributed another level of complexity to the deep sense of outrage felt and expressed by many mill workers when the Coopers launched their assault on the union.

Despite union members' perception that unionization had significantly improved their standing within their community, economic developments in Vance County and the entire region had undercut the potential power these workers would hold in any strike. While contemplating whether or not to strike, union members had little control over and quite possibly minimal awareness of the consequences of these changes. Throughout the South, the years following World War II saw enormous shifts in employment opportunities. Between 1945 and 1959, mechanization in cotton production and the general unprofitableness of tobacco farming forced some 462,000 white tenant farmers and sharecroppers and nearly 400,000 white farm owners and managers out of agriculture. There were not nearly enough low-wage jobs available in the South to absorb that many potential employees. Many of these unemployed and underemployed whites coveted cotton-mill jobs, which often looked stable and lucrative compared with agriculture.[25]

Despite the steep decline in farm profitability, businesses in Henderson still relied heavily on the income generated from the county's agricultural production.[26] Even during 1957, a disastrous year for tobacco, the area's major crop, farm income in Vance County was nearly $7 million, over twice as much as the cotton mills' payrolls.[27] Raising tobacco, however, had been a risky business throughout the 1950s. Land committed to tobacco production in Vance County had been declining steadily, from nearly 12,000 acres in 1954 to just over 7,600 acres in 1957. Although 1958 proved to be a better year for tobacco growers, many had either already left farming or had serious doubts about their futures.[28] It was possible for farmers in the Henderson area to consider growing cotton as an alternative to tobacco. In any given year, between 2,000 and 4,000 acres of county land were devoted to that crop. Throughout the 1950s, however, imported cotton became available in relatively cheap abundance, undercutting the livelihoods of many domestic producers and causing a drastic reduction in acreage committed to cotton. Moreover, most of the nation's 1957 crop was rated inferior in quality because of weather damage and therefore sold at low prices, driving more farmers away from cotton. Vance County farmers who were disillusioned with their prospects in tobacco during the 1950s could hardly have viewed cotton as their savior.[29] Hundreds of farmers in Vance County, and thousands in the immediate vicinity, including southern Virginia, existed precariously on the land and searched for alternatives.

This pressure intensified during the recession that began in late 1957. On 31 January 1958 the Vance County office of the State Employment Security Commission held 1,047 active applications for work, while it listed only 16 job openings. At the end of March, 1,172 job applicants sought 21 positions. Although by October 1958 the *Henderson Daily Dispatch* reported a "much brighter" employment situation because of the seasonal increase in demand for agricultural labor, there were still 596 people actively seeking jobs in the Henderson area. It is likely that many more were looking for work but had not bothered to file applications with the SESC.[30] Even without the recession, it is doubtful that Henderson businesses could have absorbed the large numbers of unemployed residents and those leaving the land in search of jobs.

Besides the Harriet and Henderson Cotton Mills, there were limited job possibilities for whites in Henderson. With the exception of three small hosiery mills, which employed from forty to fifty people each, the only other significant industrial employer of whites in the early 1950s was the Corbitt Company, which produced trucks for the federal government. Corbitt employed less than one hundred people in production jobs, however, and by the mid-1950s it had been sold and was no longer producing vehicles.[31] In 1956 a department store chain based in Henderson, Rose's 5-10-25 Cent Stores, began a major expansion, but significant numbers of warehouse jobs did not materialize until the 1960s.[32] The only significant nonagricultural employer of whites in Vance County, outside of Henderson, was a tungsten mine near the Virginia border that provided jobs for four hundred to five hundred people. First developed in 1943 for its usefulness in war production, this tungsten deposit shortly became the largest source of the metal in the United States. By 1958, however, the federal government had stockpiled nearly six years' worth of tungsten and could import additional supplies cheaper than having the metal mined in Vance County. By late June 1958, the tungsten mine had laid off four hundred workers, awaiting the outcome of pending federal legislation that would have authorized either a tariff on imported tungsten or a subsidy to continue accumulating domestic production of the metal. When Congress defeated both proposals in August 1958, the mine layoffs became permanent.[33] In late 1958, then, large numbers of farmers and laid-off mine workers sought jobs with very few employment opportunities in the area. This was not a labor market that boded well for the success of any strike.

It also remained unclear whether or not a strike would spur Harriet and Henderson managers to break the decades-old racial barrier to production jobs in the mills. In 1958 over 40 percent of Henderson's 12,000 residents were African American. Industrial jobs for blacks were limited to the Carolina Bagging Company, which employed some seven hundred people, and several tobacco companies, most notably J. P. Taylor, which alone employed up to eight hundred for seasonal work.[34] Many black women worked as domestic help for wealthier white citizens. As in most southern towns, there were also a number of black business owners and professionals, serving mainly the black community. Only about two dozen blacks, however, worked at the Harriet and Henderson Cotton Mills, and none held production jobs. Nevertheless, Henderson's large underemployed black population could have been a potential weapon at the Coopers' disposal if union members at their mills went on strike.

White cotton-mill workers had done little to foster any formal connections with Henderson's African American community. This was, after all, the American South in the 1950s. "Back there then it was segregated, and that's the way people growed up," recalled Joseph Braswell. "You couldn't undo it back then." Several black neighborhoods were adjacent to the mill villages, but very few blacks ever ventured into white residential areas. In retrospect, it seems that Locals 578 and 584 might have tried to establish some kind of relationship with the predominantly black union at the Carolina Bagging Mill—United Furniture Workers of America Local 265, which had 350 members. The very idea, however, was nearly unfathomable to white union members at the time. "There weren't much togetherness," recalled Joseph Braswell, referring to relations between white mill workers and black union members at the bagging mill. "As far as voting or stuff like that, there was never no all the unions banding together and so forth." Former Local 584 president Luther Jackson, who possessed a keen memory, could recall the white union local at the Corbitt company in the early 1950s but did not recall the black bagging-mill union, which remained strong in 1958.[35]

There are other reasons, however ahistorical, why white mill workers and blacks in Henderson might have found common ground in the 1950s. Some members of Henderson's black community were testing the limits of democracy during the same period that local textile workers were challenging managerial power in the cotton mills and exercising their own political rights.[36] Over six hundred Vance County African Americans successfully registered to vote in 1950. Although this number was modest in an absolute sense—blacks represented 45.5 percent of the county's population but still only 7.9 percent of its registered voters—it was the first upsurge in black political activity in decades.[37] In 1955, an African American man, Pompey Jones, ran for a seat on the Henderson City Council. Although Jones campaigned as an advocate of growth, hoping "to make Henderson so desirable that business and industry of every kind will want to come to Henderson," he also believed it necessary to pay "good wages to all workers, and to grant raises as necessary to uphold a good standard of living and make all of our people more happy and contented."[38] Jones's empathy for workers distinguished him from Henderson's white boosters but garnered him only 170 votes, compared to Third Ward winner Andrew Finch's 2,141 and second-place finisher Irwin Baker's 316.[39] Three years later African Americans staged a "swim-in" at a popular "public" beach on nearby Kerr Lake. The beach at Satterwhite Point was owned by the federal government, having been leased for public use by the U.S. Army Corps of Engineers. Because it was federal property, the beach could not legally be segregated. In practice, however, it had been reserved for whites, while another area was allegedly being developed for use by blacks. Shortly after a small group scouted the area, nearly one hundred blacks entered the beach. In a display of fair-mindedness that any student of the civil rights movement would find amazing, Vance County Sheriff E. A. Cottrell refused to make any arrests, explaining that the swimmers weren't breaking the law. A few days later, however, the *Henderson Daily Dispatch* noted that there would be officers on hand to protect people, presumably whites, who went to the beach.[40]

There is no evidence, however, of any support for Henderson's black civil rights activists by white members of Locals 578 and 584. If anything, it seems likely that black political involvement inspired many millhands to vote for segregationist Willis Smith against Frank Porter Graham.[41] Locals 578 and 584 took no public stand on these emerging racial issues, and it remained to be seen what role, if any, the lack of connection between the white union members and the community's black workers would play in a strike at the cotton mills. It is doubtful that Harriet and Henderson union members seriously contemplated the threat of black strikebreakers in their assessments of their prospects for success.

It is far more likely that mill workers focused instead on their role in the increasing prosperity of Henderson during the 1950s. Henderson's economy in 1958 still depended to a great extent on the Harriet and Henderson Cotton Mills, which remained the community's largest single industrial employer.[42] In 1951, for example, the company's $50,000 weekly payroll amounted to 40 percent of Henderson's industrial earnings. In 1957 the cotton mills' average weekly payroll of $60,000 provided over $3 million annually, nearly 9 percent of Vance County's "effective buying income."[43] With the mills as the primary economic generator, Henderson had displayed signs of growth throughout the 1950s. The town itself experienced a population increase of nearly 16 percent, from 10,996 in 1950 to 12,740 in 1960. Since the population of Vance County remained virtually the same during the decade—declining slightly from 32,101 to 32,002—it seems likely that part of the increase was the result of an influx of new residents, mostly white, from the surrounding countryside.[44] Henderson also grew spatially and took on a more modern appearance during the postwar years. The city more than doubled in area as its limits were extended to include many of the newer residential neighborhoods, especially the relatively expensive homes under construction on the west side of town. More streets were built, old ones were paved, and new sewer lines were installed.[45] In the early 1950s, Henderson residents voted to issue nearly $1 million in bonds to improve the city's water supply and distribution system. The town also formed its first modern fire department and organized an ambulance service.[46] Mill workers knew that their elevated economic standing in the community paralleled, and indirectly helped to finance, the general improvement in Henderson's quality of life.

Despite periodic recessions and fluctuations in agricultural earnings, most Henderson businesses flourished during the 1950s. Higher wages, especially at the cotton mills, fueled growth in retail and service-sector jobs. By 1948 the number of jobs for whites in "wholesale, retail and trade" in Henderson surpassed the number of jobs available in the Harriet and Henderson Mills, 1,200 to 1,156.[47] Benefiting from the community's relative prosperity, there was an increase in the number of appliance stores, television dealers, beauty shops, barbers, restaurants, drugstores, insurance companies, automobile dealers, and, especially, filling stations during the 1950s.[48] Between 1953 and 1955, service jobs, mainly for whites, were also created at several new supermarkets, like the Save-Way and the Colonial Store; at the city's first Woolworth's department store; and at a new Walgreen's drugstore.[49]

Union members accurately perceived their own importance in the community's prosperity. They could feel it in their interactions with local merchants. In contrast with the 1920s and 1930s, in the 1950s store owners in Henderson welcomed the business of millhands and readily extended them credit for major purchases. "After they knew that we was making a good salary," Edith Adams recalled, "they wanted to get their fair share. So they started paying a little more attention to you." By no means did condescension toward mill workers end, but the union members' increased earnings brought them a measure of respect within the community that they, in turn, associated with unionization.[50] As union members contemplated a strike, they knew that many local business owners depended greatly on the mills' payrolls for survival and might be sympathetic with the workers' concerns.

Yet a significant group of city leaders, strongly opposed to unions, was concerned about Henderson's lack of new industrial jobs.[51] "When one gets about over the State," noted *Henderson Daily Dispatch* editor H. A. Dennis, "the fact is brought home with stunning reality that we are still small and that there is a long way to go to climb into the class with some communities which once were in about the same category as we were years ago."[52] As early as 1950 Dennis and others had been urging reluctant businessmen to revive the city's long-dormant chamber of commerce and seek new industries. Unlike their predecessors in the 1890s, the 1950s boosters rested their hopes not on homegrown industry but on luring employers to their community. "A town without a Chamber of Commerce makes little impression upon an outsider," Dennis argued, "and particularly one who is interested in what a community has to offer if a business were located within its borders."[53] Once reorganized, the Henderson Chamber of Commerce considered forming an industrial development corporation that would "permit an aggressive approach to seek out new industries which never thought of coming to Henderson."[54]

Henderson's economic vulnerability became even more apparent in 1951, when Locals 578 and 584 joined the TWUA's unsuccessful regional strike for higher wages. While the five-week strike cost union members at the Harriet and Henderson Mills nearly $300,000 in lost wages, the economic impact, according to newspaper editor H. A. Dennis, was "felt by everyone," highlighting "the interdependence of all elements one upon the other, and the concern of each for all others."[55] According to boosters like Dennis, the strike highlighted the need for economic expansion and diversification to soften the impact of any similar disruption in the future. Mill workers, on the other hand, could see concretely how vital they were to the town's prosperity.

Throughout the South during the 1950s, local efforts to attract new industry became increasingly common, especially in small towns like Henderson. Usually communities would offer potential employers various subsidies—like free land, free buildings, interest-free loans, or tax exemptions. Boosters also trumpeted whatever virtues, in addition to cheap, available labor, that they could perceive in their particular communities or surrounding countryside. Local development corporations usually worked closely with state government organizations. State developers would promote their state in general, or a particular area within it. Once a prospective business voiced an interest, local officials competed to close the sale for their communities.[56]

Beginning in 1953, when he assumed office on the death of William Umstead, North Carolina governor Luther Hodges became one of the most aggressive industry hunters in the South. After graduating at the top of his class from the University of North Carolina in 1919, Hodges went to work for the Marshall Field textile conglomerate; he eventually served as a corporate vice president before making a successful career shift to politics.[57] As governor, Hodges sent delegations directly to northern cities, and eventually to Europe, to discuss the benefits of relocating in North Carolina, including what he portrayed as a strong antiunion consensus. He also competed fiercely with other southern states interested in the same prospects. In one instance, Hodges tried to convince a rubber company to choose the long-term benefits of North Carolina's infrastructure over the even lower wages being offered in Mississippi.[58] Hodges claimed that North Carolina's efforts to attract new industry resulted in 617 relocations between 1 July 1954 and 1 July 1958.[59]

Henderson's boosters sought new industries in the midst of this statewide campaign, yet by early 1955 they had failed to experience a single success. Ever optimistic, H. A. Dennis hoped that by the end of that year Henderson would "break the ice with one or more new industries," which would be "the turning point for greater growth to which all good citizens here have looked for so long with anxious eyes."[60] Leading the pursuit of growth was Henderson native Carroll Singleton, born in 1919, who studied business administration at the University of Alabama, served in World War II, and worked for a life insurance company in Virginia before returning to his hometown around 1950. In addition to promoting the relocation of industries to Henderson, Singleton was an entrepreneur who had grown frustrated with the difficulty of obtaining loans from established banks for new local projects. Responding to this need, another young advocate of growth, Junius Tillery, transformed a traditional savings and loan in 1954 into a commercial bank willing to take much greater risks than the community's leading lending institutions. Tillery, a native of Halifax County to the east of Henderson, graduated from the University of North Carolina at Chapel Hill, served in the Navy during the war, and moved to Henderson in 1946; he worked at Citizen's Bank for eight years before leaving to compete with his former employer.[61]

As Singleton's and Tillery's career paths indicate, Henderson's business community was not united in the quest for economic growth. It was "the youth of the community versus the old folks of the community," recalled W. D. Wester, who actively promoted growth in the 1950s. "It was the establishment as opposed to the postwar youth that had come back after the war."[62] The youth faced a strong challenge: the leading opponents of growth were John D. and Marshall Cooper. Wary of any local development that would disrupt their labor supply or possibly increase wage expectations, the Coopers opposed any plan to lure new industries to the area. Moreover, Marshall Cooper was the president of Citizen's Bank and dominated its board of directors, which consisted largely of older, well-established Henderson businessmen. The advocates of growth saw the Coopers' opposition as a major obstacle.[63] Marshall Cooper "was a very strong man with a very strong ego," W. D. Wester recalled, "and Carroll [Singleton] was a young man with a strong ego, and they just clashed. . . . Marshall Cooper fought him tooth and toenail."[64] In the contest to attract new industries, it was considered important to present at least the appearance of a unified community welcoming businesses with open arms. Before deciding on a particular community for relocation, business executives often asked to meet with leading local industrialists, something that would have been disastrous in Henderson. Communities were known to try to sabotage a competitor's chances by fostering such local frictions.[65]

To the further dismay of local boosters, the Coopers also seemed to be responsible for blocking the physical expansion of the city to include the mills and some four thousand mill village residents. The mills, if not the mill villages, had long benefited from city services without paying taxes for them. Most local boosters had hoped that an annexation initiative would succeed and blamed the Coopers for the proposal's defeat, claiming that the mill owners were protecting their own interests by frightening voters with the prospect of high residential property taxes. Whatever the Coopers' influence, in January 1955 more than nine hundred mill villagers signed petitions asking to be annexed, but just over two months later, the total vote showed only 440 in favor, with 524 opposed.[66] Noting that nearby Roanoke Rapids had recently increased its population by four thousand through annexation, the *Henderson Daily Dispatch* lamented that its neighboring town was "another of the live, growing communities in the State that are forging ahead of Henderson."[67]

Disappointed with the outcome of the election, the advocates of growth backed Carroll Singleton's challenge to the incumbent mayor, attorney Henry T. Powell, who had held office since 1937. After Singleton's narrow defeat, 1,389–1,330, boosters voiced disappointment once again that Henderson seemed to be stagnating. A few weeks later Henderson lost in its bid for a new industry to distant Albemarle, near Charlotte.[68]

Given the strong local opposition to attracting outside businesses, it is not surprising that the first successful development effort involved the diversification of the Harriet and Henderson Cotton Mills. Hoping to make some money from the large amount of cotton waste generated by the mills, the Coopers planned to construct a plant to handle low-grade scraps. They estimated that the new facility, including machinery, would employ fifty people, providing an annual payroll of $125,000. According to the company's plan, Henderson boosters would launch a stock subscription campaign to pay for the waste mill building, estimated to cost $130,000. Eager for progress of any kind, H. A. Dennis pleaded, "The community has an opportunity to lift itself by its own bootstraps, as it were, and cannot afford to pass up the chance."[69] Indeed, the boosters raised well over the $65,000 in cash deemed necessary for success, and the new mill began production in mid-1956.[70]

Two years later, however, no outside businesses had yet relocated to Henderson, and local growth had failed to generate substantial numbers of jobs. Listing economic highlights during 1957, the *Henderson Daily Dispatch* noted only a new wing on a small local hosiery mill, an addition to a local church, breaking ground on a new hospital for blacks, and the Rose's Stores' new warehouse. Advocates of growth had been encouraged when Carroll Singleton ran unopposed for mayor in 1957, but their successful political campaign had yet to provide tangible benefits. To these boosters, the nationwide recession that hit full stride in early 1958 only made the goal of attracting new industries seem more urgent and the competition with other communities more fierce.[71]

Moreover, Mayor Singleton and his supporters faced another roadblock at least as imposing as the Coopers. The very existence of Locals 578 and 584 at the Harriet and Henderson Mills gave Henderson the reputation of being a union town, which eliminated the primary attraction for most outside industrialists. Business representatives investigating Henderson learned about the five-week strike at the cotton mills in 1951 and the seven-week strike in 1954. They also learned about a strike by organized workers at the Corbitt Truck Company in 1950. Although the Corbitt Company had survived precariously in the postwar years and would probably have been unable to compete much longer with General Motors, Ford, and Chrysler for government contracts, the truck manufacturer was sold within two years of the unsuccessful strike, and some business leaders drew the conclusion that unions destroy good companies.[72] While Henderson boosters had no choice but to acknowledge the union presence in their town, they repeatedly emphasized the peacefulness that had been displayed by organized workers even during these postwar conflicts. Nevertheless, as W. D. Wester noted, "industrialists don't want to come to a union town." In the 1950s, according to Wester, numerous potential businessmen who considered relocating to Henderson "would say absolutely not, because it had a strong union flavor."[73]

Despite all obstacles, in early 1958, Henderson boosters negotiated an agreement with a potential new industry, the Perfect Packed Pickle Company. If local residents could raise $150,000 toward a new $300,000 food-processing plant by 29 March, the pickle company would relocate to Henderson and provide an annual payroll of between $400,000 and $500,000.[74] Although Henderson boosters collected pledges totaling $50,000 within a week, they still lacked the support of the Coopers. In a thinly disguised attempt to shame the cotton-mill owners, with only $96,000 raised campaign leaders published the names of individuals and businesses that had made contributions. Included were the town's leading boosters and banks, each of which sought a share of any mortgage that would be necessary to complete the facility. John D. and Marshall Cooper and the Harriet and Henderson Mills, however, were not on the list. Responding to this public revelation, Marshall Cooper contributed on his own behalf, and for the Harriet and Henderson Mills, but John D. Cooper adamantly refused to participate. At this point the campaign still needed $18,000 within three days.[75]

Racing against the deadline, Henderson boosters reached their goal of $150,000 and even raised an additional $16,000 three months later when construction bids were higher than expected. In July 1958, the pickle company signed a contract to use the new facility, to be built in part with the locally generated funds.[76] In an editorial entitled "An Industry in the Bag," H. A. Dennis celebrated: "This is a magnificent beginning which could blossom into still greater accomplishments."[77]

The campaign, however, was not home free. By early October, over $50,000 pledged to the cause had not been paid. "Think of what a disgrace and what a black eye the community will receive," Dennis wrote, "if this movement should fall by the wayside at this stage of the project."[78] A month's worth of cajoling still left the boosters with over $15,000 uncollected.[79] The shortfall seemed especially crucial because at the same time two new industries, a candy manufacturer and a glass plant, were seriously considering moving to Henderson.[80] After years of fruitless effort, Henderson boosters appeared to be tantalizingly close to several successes. At precisely this time, however, the stalled and highly contentious contract negotiations at the Harriet and Henderson Mills burst into public view.

The emerging conflict at the cotton mills highlighted the divisions between the community's business leaders and revealed competing strains of antiunionism. On the one hand, the Coopers had become thoroughly disenchanted with Locals 578 and 584 and actively sought a strike in order to greatly diminish, and possibly eliminate, the union's influence. On the other hand, although the boosters also detested unions, especially the debilitating effect the TWUA locals had on industrial recruitment, they abhorred overt labor conflict even more. It was far better, they thought, to have peaceful, functioning union locals in town than to have any kind of strike that would call attention to the union presence and cast doubt on their claim that Henderson had a favorable business climate. "We have just begun to acquire new industry and are in the midst of negotiating for one that would be very beneficial to us," appealed Mayor Singleton. A "show of poor employer-employee relations at this time would do untold damage to our chances."[81]

Governor Hodges was also at some risk because he had invested himself personally in the effort to attract the Perfect Packed Pickle plant to Henderson. Hodges had been criticized by many people in agriculture for expending large amounts of energy seeking new industries while paying less attention to the difficulties faced by farmers. Seeking to link constituencies, Hodges had promised to pursue new food-processing facilities. Vance County farmers, for example, could possibly switch from tobacco or cotton to cucumbers if the pickle plant materialized. In this effort, Singleton and Hodges became friends, with Henderson's mayor joining the governor on northern recruiting ventures. Although the Henderson pickle plant was not the only food-processing project being monitored by Hodges, he had more than a casual interest in its success.[82] Moreover, Hodges also feared the unfavorable publicity inherent in any strike, because any evidence of labor conflict undermined his administration's credibility when promoting the state's hospitable business climate.

As a strike at the cotton mills appeared increasingly inevitable, threatening to tarnish the image of Henderson's and North Carolina's business climate, the allegiances of local business leaders and state officials became more crucial. Would Henderson's progrowth faction, despite its antiunionism, oppose the Coopers' hard-line tactics in hopes of ensuring labor peace? Would the city's old-guard leaders respond to the boosters' sense of what was in the community's best interest? Would union members make concessions for the sake of luring new industries to town? Would Governor Hodges work either publicly or behind the scenes to foster a settlement, even if it meant having the company make some concessions to the union? Or would he welcome the opportunity to help smash a union, preferably quickly, to prove his probusiness credentials? Perhaps even more important, would unemployed whites or embattled farmers seek to replace striking millhands? And would the company be willing to break with tradition and destroy the union with black strikebreakers?

As local union members contemplated whether or not to work without a contract, they undoubtedly focused mainly on the material and emotional gains they had experienced inside the mills and in the community since unionization. If they bothered to consider the larger economic and political contexts, they would probably have been humbled, if not deterred. In the midst of a national recession and a shifting regional economy, thousands of white southerners sought jobs in a tight market. Thousands more African Americans in the region were also looking for work, and it is likely that most would have considered positions in a cotton mill if racial barriers were removed. Local and state political leaders opposed unions, and the company had adopted a position of outright intransigence. The union members' only hope for support from those in power seemed to rest on the desire of boosters at all levels for a strike-free business climate—a desire that could conceivably lead some antiunion activists to exert covert pressure on company officials to make concessions. Henderson boosters, however, were hardly on speaking terms with the Coopers. Despite these ominous contexts, and possibly unaware of them, Harriet and Henderson workers scheduled their referendum on what unionization had meant to them and whether or not union power was worth defending.

9   Striking for the Grievance Procedure, 1958–1961

Members of Locals 578 and 584 met together at a Henderson warehouse on Sunday evening, 16 November, to decide whether or not to strike. The place "was just packed," Esther Roberson recalled. Luther Jackson, who chaired the meeting, outlined for the members exactly what the company had offered. Then, Jackson recalled, he had some of the older workers speak about the changes they had seen in their working lives. One of the few younger hands, Clifton Carter, recalled hearing them defend "something they believed in, something they'd worked on all their lives." The nearly nine hundred union members in attendance voted unanimously to strike.[1]

There were still a number of union members, probably as many as one hundred, who did not attend the meeting. Undoubtedly there were some hands who for various reasons disliked the union and belonged to it only to keep others off their backs. Also, a number of union members were the spouses or close relatives of second hands and foremen. Management put pressure on these workers not to participate in such a potentially divisive act. Other union members did not depend enough on mill work to risk involving themselves with a strike.[2] A few were too unsure to commit themselves. Despite serving as Local 584's financial secretary, Edith Adams remained timid about stepping out too far on a limb. She and her husband had voted no in the original union election, and they abstained from this vote, she remembered, "because we didn't want to strike." Yet if they had attended, Adams explained, "we wouldn't have voted against it," because "we felt like we'd be betraying our neighbors and our fellow workers."[3]

Despite ambivalence among some of its members, the local unions appeared to be just as willing as the company to hold firm. Strikers organized picket lines at both mills, and there seemed to be little pressure to reach a quick settlement. After the strike's first week, union representatives and company officials rarely met, because no one would budge on the crucial issue: the union demanded the old arbitration clause, while the company would not consider it.[4]

After receiving their final paychecks on 19 November, however, union members faced an uncertain future with many practical problems to solve. In early November, Luther Jackson and Charlie Ranes had met with TWUA general president William Pollock, who promised that the international union would "see that the workers are not starved back into the plant."[5] With this pledge of support, union members organized commissaries to provide food. Trucks carrying items like flour, corn meal, eggs, cheese, and beans arrived regularly at the two local union halls. Many union members recalled that although during the strike they were not "eating fancy," they always had plenty of food.[6] Because the dispute was legally a strike and not a lockout, the North Carolina Employment Security Commission ruled in early December that union members were not eligible for unemployment benefits.[7] At this point the international TWUA agreed to send additional money to purchase heating oil for the strikers. Eventually the international union would also assume the strikers' house payments, rent, utility bills, insurance premiums, and installments on merchandise purchased prior to the strike. Local union officers handled the allocation of the strike relief funds, which covered almost everything except alcohol and cigarettes.[8]

Throughout November and December, however, as the labor conflict became a topic of public concern, the central issues of the strike slowly began to shift. There was little serious public discussion about issues like workloads, arbitration, and absenteeism. Instead, union members were forced to defend themselves against community leaders' charges that strikers were threatening the future of Henderson. Henderson's pro-growth boosters, led by Mayor Carroll Singleton, continued to view the strike primarily as a hindrance to Henderson's ability to attract new industries. On the first day the mills were closed, Singleton asked local union leaders to continue working without a contract so that the new pickle company would not be dissuaded from relocating to Henderson.[9]

The chamber of commerce, whose members benefited immensely from Harriet and Henderson's $60,000 weekly payroll, also pressured the union to accept management's demands. Chamber president Cecil Lewis warned union officials that there was a "50–50" chance that management would either move or liquidate the mills. Union leaders recommended instead that Governor Luther Hodges and the state commissioner of labor appoint a three-man fact-finding panel to settle the dispute. The company refused, but it was clear that the local unions would not be easily intimidated.[10]

Town leaders, however, had not exhausted their arsenal of strategies to tame the strikers, as demonstrated when Mayor Singleton blamed the strike on outside agitators. The "outsider" theme received reinforcement when the local paper printed excerpts from an editorial first published in *America's Textile Reporter*, an industry-funded publication, warning that many towns had been destroyed by "the intrusion of outside professional union organizers." The Henderson strike, claimed the *Reporter*, was "a prime example of how unionism eventually wrecks companies and communities."[11]

Confronting the charge of outside influence, union members characterized their regional TWUA representatives as "honest and conscientious men" who had made no recommendations on whether or not the locals should strike. In addition, the local unions called the excerpts from *America's Textile Reporter* "unfair, biased and prejudiced propaganda." In language that underscored what unionization had meant, a union writer argued in the local paper that "the full extent of the warped mind behind the editorial is revealed in its question, 'Who, but management should determine how the business shall be operated?' and its answer, 'no one knows as well as management what workloads should be; what pay rates should be.'" Whereas in 1927 workers had carefully avoided showing any "disrespect" toward managers, in 1958 union members displayed few signs of public deference.[12]

As the New Year approached, the union became frustrated that there had been no formal negotiations since the week before the strike vote and none were scheduled until 30 January.[13] Throughout December and January, however, the company made no effort to produce any yarn. Managers had anticipated a strike, and given the poor market conditions in 1958, the shutdown might have been good business. According to Marshall Cooper, as of late January 1959 the company had suffered "very nominal" losses from the strike, because they "had shipped a good portion of the inventory" and had not paid workers their Christmas bonus, which saved "about $25,000."[14]

As the strike dragged on, local business leaders grew increasingly restless and confused. By mid-January the *Daily Dispatch* had stopped blaming the union for wanton community-wrecking and had begun to plead that "something should be done if anything at all can be."[15] This perplexity suggests that to this point the union had succeeded in maintaining relatively favorable public relations. Although it is doubtful that many people outside the mill villages understood or agreed with the workers' positions on issues like workloads, it seems that the union benefited from not being the aggressor. As Henderson Mill hand Lloyd Wilkins put it, "We didn't ask for nothing but just for what we had."[16] In addition, the union members' behavior was impeccable. Picket lines had been quiet except for card games and conversation.

In early February, however, company officials altered the terms of conflict by deciding to resume production without a union. Before announcing their intentions publicly, managers sent labor recruiters into the North Carolina and Virginia countryside looking for potential strikebreakers. Then, on 9 February, management had a local businessman, Charlie Rose, attempt to cross the Henderson Mill picket line with a load of cotton. As the delivery truck crept slowly toward the mill's gate, pickets swarmed around it, opened the passenger door, and pulled Rose from the cab. Although union members believed that the company had orchestrated the affair, they nevertheless refused to allow any nonmanagement personnel to cross their picket lines.[17]

On the basis of this incident, mill officials obtained a temporary restraining order from Superior Court Judge William Bickett that legally prohibited strikers from "interfering in any manner" with "free ingress and egress" to and from the mills. The judge limited the number of pickets to eight and ruled that they had to remain at least seventy-five feet from any gate. Strikers were also ordered not to direct "vile, abusive, violent, or threatening language" toward managers or strikebreakers.[18]

Once they were certain that Judge Bickett would issue a restraining order, Harriet and Henderson executives formally announced their intention to reopen both mills. On Thursday, 12 February, the company placed a notice in the local paper inviting all striking union members to report to work the following Monday. Management also claimed that there would be "adequate police protection against interference with those who desire to work."[19] Not content with local protection, managers recruited state troops to guard the mill entrances. In compliance with state law, Sheriff E. A. Cottrell and Police Chief C. C. Harris made the formal request, arguing that if the mills reopened, their forces "could not cope with possible violence." Two days later, however, Sheriff Cottrell told a *Raleigh News and Observer* reporter that John D. Cooper "was the man that wanted them here, and they done got here." Governor Luther Hodges quickly sent thirty highway patrolmen to Henderson.[20]

Newspaper coverage of these developments shows how easily the strike's central issue could be shifted. The *Henderson Daily Dispatch* praised the governor's decision, arguing that the troops had come "solely to impartially enforce provisions of a court restraining order."[21] Yet from the strikers' perspective, the restraining order could hardly have been considered impartial. It enabled the Coopers to run the mills with whatever workforce they wanted, and if the company successfully reopened with nonunion strikebreakers, there would be no pressing need for managers to negotiate with striking workers. Since union members would have to break the law to prevent the mills from operating, the conflict's central issue, at least in public debate, became whether or not strikers would take that risk. The *Raleigh News and Observer* acknowledged that the governor's directive was "a dangerous suggestion that the patrol might seem to be available as an anti-labor police force." The troopers appeared to be "the armed force of those with the power to ask for it and get it." Yet despite this analysis, the *News and Observer* argued that "strikers must obey the law. Order must be preserved."[22] Outside the mill villages the conflict had been redefined as a battle between managers as law-abiding citizens and strikers as potential criminals.

Management had acted well within the law. Any company in the United States had the legal right to operate with strikebreakers as long as it had not been found guilty of engaging in unfair labor practices, as determined by the National Labor Relations Board.[23] State courts could readily issue injunctions and restraining orders as part of the government's police powers, and state and federal government troops had long been deployed in strikes to enforce injunctions and the right to operate with strike-breakers.[24] Nearly nine years earlier, TWUA general counsel Isadore Katz had outlined this familiar dynamic before a committee of U.S. senators. "The tactic of an employer is always to convert the economic battle into a legal battle where the courts grant relief wholly irrelevant to the dispute between the parties," he testified. "The employer may then appear before the community as the upholder of law and order and the strikers are reduced to the position of criminals who have had a decree of an equity court entered against them."[25]

Undeterred by these parallels, TWUA representatives worked closely with local union leaders as the company prepared to resume operations. The TWUA's Julius Fry was in charge of overseeing strike activities in Henderson. Raised in a family of millhands in Durham, North Carolina, forty-six-year-old Fry began working for the TWUA in 1943, assisting local shop committees throughout the Carolinas. Because Fry still had his wider regional responsibilities, the TWUA assigned Boyd Payton to remain in Henderson on a daily basis.[26] Born in West Virginia, fifty-one-year-old Payton also began working for the TWUA in 1943. From 1943 to 1953 he had served as the Upper South director, responsible for overseeing union locals in Virginia, West Virginia, and Maryland. From 1953 to 1955 Payton had directed organizing efforts throughout the South from his base in Charlotte, North Carolina. Since 1955 he had served as the southern director in charge of handling local unions' administrative problems.[27]

Payton felt that the strike would be won or lost the Monday morning the mills reopened.[28] "[We] didn't have no intention of going back," recalled Joseph Braswell, "because the people weren't really hurting for nothing."[29] Union members also derived a measure of confidence from their certainty that the Coopers could not operate the mills profitably without the strikers. The company had forced a competent, experienced labor force out of the mills. Union members believed that they could not be replaced unless the company was willing to endure a costly, lengthy period of training new workers. As a picket sign announced, "Jesus Leads Us, the Union Feeds Us, and John D. Needs Us."[30]

At least 300 workers were required in order for the company to operate first shifts at both mills, but at most, 61 of the roughly 1,000 members of Locals 578 and 584 returned to work that first day. In addition, all union members strictly obeyed the terms of Judge Bickett's restraining order. Between 700 and 800 strikers met that evening at the city's National Guard Armory to ensure that everybody understood and would continue to obey the terms of the injunction.[31]

Ominously for union members, however, a stream of nonunion strike-breakers had begun to enter the mills. John D. Cooper claimed that even though only 50 or 60 union members had crossed the picket lines, 165 workers in all had reported for jobs on Monday morning.[32] The regional economy indeed undermined the union's power. As over one hundred strikebreakers explained, "We non-union workers took jobs in the Harriet Cotton Mills not to defeat the Union, but because most of us had been out of work for many months and it was a matter of absolute necessity. We still need the jobs so that we can support our families."[33] At this point, however, many union members believed that the company was simply "putting on a show."[34] Strikers claimed that many of their replacements had been discharged from the mills earlier for reasons of health or ineptitude.[35]

Significantly, one week after reopening the mills, management turned away carloads of black job-seekers when there were still plenty of first-shift production jobs available. The company claimed that all positions reserved for blacks had already been filled. Despite their obvious need for strikebreakers, managers refused to violate the industry's racial barriers and hire blacks for jobs traditionally held by whites.[36]

The very presence of strikebreakers, however, brought an end to the strike's peacefulness. There were several bomb blasts in the mill villages the second night after the mills reopened. The most significant was a dynamite explosion in the yard of Elmer Jenks, one of the few Local 584 members who had returned to work. Although the blast caused little damage and no injuries, it cast doubt on the strikers' methods. The company immediately offered a $1,000 reward for information leading to the bomber's arrest and conviction, and the *Raleigh News and Observer* clarified the company's suggestion: "If striking workers were guilty of this act, their cause was badly damaged by a fool among them."[37]

Union members, however, conceded nothing on the issue of violence. They matched the company's offer of a $1,000 reward to any person who could convict the bomber. Boyd Payton charged that the violence could have been "instigated by anti-union forces in an attempt to place the union in a bad light and justify the continued presence in Henderson of numerous police officers."[38] Union members were concerned that violence would become the main issue of concern for the larger public.

These fears proved justified a week later, on Tuesday, 24 February, when several pickets threw stones at strikebreakers' cars. Two events appear to have provoked this outburst. The night before, a group of anonymous assailants had knocked on Boyd Payton's hotel door and clubbed the union leader on the head with a bottle, knocking him unconscious.[39] In addition, just hours before Payton's beating, John D. Cooper had announced that on Monday, 23 February, the company would "begin to hire permanent replacements for those who have not yet returned to work."[40] Cooper also insisted that in any new contract, strikebreakers would receive seniority over strikers.[41] It seems no coincidence that the first picket-line violence occurred the following day.

But no matter what instigated picket-line incidents, violence by strikers or their sympathizers always worked against them. In this case, in reaction to the stonings, the state highway patrol began escorting strikebreakers into the mills.[42] Boyd Payton complained that the patrol's new service "cast a pall on hopes for an equitable and just settlement."[43] At first Governor Hodges deferred to Department of Motor Vehicles commissioner Ed Scheidt, who claimed, "It is not true that patrol cars are escorting workers into mill property."[44] "We have movie films which will support my previous statement," Payton countered.[45] A *Raleigh News and Observer* editorial expressed some sympathy with the union's position: "Charges that the North Carolina Highway Patrol is escorting strikebreakers to the plant are injuring, if not distorting, North Carolina's reputation for even-handed justice."[46]

Sensitive to any public criticism, Governor Hodges consulted with a friend, attorney William Womble, about a more defensible position. Criticizing what he called Ed Scheidt's "waffling" on the use of state troops, Womble recommended arguing that

their only purpose is to preserve law and order, and, without partiality, to protect against violence; that persons who want to strike have a right to do so; that persons desiring to enter or leave the mill have a right to do that also; that if persons desiring to enter or leave the premises can do so in safety only with an escort due to blockades, violence or threat of violence by pickets, then escorts will be provided, without apology.[47]

Taking Womble's cue, throughout the remainder of the strike Governor Hodges defended his actions on the basis of the impartial maintenance of law and order. Hodges's position allowed the Coopers to easily manipulate the state's police power. As the governor's assistant Robert Giles noted, Harriet and Henderson managers were making "every effort to operate the mills in spite of the union and in spite of the strike, look to the Governor to 'maintain law and order' and incidentally their property rights, and hang all other consequences."[48]

The governor's position assured a vicious cycle that brought unpleasant "consequences." The claim that state power was used impartially insulted local union members, and as Hodges learned from an assistant, "the vast majority of the employees of these two plants [union members] seem to be above average in intelligence and ability."[49] Left with no legal options for defending their perceived rights, many union members risked arrest by harassing, if not blockading, those who were taking their jobs. The unacceptable alternative was to watch passively while strikebreakers entered the mills. However, intervention resulted in arrests, criticism about the lack of law and order, and hence the involvement of state troopers on management's side. The only ones well satisfied were the Coopers.

Violence was inevitable. By early March nearly 100 strikebreakers reported each day at the Henderson Mill and over 230 at the Harriet Mill, and strikers were powerless to stop them. At every union meeting and on several local radio broadcasts, union leaders pleaded with members to remain peaceful. Meanwhile, public opinion remained riveted on the persistence of anonymous, nighttime violence. On Thursday, 26 February, forty-five windowpanes at the Henderson Mill were broken by gunfire. There was also another explosion that night. Two nights later, dynamite exploded twenty yards from a strikebreaker's home.[50] On 1 March there was an explosion less than forty feet from time-study engineer William Camp's home, and on 9 March a blast damaged the Harriet Mill boiler room. Given that they never caused physical harm to people, the bombings must have been carefully planned.

Governor Hodges responded by authorizing the involvement of the State Bureau of Investigation. Suspecting union responsibility, SBI agents kept Boyd Payton's hotel room under constant surveillance, and in mid-March Agent C. M. Horton reported that he had "developed an informant who has promised to advise us when the next bombing is going to take place." Horton also felt that he had a solid lead in the explosion at the Harriet Mill boiler room.[51] Nearly a month later, however, no arrests had been made in any of the bombings. Responding privately to a friend who criticized this lack of success, Governor Hodges wrote, "We have two-thirds of the SBI in Henderson now trying to get data on the dynamiting. It is a very difficult situation."[52] It appears, then, that to the extent union members or their supporters were responsible for the bombings, and in many instances they undoubtedly were, they were easily able to avoid detection by the state investigators. It is also possible, of course, that company sympathizers could have lit some of the fuses to discredit the strikers. Many union members were convinced of this.[53] Whoever was responsible, it also seems clear, at least in retrospect, that the intent of the bombings was to scare rather than to kill or maim. "Most of the bombings have occurred in open fields and yards of workers," concluded a State Highway Patrol report, "causing minor damages, mostly shattering windows."[54]

At the time, however, the explosions frightened many Henderson residents. "People are so full of fear and terror," wrote strikebreaker Mrs. Odell Cottrell, "they would not dare turn on a light after dark, but sit in darkness watching with guns, so they can protect their families."[55] Expressing "the feeling of peril spreading over all of us," Jeannette Bachman wrote Governor Hodges that "unions have gone far beyond their original purpose, and now seem to be infiltrated, not only with dishonest leaders but with gangsters as well."[56] The *Raleigh News and Observer* suggested that the persistence of violence negated any sympathy the union locals once might have deserved. "The striking textile workers at Henderson are threatening to break their own strike," read one editorial. "Men who have a good cause should not let any among them stain it with bad methods, means, or manners."[57]

While the violence turned many citizens against the union, newspaper editor H. A. Dennis worked feverishly to play down the severity of the situation. Dennis voiced concern that the nation had "the false impression that all hell has broken loose," accusing the *Raleigh News and Observer* of implying "that a miniature Cuban revolution has broken out in Henderson."[58] Despite the strike, neither the new pickle company nor the prospective candy manufacturer had yet backed out on their plans to relocate in Henderson. Nevertheless, the progrowth faction desired a peaceful business climate to attract an interested glass manufacturer and a new hosiery mill. "Our 'fame' is spreading," Dennis moaned as the strike wore on, lamenting that "it is a sort of notoriety . . . that is highly undesirable and derogatory."[59]

Union sympathizers offered yet another perspective on the continuing violence. Agnes Barnett, for example, argued in a letter to Governor Hodges that he "could stop all this by just requesting that the gates be closed until the contract be settled one way or the other. There was no violence until the gates were opened." She asked the governor how he would feel "if some one came up there and took your job and then shook there fist in your face after taking everything you had worked for all your life. That is what these people are doing that are coming in here to work.

That is why these people are so angry and rough." [60] Indeed, she was right: there was no violence until the mills reopened with strikebreakers.

Meanwhile, contract negotiations remained stalled. "Union representatives are 'mad' because the parties do not confer enough," noted Governor Hodges's administrative assistant, Robert Giles, while "Company representatives give the impression of resenting meetings." [61] There was a definite decrease in violent activity on the days when there were negotiations. [62] When talks broke down, however, violence increased both at the picket lines and at night. With an ever-increasing number of strikebreakers entering the mills, the daytime street battles between pickets, the highway patrol, and the replacement workers escalated. Lieutenant Robert Chadwick, who commanded the state highway patrolmen, notified his superiors that Monday, 3 March 1959, "was the first time that the crowd had advanced on the police." Later that day about thirty patrolmen and fifteen city policemen stood between several hundred pickets at the Harriet Mill. The crowd, Chadwick reported, "had reached [a] violent peak." He described the strikers as an "excited group, men and women, crying mad obviously over the fact that more people were going to work and they were losing their jobs." [63]

Later that day, Singleton requested, and Governor Hodges sent, more than 100 additional highway patrolmen to bring order to the picket lines. By the next day 146 patrolmen, over one-quarter of the state's total, were stationed in Henderson. [64] The show of force apparently succeeded. "It appears definite that when we are there in number," Chadwick concluded, "there is little or no violence." [65]

When requesting the additional patrolmen Mayor Singleton raised the charge that "outsiders" had infiltrated the picket lines and were causing much of the violence. [66] In a limited sense Singleton was correct. Union members maintained that they often comprised only about half of the pickets. Many of the "outsiders," however, were spouses, friends, sons, or daughters of union members. Others apparently were nearby residents who came to show their support. Many strikers claimed, as did the mayor, that nonunion pickets were responsible for much of the rock throwing and harassment at the picket lines. Yet when asked whether the union made efforts to dissuade townspeople from coming to the picket line, striker Joseph Braswell responded quickly, "Oh no, no, because most of them were on our side." [67] A group of women strikers argued further that blaming the union for accepting outside assistance "seems absurd when [the Coopers] have been able to get 'outside' forces of the State Highway Patrol, paid from taxpayers funds, to enter this dispute." [68]

Strikers came to believe that in order to force management to negotiate, the union had to either fight the state government or gain its support. The alternative was certain defeat, so for several weeks strikers tried to oust the highway patrolmen. For a few days in early March they left the gates alone. Chadwick learned from an informer on 5 March that union members "were waiting for the State Highway Patrol to move out." The tactic worked to an extent; Chadwick dismissed forty-six officers.[69] One afternoon pickets separated into small clusters, spacing themselves along the road. Chadwick noted that the strikers were "trying to spread the patrol out enough to enable another group to cause trouble, but we have enough patrol cars to keep down any such maneuver."[70] Pickets occasionally placed tacks on the road in front of the gates. They also piled rocks, glass, and wood on the pavement to blockade the mills. But the police always cleared the debris quickly, and the company hired a mechanic to fix flats. Once, about twenty-five women approached Chadwick's car and taunted the officer with jeers and catcalls, which he believed to be "a maneuver to get the Patrol to arrest some of the women, which would stir up the entire mill village even more." The next day women stoned strikebreakers' cars directly in front of the patrolmen. Two were arrested, and Chadwick soon reported that the pickets "were yelling 'women grabbers' at us."[71]

These episodes underscored the strikers' weakness. Management had a proxy army with legal orders to allow the mills to operate with strikebreakers. In contrast, it would have been suicidal for local union members to engage in armed conflict against the state. Union pickets often annoyed and frightened the troops, but strikers never posed a serious threat to the company's control of the mill gates. Luther Jackson recalled the brainstorming, faith, and weakness that produced the various union strategies. "You have to fight those things like they did when Christ told that man to walk around the Jericho wall so many times, and play that music loud. And the walls would come tumbling down." For two evenings in March the strikers seemed to be reenacting the Jericho metaphor. Union members drove their vehicles in a convoy around the motel that lodged the patrolmen, honking their horns and shouting at the troopers. At the request of the police, however, the strikers stopped this ritual. It would take more than blaring horns to remove the highway patrol from Henderson.[72]

The armed power of the state was especially crucial, because most local officers respected the union's cause and left the picket lines alone. Lieutenant Chadwick complained in mid-March that "the Sheriff's Department has not made any arrests, except on warrants obtained by others," for four weeks. "I have been present when violence was being committed all around them. Deputy Leonard, who is a regular deputy, openly speaks in favor of the Union." Chadwick also noted "the problem of dealing with the local Police Officers, some of which have strikers in their families."[73] Officer Sam Littleton, for example, had once been president of Local 578. Top state officials grew extremely frustrated with what they perceived to be at best lackadaisical, at worst traitorous, efforts by local law enforcers. SBI director Malcolm Seawell wrote Governor Hodges that it would be useless to hire additional deputy sheriffs to patrol picket lines because "the ones appointed would be sympathizers with the Union as have been all the deputy sheriffs employed up to now."[74]

Sheriff E. A. Cottrell became a lightning rod for opinions about local law enforcement. Even though he had received as much political support from the wealthier sections of town as he had from the mill villages, Cottrell clearly sympathized with the striking union members. Lieutenant Chadwick once reported with disgust that during "disturbances" at the Harriet Mill, Cottrell "was seen buying a rake" downtown. Governor Hodges called Cottrell "pitiful, pitiable and to be pitied."[75] Most union members, however, considered the sheriff an understanding friend. Local 578's Esther Roberson recalled that Cottrell did "everything he could to hold down peace. And he done everything he could to help the people." One time Cottrell came to Roberson's home to inform her that a warrant was about to be issued for her arrest. The charge, Cottrell said, was that Roberson had called one of the strikebreakers a "scab." Roberson recalled insisting that she had indeed called the scab a scab, to which Cottrell replied, " 'No you didn't Esther.' " " 'I called him a scab,' " she repeated. " 'No you didn't.' " She recalled asking, " 'Well what are you trying to get me to say? You know I did but you want me to say no?' So I said, 'No I didn't but yes I did!' "[76] The support of local law officers, however, was not enough to tip the balance of power in favor of the union.

While providing the company the protection needed to operate, Governor Hodges launched his own private investigation to determine who was at fault for the bargaining impasse. Shortly after the mills reopened, administrative assistant Robert Giles asked federal mediator Yates Heafner, at the governor's request, whether or not the two sides were making progress toward a settlement. Giles asked, "Within the general and accustomed framework of labor relations," did Heafner "view management's insistence on 'no arbitration whatever' as amounting to a reasonable demand?" According to Giles, Heafner responded that "the position of management must be characterized, by this measurement, as extreme, as going over and beyond what one would expect of management which wanted to reach agreement on the basis of 'give and take.'"[77] Aware of the mediator's insight, on 12 March, Governor Hodges gently prodded John D. Cooper to alter the company's negotiating position. "Offer the union something," Hodges pleaded with the mill president, "something that you can live with and something that the union will accept." The governor seems mainly to have wanted some positive publicity: he hoped the Coopers would make some recognizable effort "so that the public will not have the feeling that you are not making any."[78]

Although the Coopers presented a new offer to the union shortly after the Hodges-Cooper conversation, it appears that the company acted more from fear of unfair labor practice charges than in response to Hodges's urgings. On Tuesday, 10 March, the union had filed a grievance with the National Labor Relations Board, claiming that the Harriet and Henderson Mills were not negotiating in good faith. If the union's charges were upheld, managers would lose the right to hire permanent replacements for strikers. Despite the modified language in its new proposal, management still reserved for itself the right to refuse to arbitrate a grievance and insisted upon seniority for strikebreakers. The changes were in appearance, not substance.[79]

Although it was possible that NLRB charges could have resulted in a contract offer that the union could accept, the odds of that happening were very slim. Usually several months would pass between the filing of charges and the issuing of an NLRB directive. If the decision favored strikers, it would have to be enforced through the legal system. With delays and appeals, most cases took months or even years to settle. So even though company officials were sensitive to the NLRB charges, they were aware, as were the strikers, that the process was rarely of much use to unions in the midst of a labor conflict.[80]

Responding privately to the feebleness of the Coopers' revised offer, on 20 March, Governor Hodges exerted more pressure. "There isn't a single person in my whole crowd, including the Attorney General, that believes [John D. Cooper] has anything possible on his side in refusing to budge on this thing," he told company attorney Bennett Perry. "If Mr. J. D. isn't willing to give a little, or at least give them one thing, if he doesn't do that, I am going to have to put the whole responsibility on the mill management and 'the fat will then be on the fire.'"[81]

At the same time, Hodges was organizing support in Henderson for his public stand as the maintainer of law and order. In a meeting with state senator Charles Blackburn and state representative A. A. Zollicoffer, Hodges voiced "deep concern in the lack of local leadership in opposing acts of violence" and "strongly urged" the politicians "to start a grass roots movement among the substantial citizens in Vance County who would be willing to stand up and be counted publicly as opposing violence in any form." These prominent citizens would "make it clear that they were not taking sides in the strike but believed that the good name and reputation of Henderson and Vance County were more important than any issue, any mill or any union."[82]

As the designated point man for the governor's grassroots campaign, Mayor Carroll Singleton encountered stiff resistance, collecting only one signature from members of the chamber of commerce and the Merchants Association. In a meeting with the governor, Singleton "admitted that the people were scared, afraid to take sides, afraid of recrimination, etc. and would not take any public stand for fear of being dynamited."[83] Moreover, at least two local politicians either supported the union, feared electoral defeat, or risked a boycott by strikers if they signed the petition. County commissioner and grocery store owner J. L. Roberson had openly declared to strikers, "In my heart, God has shown me you are right."[84] Another commissioner and grocery store owner, Furman Satterwhite, also refused to support the governor. "Never in my life have I seen such abject surrender and fear on the part of public officials," Hodges complained. To Satterwhite the governor responded, "I would rather be a courageous citizen and leader than to be a successful groceryman."[85]

Under intense pressure from the governor, within a week Singleton was able to collect signatures from most members of the town's leading business organizations.[86] He then purchased a full-page *Henderson Daily Dispatch* ad announcing the creation of the Vance County Committee for Law and Order in words that parroted Hodges's position on state activity: "We, who are signing this statement, take no stand on either side of this dispute. It seems to us, and we understand it to be the law, that all who want to strike, have a right to quit work and strike—*in peace*. It equally seems, and we understand it to be the law, that all who want to work, have the right to work—*in peace*."[87]

Largely unaware of the governor's private investigations and manipulations, union members both detested Hodges's deployment of state troops and encouraged him to become directly involved in negotiating sessions. "We always had hope," recalled TWUA representative Julius Fry. It was possible, Fry thought at the time, that mediation by the governor would allow the company to make an offer that it would not make directly to the union.[88] On 6 March a delegation of women strikers met with the governor in Raleigh to encourage him to mediate the conflict. Edith Adams, a member of the delegation, recalled her frustration with the governor's response: "He did all the talking. He didn't give us an opportunity to say anything."[89] Union members' anger with the governor could also be seen on the picket lines, on the signs strikers held: some of those signs called Henderson "Governor Hodges' Russia," and others asked, "Is this Democracy?"[90] Lieutenant Chadwick reported to his superiors that on 9 March "the crowd in the picket line was yelling at us for the first time as 'Hodges' Boys.' "[91] Yet despite their ambivalence, union members had no viable options besides asking for the governor's assistance.

Persistent violence and negative publicity, however, were far more effective in gaining the governor's attention. The bitterness in the mill villages intensified on 15 March, when mill foreman Garland Cash shot the son of a striking union member. Cash contended that the victim, Jim Manning—who suffered minor injuries—had intended to bomb his home. Union members claimed that Manning, having just returned from military service, had been walking innocently down the street with a friend. No explosives were found.[92] Union members' frustration spilled out the next day in a show of force at the Harriet gate. A few dozen pickets threw bricks, rocks, and bottles at strikebreakers' cars, while several hundred more congregated in the vicinity. The highway patrol arrested twenty-four strikers, and Lieutenant Chadwick feared that "if the crowd becomes much larger and angrier, a sizable number of patrolmen will be needed in addition to the forces now here."[93] Meanwhile, the anonymous nighttime bombings continued, including two blasts near Cash's home.

Aware that the company was maintaining an unreasonable negotiating position and that at least one TWUA official had called Henderson a "powder keg," the governor called for negotiations in his office to begin Monday, 23 March. If Hodges could force the two sides to agree, he could turn a public relations embarrassment into a personal triumph. Before announcing his increased involvement, however, Hodges checked with Boyd Payton to be sure the union leader "had the authority to make complete settlement without submitting the thing to the national authorities." Hodges reported that Payton "had full authority" and was willing to "make a lot of concessions if we can get anything on arbitration out of the mills." Hodges also insisted "very strongly" that if he were to mediate he did "not want any delegation of busloads of strikers nor anybody picketing or making any demonstrations in Raleigh."[94]

The strikers' reaction to Hodges's decision reveals much about the relationship between power and violence in labor conflicts. Boyd Payton announced that the TWUA would "welcome the opportunity to present our case to the Governor" and pledged the union's "full co-operation," On the morning of the first session at the governor's office Lieutenant Chadwick remarked from the picket lines that "the attitude of the strikers seems to have changed for the better, as they evidently are very hopeful about the results of the conference today." There had been no strike-related violence in Henderson, Chadwick reported, since the governor announced his intervention.[95] In contrast, company officials had little to gain from these sessions, and John D. Cooper commented that "through courtesy, if nothing else, I'll be there." In his memoirs, Hodges mentioned that "it was evident to management then that it could operate the mills without the union and that it did not have to give in on the arbitration clause."[96]

Unfortunately for the union, however, the governor made no substantive effort to break the deadlock. According to his personal diary from the sessions, Hodges told mill managers "very frankly" on the first day "that they didn't have a leg to stand on so far as the public was concerned" and that he "felt the same way." The governor insisted that the company offer "some kind" of arbitration. The next day the Coopers offered arbitration by mutual consent only. When the union suggested limiting the number of cases each year that could be subject to the "mutual consent" provision, the company announced that it would refuse to consider any counterproposals. The two sides met several more times, but each session produced the same result. After a meeting on 1 April, Hodges concluded that "the prejudices and positions were so well entrenched that there wasn't much chance" for a settlement. On 2 April, both sides agreed that the governor could withdraw from his mediating role. Hodges expressed "surprise and disgust" that there had been no settlement.[97]

Union members were bitterly disappointed, if not completely surprised, by the governor's failure to mediate a settlement. Boyd Payton chided Hodges for his naiveté, stating that the governor "very quickly got a taste of what we have been facing since last November." "He wasn't really putting any pressure anywhere on them," Julius Fry recalled. "He wasn't going to stick his neck out." With the governor unwilling to intervene seriously, Fry concluded, "there wasn't anywhere the union could go."[98]

Highly regarded antilabor attorney Whiteford Blakeney consulted with Hodges about the precise language to use when explaining to the general public the governor's failure to resolve the strike. Blakeney had already sent the governor a prepared statement, claiming that he could not see "how either contestant in the controversy—nor any present or future adversary—could rightly or effectively criticize it."[99] When Governor Hodges announced that he was withdrawing from his role as mediator, he used virtually every word suggested by Blakeney. "It is my authority and my duty to enforce the laws of North Carolina with respect to violence and to maintain peace and order within this State," Hodges explained. "The Textile Company has the right to operate and to continue operating its mill—so long as it does so within the law. The Union and the striking employees have a right to strike and to continue striking— so long as they do so within the law. Neither side has any right whatever to resort to violence."[100]

Hodges worked in close association with one of the South's leading antilabor attorneys, yet he still claimed to be taking a neutral stance in the Henderson strike. It appears, moreover, that the governor truly believed he was the voice of impartial reason. In a letter to *Charlotte Observer* editor J. E. Dowd, for example, the governor explained that "it is neither black nor white and it is a difficult problem and I find myself 'in the middle.'" Commiserating with textile executive J. Spencer Love, Hodges complained that "the public relations and any other kind of relation on the part of the Coopers is very bad. On the other side you have a completely irresponsible union leadership. So the State is caught in the middle." To his friend Stark Dillard, Hodges declared, "If anybody has refrained from playing politics, it is I."[101]

More than merely an intellectual posture, Hodges's conception of the proper use of state power was essential for him politically. Throughout the strike the governor received an abundance of support for his efforts to maintain law and order. Of the nearly 600 letter-writers who commented on the strike, 411 were either solidly in favor of Hodges's actions or at least candidly opposed to unions. A large proportion of these correspondents, 185 out of 411, identified themselves as businessmen, and many of them were on a first-name basis with the governor. Among Hodges's personal friends were textile leaders William Ruffin, president of Erwin Mills in Durham; Charles Cannon of the giant Cannon Mills corporation; Ceasar Cone of the Cone Mills chain; J. Spencer Love, chairman and president of Burlington Industries in Greensboro; and P. Huber Hanes of the Hanes Knitting Company in Winston-Salem.[102] Numerous letter-writers emphasized the adverse impact the strike in Henderson was likely to have on North Carolina's efforts to attract new industry. Martin Foil, president of the Tuscarora Cotton Mills in Mt. Pleasant, argued the case succinctly. "I hope you will stand squarely behind the Coopers in their rights," he wrote the governor, "and not give in to the unions in our state, else all the good, hard work you have done during your administration to attract industry to North Carolina will have been in vain, and you and I will see an exodus of industry from our state."[103] There were also several letters criticizing the governor for using too little force in crushing the Henderson strike.[104] Given this strong support for "law and order," it was virtually inconceivable for the governor to alter his position.

Eager for total support from the state's business community, Hodges reacted with apparent shock in the rare instances when self-identified businessmen questioned his handling of the strike. Responding to criticism from a businessman in Southern Pines, Hodges felt compelled to learn more about the letter-writer: "Is he a foreigner, an invader, or is he a native Sandhillian?" Hodges asked his friend Voit Gilmore, a Southern Pines resident.[105] Hodges also researched the character of one of the other businessmen who criticized him for anything other than not going far enough to protect the Coopers. A friend of Hodges, Grady Rankin of Gastonia, wrote that the governor's critic "is not well known locally and so far, I have been unable to find out where he came from. I can only suggest that you reply to his letter in your usual tactful manner without any thought to the consequences."[106]

Governor Hodges received at least 133 letters criticizing his handling of the strike as unfair to the union. Of the nearly 30 correspondents who identified themselves by profession, 22 represented either international unions or union locals from throughout North Carolina. Whereas Governor Hodges frequently poured his heart out in replies to his business friends, it appears that very few of his union critics received anything more than a standard form letter. In a rare personal response to a self-identified union member, Hodges's assistant, Robert Giles, chastised Lenora Hall of Local 91, Amalgamated Clothing Workers of America, in New Bern, for asking the governor to close the mills until a settlement was reached. "The Governor does not believe," wrote Giles, "that the union you represent intends to take a position *against* law and order, regardless of who may be involved."[107] It seems apparent that Governor Hodges would not take seriously the opinions of those in the politically insignificant North Carolina labor movement.

Despite Hodges's irritation with those who criticized his efforts to maintain law and order, privately he voiced disgust with Harriet and Henderson management for provoking the violence that was bringing negative publicity to the state. Recording his thoughts after a meeting with the Coopers, Hodges wrote that the mill owners were "practically sick, determined, and in my humble opinion without a scintilla of public relations point of view."[108] Although Hodges seemed genuinely irritated with the Coopers, given his own political base and personal animosity toward unions he could not reduce his commitment to deploy the power that allowed the Harriet and Henderson management to maintain its steadfast course. The Coopers, therefore, could be fairly certain that Hodges was bluffing when he threatened to blame them publicly for prolonging the strike and provoking violence.

There is evidence, however, that the Coopers were not as firmly in control of the strike's progress as it might have seemed. In early March, Governor Hodges's personal secretary, Ed Rankin, spoke with Thomas Morgan, a Vance County native who had gone on to serve as an executive with the Sperry Company and as an adviser to Presidents Roosevelt and Truman. Morgan had returned to Henderson to learn more about the strike. According to Rankin, Morgan had concluded, after talking "with some of the stockholders of the company, and with others close to the situation," that "'[John D.] Cooper has a 'bear' by the tail and doesn't know how to handle it.'" In Rankin's words, Morgan recommended that the governor "should do what you can to help management to save face and escape somehow from the situation."[109] A month later, Rankin discussed the strike with the governor's good friend Voit Gilmore, who had been active in recruiting new industries to the state. In Rankin's words, Gilmore maintained that "according to reports in the trade, Cooper is producing a very poor grade yarn at this time and will lose money steadily until and unless he can improve his quality." Gilmore suggested that "Cooper should be persuaded to relinquish active management for reasons of health and could go to Florida . . . leaving control in the hands of a management team which would take over, run the mill and settle with the union on the best basis possible."[110]

The assessments of Morgan and Gilmore indicate that the Coopers were by no means certain of the strike's outcome and that they were apparently acting alone, without the material assistance of other textile manufacturers. Although some TWUA leaders suspected that erstwhile competitors were secretly filling orders for the Harriet and Henderson Mills, the market for yarn had been so tight that few textile executives would even have considered foregoing their own profits for the benefit of a beleaguered colleague. Even personal friends were only willing to offer the Coopers their sympathy. "Although Marshall and I are competitors in business now, we were good friends at Carolina," wrote R. H. Griffith, "and I hate to see a fine outfit and fine people like the Coopers being put through such an ordeal."[111] Indeed, Harriet and Henderson managers had reconciled themselves to relatively enormous net losses with their strike-breaking workforce. The Henderson Mill lost $103,000 in the second quarter, while the Harriet Mill lost $58,000.[112]

When Governor Hodges withdrew from his mediating role, management's total intransigence became even more apparent and more disturbing to strikers, who had no more viable options for pursuing an acceptable settlement. The company refused to consider any union proposal, including Boyd Payton's suggestion that the mills operate three days a week with strikebreakers and three days a week with returning union members, which would have meant the loss of hundreds of strikers' jobs.[113] On 10 April, a week after the negotiations with Hodges were abandoned, Lieutenant Chadwick reported that "the strikers have built up strong animosity toward the Highway Patrol. . . . They have proclaimed to me on numerous occasions that they would keep all scabs from work and end the strike in two days if we would only leave. The people in the mill area hoot, yell, and threaten the troopers nightly on their patrols." At this point, Chadwick noted, "the strikers seem to be waging a war with us more so than with the Mills." Despite the union members' powerlessness, he continued, "their determination appears just as strong as on 16 February 1959 when the mills opened."[114]

Meanwhile, community leaders feared an increase in nighttime bombings and formed a citizens' committee, called Night Watch, to patrol local streets after dark. The unarmed Night Watch volunteers reported to a central location that was linked by telephone with the various law enforcement offices. Mayor Singleton also called for a voluntary 10:00 P.M. curfew, while state representative A. A. Zollicoffer proposed a law, apparently in earnest, that would have allowed the sale of dynamite only if the purchaser explained why it was wanted.[115] Despite these efforts, on Friday, 3 April, Henderson was rocked by two blasts, including one near the Harriet Mill, and on 5 April, another explosion damaged a strikebreaker's home. Aware that the bombings were counterproductive, many union members offered their services for the Night Watch, but Mayor Singleton failed to respond.[116] Whether or not such a snub was justified, it was true that no bombings had occurred near the homes of strikers, and a number of union members openly scoffed at the larger community's fear and the mayor's curfew request. Annie Journigan wrote a letter to the local paper asking, "Why should we give up what we want? No movies or dances for us and our children, just to be in bed with lights out so the scabs can sleep. Well, we don't have to go to bed early, we are not working, so why not dance and be merry, we have nothing to hide nor fear."[117]

Editors of both the *Raleigh News and Observer* and the *Henderson Daily Dispatch* voiced increasing despair with the strike's persistence. A continuation of the status quo, wrote Henderson's H. A. Dennis, "will likely be accompanied by more violence, which could become worse, especially if another shift goes on the job." Dennis saw no acceptable way out of the mess, fearing the sale or liquidation of the mills as much as an intensified police presence or, worse, martial law, which in his opinion would have been "a terrible black eye." "What then is the answer?" Dennis asked. "We do not know much about labor relations, and hence have no formula to offer." [118] The *News and Observer* called for Luther Hodges to "insist with all the moral power of his office that this matter be arbitrated and settled." [119]

This sense of desperation only intensified, however, when the Coopers announced publicly on 15 April that they intended to begin operating second shifts at the mills the following Monday, 20 April. Boyd Payton declared that if the company succeeded, "the strike would be lost." John D. Cooper threatened either to liquidate or relocate the mills if he failed to start the new shifts. According to Lieutenant Chadwick, immediately after the company's announcement "a group of about 40 men" near the Harriet Mill threw "a barrage of broken bricks" at highway patrolmen, injuring two. On being arrested, one woman picket bit a patrolman. Another woman screamed at the troopers, "It's you that we hate." [120] One night later a bomb blast shattered windowpanes at the home of Marshall Y. Cooper. [121]

In response to this violence Governor Hodges once again increased his involvement in seeking a settlement. "While your legal right appears to be clear and undisputed," Hodges wrote John D. Cooper,

it is also my duty to call to your attention that your decision to begin a second and third shift at your mill will definitely heighten existing tensions in Henderson and Vance County and may actually result in bloodshed in spite of the best efforts of law enforcement personnel. This is an unpleasant and harsh reality which you must face.

Sometimes a person is confronted with a citizenship responsibility which transcends any strict legal rights, and on such occasions it can only be hoped that the individual who holds the power of decision will somehow be able to reconcile his personal and private rights with those greater interests of the community at large. [122]

In a phone conversation early on Thursday, 16 April, Hodges also told Boyd Payton that when union members "start throwing bricks and hitting Patrolmen, you are getting down to the last ditch." "You will have to realize these people are beaten down to the last ditch," Payton answered, "and feel everything is against them; no law, no government on their side." "The law protects everybody," Hodges replied. "There is law on their side, but what your people are doing is taking law into their own hands."[123]

Privately, Hodges conceded that the strikers "have provocation because of the way the mill has handled the situation and the fact that they had brought in four or five hundred people from the outside." Yet despite his understanding of the strikers' sense of outrage, the governor remained somewhat perplexed by the union members' tenacity. After confirming that as of 17 April only fifty-eight of over one thousand union members had broken ranks, Hodges noted that "usually in a situation of this character, from a third to a half of the strikers go back to work and the situation is easy to handle because there isn't the same balance."[124] Perhaps this had been the governor's private desire all along, but the Harriet and Henderson strikers refused to simplify Hodges's job by crossing the picket lines en masse.

At this point the governor's private sympathies, business ideology aside, seemed to lie with the strikers. The Coopers antagonized Hodges further by claiming to newspaper reporters that the company had been assured of adequate police protection for second-shift strikebreakers, although the governor had not authorized the deployment of additional troops. "I knew the Sheriff and his group would make no promises as they had done nothing yet," Hodges wrote in a private memo. "I checked carefully with the Patrol and found that nobody had made any assurances whatever."[125]

Law enforcement personnel were especially concerned with the logistical problems posed by management's plan. The company would now require protection when second-shift workers departed at 11:00 P.M., well after sunset. Sheriff Cottrell and his deputies wanted no part of nighttime picket duty. According to Hodges, the sheriff had stated at a meeting on Monday, 13 April, that "he was sure that when the mills opened . . . for a second shift that somebody back in the dark would shoot and somebody would get killed and they didn't want to take a chance on it."[126] Lieutenant Chadwick was concerned that his patrolmen would receive little or no help from either the sheriff's department or the city police.[127]

Fearing the consequences if the company persevered, the governor met with John D. Cooper on Thursday, 16 April, and extracted a proposal that he was certain the union would accept. As soon as he received the offer in writing, Hodges contacted Boyd Payton, who told the governor that, subject to a vote of the local membership, he would indeed accept it. While rumors of a settlement circulated through the mill villages, Hodges learned that the company had changed its mind. This news provoked the governor to make more threats: he told John D. Cooper that the company would "have to take the consequences." Indicating that he might withdraw the patrolmen, the governor warned, "I will go to the public with this and you may have to ride this thing by yourself." That prospect, however, did not seem to faze Cooper. According to Hodges, the mill executive replied, "I am going to start the second shift at 3:00 o'clock on Monday, April 20, even if I don't run one hour. I am going to start it whether there is a city policeman, county sheriff, or a single highway patrolman there. If in starting it general warfare breaks out, let it be general warfare. I will then shut the damn mill down and sell it out piece by piece."[128]

At a regularly scheduled negotiating session in Henderson on Friday, 17 April, however, the company appeared to be willing to bargain seriously. Governor Hodges arrived at 4:30 that afternoon and immediately met with company officials, conveying his frustration "in no uncertain terms." Hodges then "sent for the union people and met them separately and then together, and then separately and then together, etc., for the next three or four hours." After an hour's recess at 7:15, "Payton announced that the matter had been settled."[129] A few minutes later, Hodges emerged from the room waving the signed contract high above his head while reporters and photographers recorded the triumphant moment.[130] The morning after the settlement the governor wrote in a personal memo, "I had a good night's sleep. A train is off my back. . . . I am overjoyed."[131]

The union had made severe concessions; the most significant of these was their agreement to arbitration by mutual consent only. In return management conceded to workers the unlimited right to strike whenever the company refused to arbitrate. Also, all first-shift jobs would go to strikebreakers. It was understood that most of the remaining positions would go to strikers, with their seniority preserved, but no one who had been convicted of violating the restraining order would be rehired. Jobless union members would be placed on a preferential hiring list. In addition, there would be no checkoff of union dues, although collection booths could be placed near the mill gates.[132] Despite these compromises, most strikers were elated. Lloyd Wilkins recalled that there was "a whole lot of celebrating around." Many strikers held prayer sessions at their churches, giving thanks for the settlement. Union members and sympathizers danced in the streets and paraded around town in their cars honking their horns, this time for joy. The local paper said that "the jubilation in the mill villages" was "comparable to that at the end of World War II."[133]

On Saturday morning, 18 April, however, when union members reported to confirm their new work assignments, supervisors remained noncommittal. Lloyd Wilkins recalled that his foreman said only, "We'll send for you."[134] Many of the hands perceived this as a mix-up that the company would correct Monday morning. Demonstrating their continued confidence, at a meeting on Sunday afternoon, union members ratified the new contract by an overwhelming margin.[135]

Governor Hodges phoned Boyd Payton on Monday to ask how the new arrangements were working. "Not so good," Payton answered. "We are getting the story that everybody is being told their jobs are already filled. Governor, we have got a furious bunch of people here." "Are they actually saying all jobs on the second shift are filled?" Hodges asked. "About 50 people have already been told that the second shift has been filled," Payton reported.

Hodges, however, still had faith in management. "Of course, Boyd," he said, "you can't afford not to go on through with this thing now. The company, I am sure . . . will go along and do the right thing. You and your people will have to be patient."[136] By day's end, however, the union learned that the Coopers had reserved only about thirty jobs for the 950 union members who were still on strike when the agreement was signed.

Company officials explained that at the session during which the contract was signed, they had promised only that all positions on the second shift that had not yet been permanently filled would go to returning strikers. They had not disclosed the absolute number of jobs available, and the union had not demanded such a number. Managers explained that in the discussions leading to the agreement, they had claimed, honestly, that no second-shift jobs had as yet been filled. They failed to mention, however, that they had already hired 698 permanent strikebreakers—double the number necessary for operating the first shift. Shortly after signing the contract, management officially transferred the redundant first-shift strikebreakers to the second shift. Therefore, when union members reported to work, the company informed them that only thirty jobs were available.[137]

Union leaders and Governor Hodges both felt betrayed. Significantly, Julius Fry had been sick with the flu and had missed the contract-signing session. On returning to Henderson, Fry was very upset with Boyd Payton, and with the governor, for failing to make the company give specific figures.[138] Hodges complained that the Coopers "let us deliberate for several hours and then come to a 'glorious agreement'" when it was obvious that "no contract would have been signed by the union" had the company been forthright.[139]

Embittered by the company's bad-faith bargaining, strikers reached new levels of rage. On Monday afternoon, 20 April, an officer at the picket line noted that "the crowd had been threatening [the strikebreakers], saying they were going to shoot them after they got off work." Pickets also shouted "shoot the Patrol" or "kill the Patrol." When the company erected floodlights to brighten the mill area for departing second-shift workers, union sympathizers shattered the lamps with rifle fire. Thinking that the strike was over, Governor Hodges had removed most of the highway patrolmen from Henderson, and because they had no armed opposition, strikers were able to force the second-shift strikebreakers to spend the night inside the mills.[140] From his home "one half mile from the mill," local historian S. T. Peace wrote Governor Hodges late Monday night that "three hundred fifty people are under direct small arms fire."[141] A full complement of patrolmen quickly returned and fired flares into the night sky, trying to expose the snipers.[142] If the strikers had aimed to kill, the casualty count could have been enormous. Indeed, a few days later a *Raleigh News and Observer* reporter noted that "several members of the crowd that nightly heckles the workers had advised newsmen where to stand so as not to be in the line of fire."[143]

The increase in violence and the Coopers' grim determination once again revealed strains in the antilabor alliance. On 22 April Governor Hodges released to the news media a copy of a telegram he had sent that day asking John D. Cooper to shut down the second shift.[144] The mill president responded, shrewdly, that to do so "would be an absolute surrender to force and violence." Although Hodges strongly disagreed, explaining to Cooper that his request was based "on your personal responsibility for the present difficulty," given his commitment to a particular type of law and order the governor had no room to maneuver.[145] Indeed, Hodges had already sent a telegram to Boyd Payton stating that he would hold the union leader "responsible for any further violence."[146]

On the local level, several Henderson leaders split with the Coopers over the virtues of continuing operations without hiring striking union members. Despite his strong antiunion feelings, Mayor Carroll Singleton feared even more the economic consequences for Henderson if nearly one thousand residents permanently lost their jobs to others, most of whom lived out of town, some as far away as Virginia. "It is realized that you yourself are more interested with the present than with the future," Singleton wrote John D. Cooper. "If the Mill is successful in resuming full operation without re-employing any of the employees who are now on strike, the community is faced with an enormous social problem for many years."[147] City school board chairman W. Y. Bryan voiced similar fears: "A mass exodus of strikers seeking employment elsewhere would be disastrous to our school census and would require a long time to recoup our losses."[148] Just like the governor, however, these community leaders were also committed to the continuing presence of state troops around the mills.

Most of the town's business leaders continued to strongly support the use of state troops to protect strikebreakers. The intensity of the violence following the false settlement only seemed to solidify the revulsion many of these citizens had for unions in general and Locals 578 and 584 in particular. Representing "the better citizens of Henderson and Vance County," Mrs. C. F. Finch asked Governor Hodges to "imagine ignorant people and gangsters completely taking over your business, you standing on the sidelines painfully waiting for the tragic end."[149]

The false settlement and subsequent violence, however, also inspired nearly one thousand Henderson-area residents to sign a petition calling for Governor Hodges "to remove the cause of violence in our community" by utilizing "the police power of the State to close the mills and keep them closed until such time as the management deals fairly and honorably with the more than 1,000 citizens of our county who constitute the skilled labor force which has made the mills successful and profitable." Closing the mills, the citizens argued, would restore "a balance that will make a fair settlement possible."[150]

By matching names on this petition against city directory listings, it is possible to identify some of the general fault lines that cut through the community during the strike.[151] Support for strikers tended to come from small business owners who depended on mill workers for business; from waitresses, plumbers, carpenters, construction workers, and other blue-collar employees; and from a handful of white-collar workers, most of whom were probably in contact with mill hands on a regular basis. Several other Henderson residents wrote personal letters to Governor Hodges asking him to reconsider his position on law and order. One correspondent, Mr. C. F. King, had been a foreman at the Harriet Mill until the modernization movement of the late 1930s. By 1959 he had been a grocery store owner for twenty years and was threatened by the loss of the strikers' paychecks. "I know the South Henderson people," King explained.

I know them to be good people, who are willing to cooperate with anyone as long as it is worthwhile. If only you could use the high influence of your office to encourage Mr. Cooper to close the mills until justice is accomplished I believe it would restore peace and progress to the whole community more quickly. These people, may I emphasize, want justice. They have never had it in the truest sense.[152]

There is little documentary evidence to indicate the ways in which Henderson's African American community viewed the conflict. All but one of the roughly two dozen black members of Locals 578 and 584 remained committed to the union cause throughout the strike and regularly attended union meetings. A newsletter published by Locals 578 and 584 noted that "our Negro members . . . have been exemplary in their steadfastness."[153] It is likely that the families of these strikers supported the union, and it is possible that some friends and neighbors were sympathetic. The one black striker who crossed the picket line had his yard bombed, which could have caused a ripple effect of antiunion sentiment among others in the black community. Very few blacks were hired as strikebreakers, and it is not clear whether or not those who crossed the lines came from Henderson. Perhaps a number of black residents had feelings similar to those of an anonymous letter-writer: "We are really enjoying this Henderson Ball," this person wrote Hodges. "You all studied so many ways to stop integration, let me see you all work this strike out. . . . All the South know to do is to take advantage of the Negro minority, but when it come to white for white, their hands are tied."[154] No matter how passionate or indifferent Henderson's African Americans were, race played at best a marginal role in determining the course of the strike and its ultimate outcome.

Within the white community, one of the most difficult splits involved church congregations. Edith Adams recalled that many fellow members of her City Road Methodist Church congregation refused to speak with her or even acknowledge her presence during and long after the strike. Although Adams remembered that her pastor, David Bercaw, empathized with all church members' feelings at the time, in private he strongly supported the use of state troops in Henderson.[155] Several pastors at churches serving the mill villages openly supported the strikers. Reverend Effert Snodderly of the Second Baptist Church, across the street from the Harriet Mill, wrote the governor that "having been closely associated with both strikers and non-strikers as their pastor I have come to the conclusion that there would be no violence if the issues had been left between management and those employees who were at work in the mills when the strike began."[156]

On the other hand, it appears that in those churches less frequently attended by mill villagers, ministers tended to support the governor's actions with equal fervor. David Guthrie, pastor of St. John's Episcopal Church, commended Hodges "for the dignified and effective way in which you have met the strike situation here. I am indeed grateful for your sending the Highway Patrol; conditions would otherwise be intolerable."[157]

The conflict also affected children in the city's schools. As W. Y. Bryan, chairman of the city school board, wrote the governor, "The 'powder keg' hysteria of our town has been transfused to the youngest child; teachers report unfavorable results of the strike upon the physical and mental well being of their students; actual violence has been witnessed between children of scabs and strikers."[158] "I prayed every night that it might be settle[d]," seventh-grader Betty Jo Oakley wrote the governor after the 17 April agreement. "Because of you we will have to argue no more."[159]

Many adult relationships were also strained. In some cases family members and relatives differed in their allegiances, causing great pain and hostility. When a friend of hers considered taking a job as a strikebreaker, Esther Roberson recalled saying, "'I love you. But if I'm on that picket line and you come up there and cross that picket line we're going to have a fight right down on the street. I'm gonna whip you or you're gonna whip me.' And I meant that, because I was out there striking for what I thought was right."[160]

Union members did not give up easily, even after the successful reopening of the second shift. But by the end of May 1959, strikebreakers operated three full shifts at each plant. In mid-May the state's presence took on an even more overtly militaristic appearance. Hodges had been under pressure to return the highway patrol officers to the state's roads because it had been revealed that compared with the previous year, through 25 April, traffic fatalities in North Carolina had increased over 33 percent—from 257 to 344.[161] The governor's own commissioner of motor vehicles, Ed Scheidt, told reporters that "keeping a large part of the Highway Patrol on strike duty at Henderson" was "partly responsible" for the large number of deaths. Responding to harsh criticism, Hodges announced on 8 May, after a week of relative calm in Henderson, that the highway patrolmen would leave. But as soon as the patrolmen left, strikers blocked mill gates with railroad ties and threw rocks at strikebreakers' cars. In response, on Tuesday, 12 May, Hodges ordered National Guard troops to protect the Harriet and Henderson Mills.[162]

The following morning, several hundred troops with bayonet-tipped rifles stood between pickets and the mills, snuffing out any remaining hope for an agreement. "When they brought the National Guard in that liked to broke my heart," recalled Local 584's Edith Adams. "It looked like war." "They was trying to make the union look like they was a bunch of invaders or something," Joseph Braswell remembered.[163] Indeed, the presence of troops in army uniforms seemed to highlight the relationship between the strike's central issue and the meaning of patriotism. As one TWUA representative noted, "Distinguished and many-times bemedalled war veterans, like Warren Walker, have ruined their best shirts by pinning their military decorations on their breasts and parading past the Guardsmen carrying signs reading, 'Is this what we fought for?'"[164] Verbal expressions of anguish, however, proved as ineffective with the National Guard as they had been with the highway patrol. Relatively quietly, the company began third shifts at the mills on 25 May as formal opposition by union members gradually diminished. Taking no chances, Governor Hodges stationed National Guard troops in Henderson until 9 August 1959, completing nearly six months of armed protection for Harriet and Henderson strikebreakers.

Meanwhile, state power in a different form made the union's slow death even more painful. A special session of superior court was scheduled in early May to determine the fates of those arrested for violating the restraining order.[165] In prosecuting these cases, the state received little assistance from local law enforcement officers; as Attorney General Malcolm Seawell complained, "The sheriff and his deputies have appeared as witnesses (usually character witness) in behalf of all those tried in court."[166] Nevertheless, more than sixty union members and sympathizers were convicted and received jail sentences, fines, terms on county road crews, or some combination of these punishments.[167] Addressing eleven people convicted of engaging in a riot—all of whom were arrested the day after James Manning had been shot by a foreman—Judge Raymond Mallard lectured, "I want to tell each of you that someday you are going to face your Maker, and then you are going to be punished for your attitudes, for your motives, for your lack of love." According to Mallard, "You and the likes of you have been prompted by the Devil."[168] It is small wonder, then, that so many union members considered the court session to be a farce.[169]

By far the most spectacular trial, however, came later that summer. On 15 June 1959 the state indicted Boyd Payton and seven others for conspiracy to bomb both the boiler room and the office at the Harriet Mill and to destroy a substation that delivered electricity to the plants. The defendants included regional TWUA representatives Lawrence Gore and Charles Auslander and five local members. Judge Raymond Mallard returned to Henderson in mid-July to conduct the trial. The state's case rested on the testimony of Harold Aaron, a former textile worker and union member—although not in Henderson—who had been working as an undercover agent for the State Bureau of Investigation (SBI). Under the SBI's direction, Aaron promoted the conspiracy and discussed it with several of the defendants in a bugged motel room in Roanoke Rapids, about thirty miles from Henderson. The state linked Payton to the conspiracy because the union leader answered the phone one day when Aaron called the Henderson motel room where several TWUA officials stayed during the strike. Aaron had been associating with union members, and Payton acknowledged on the phone that he knew who Aaron was.[170]

Defense attorneys contended that without Aaron there would have been no plot. The *Raleigh News and Observer*, too, suggested that the union defendants had been entrapped. The Payton trial "has put a stain on the reputation of the State Bureau of Investigation," the paper editorialized. "The function of the SBI is to obtain evidence, not to manufacture evidence."[171] Under the terms of the state's conspiracy law, however, that did not matter. After a three-day trial the jury returned guilty verdicts on all three charges against each of the eight men. Payton received a sentence of six to ten years in Raleigh's Central Prison, beginning in November 1960. After serving nine months, Payton was paroled by Governor Terry Sanford. On New Year's Eve, 1964, the day his term in office expired, Sanford issued Payton a pardon. The damage had long since been accomplished, however. The state had both defended the mills and concocted a successful plot to discredit all unions and union leadership.

Over 90 percent of the Harriet and Henderson workers who struck in 1958 never worked another day in the Coopers' mills. The company successfully destroyed the union locals and regained control over the production process. Although they no longer had a presence inside the mills, Locals 578 and 584 remained in existence until May 1961, when, citing "the need to face up to the harsh facts of life," the TWUA's executive council officially terminated the Henderson strike.[172]

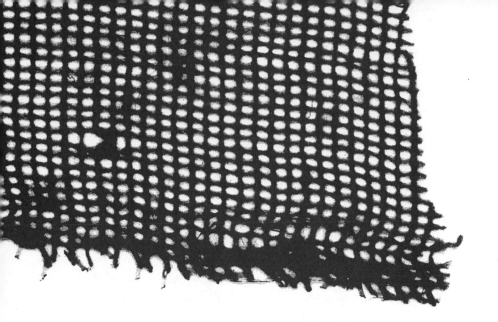

Conclusion

From the signing of contracts in 1943 until the strike of 1958, unionization meant enormous improvements in the lives of workers at the Harriet and Henderson Cotton Mills. By itself, the ability to speak up without fear of retribution had been a monumental achievement. In addition, members of Locals 578 and 584 made great strides, often against bitter opposition, toward achieving the following ideals:

1. Workers deserve to be treated with respect.
2. Workers require secure access to a livelihood.
3. Workers ought to have enough autonomy and flexibility to decide when to take time off for rest, recovery, errands, chores, or play,

within acceptable limits determined and enforced by the union members.

4. Inside each mill, workloads ought to be reasonable, as defined by workers on the basis of their experience on the job, allowing for variations in the abilities and health of each individual.

5. Technological changes and some modernization-induced layoffs were inevitable and were out of the workers' control, but no matter how dire, pleas about market pressures could not be used to justify excessive workloads.

The strike of 1958 was an awkward, thoroughly undemocratic referendum on those principles. To outside observers, the concrete meaning of unionization remained obscure throughout the conflict. The central issue of the strike, as well as for the entire era of unionization, was the locus of power in the workplace. Although workers desired even greater influence, company officials, under immense pressure from fierce competition and market fluctuations, determined that the union had already encroached far too deeply on traditional managerial prerogatives.

If managers had been primarily concerned with profits, as opposed to power, they might never have provoked the strike, and they should certainly have conceded after a few months operating with strikebreakers. In an intensely competitive market, the Harriet and Henderson Mills had remained profitable throughout the 1950s. As late as 1957, Marshall Cooper had announced to the board of directors that Harriet and Henderson's earnings "would compare favorably with any other company in our particular segment of the industry."[1] Productivity plummeted, however, when nonunion strikebreakers entered the mills. Near the end of 1959, company officials complained of their first annual losses since the Great Depression, attributing them to "a tremendous turnover in labor" and the costs incurred "to train people." As a result of the strike, the company lost nearly $600,000, roughly the same amount as the three previous years' net incomes combined. Government tax policies allowed the firm to recoup over $250,000 of its losses, but that windfall failed to solve the problem of continued high operating expenses. As late as March 1960, mill officials hoped that they would "eventually have a lower labor cost than we had when we had a Union."[2] Workers had virtually no leverage against a determined management: a strike made no difference when managers were willing to accept months of inefficiency on a scale that would never have been tolerated with a union.

If solidarity could have produced a union victory, these locals would have survived. Of over one thousand union members, no more than sixty crossed the picket lines, yet striking workers were unable to force the company to negotiate seriously. Nor could the locals' defeat be blamed on a lack of support from the international union. Sensitive to longstanding complaints among southern mill workers that unions could not be counted on for the duration of a struggle, the TWUA offered Locals 578 and 584 unlimited support. Long after the National Guard had left and the strike was effectively over, TWUA representative David George informed international union officials that it would still be "utterly disastrous to the future of organized labor in the South . . . to take any action that could be described as selling the Henderson freedom-fighters short."[3] The TWUA spent over $1.5 million on the strike, and according to local union leaders, no one went hungry and none of the members' bills went unpaid. In April 1960, seventeen months after the strike began, the commissaries still served 690 union members and their families.[4]

For local union members, then, the strike was tumultuous and agonizing for two reasons. First, the union did everything it possibly could and still had no trump cards to play. Helplessness alone, however, would not have sparked the public displays of despair on the picket lines. Union members hung on so tenaciously because they had so much to lose. The internal history of unionization made no difference in determining the outcome of the strike. There were no public debates over the relative justness of labor relations with and without a union. The very lives of the striking workers did not seem to matter. It was inconceivable to union members, at least at the beginning of the conflict, that the gains of unionization could truly be so fragile. Nevertheless, the Harriet and Henderson Mills rejoined the ranks of the industrial dictatorships that pumped out textiles across the South.[5]

From 1943 to 1958, labor relations at the Harriet and Henderson Mills represented a best-case scenario for southern cotton-mill workers. Fewer than 10 percent of southern millhands were organized, and of the small contingent of union outposts, Locals 578 and 584 were among the strongest. Given their toleration of an organizing campaign, there is reason to believe that Harriet and Henderson managers, at least in the mid-1940s, were more reasonable than many of their southern counterparts. By the mid-1950s, however, company officials wanted workers to submit to any proposed workload and obey any order without protest. It seems highly probable that such autocratic conditions were the norm in the vast majority of unorganized southern cotton mills, which employed hundreds of thousands of people in the region.

It has been a common assumption that given the harsh working conditions in southern mills, usually expressed in terms of inadequate pay, the low rate of unionization among southern millhands demonstrates that they were almost irrationally opposed to organized labor. The evidence from Henderson, however, strongly contradicts any notions that southern workers were intrinsically antiunion. Harriet and Henderson workers were born and bred in mill villages, and most were devoutly religious and undereducated, just like the workforces in every other southern cotton mill. It was Harriet and Henderson management that had been unique, first by allowing an organizing campaign and then by operating for fifteen years with a unionized workforce. Rarely, however, have southern textile workers considered the option of organizing as simply a question of whether or not they would appreciate particular positive changes in their lives. Southern millhands have always had good reason to fear military defeat, permanent dismissal, or a runaway plant if they participated in organizing efforts. It is not surprising, then, that so many mill workers have been unwilling to throw caution to the wind, vote for a union, and possibly lose everything.

Events in Henderson only confirmed the rational fears of southern textile workers. The strike of 1958 appeared to prove once again that labor unions bring nothing but trouble to workers, mills, and communities. From public sources of information about the strike, one could easily have inferred that unions drive companies to the brink of bankruptcy and that union members eagerly engage in violence and illegal conspiracies to achieve their goals. When organized labor comes to your town, the argument went, companies lose profits, communities are torn apart, and union members inevitably lose their jobs.

This analysis has considerable merit. It would be more accurate, however, if it emphasized the extraordinary efforts managements made to ensure that there would be enough chaos and despair to force unionized workers to behave in ways resembling the negative caricature. The Henderson example showed that towns explode when managers demand that union members meekly obey any command after the workers have experienced a more dignified existence.

The failure of the TWUA in Henderson did nothing to improve its already dim prospects for organizing in the South. It appears that the Henderson strike of 1958 had an immediate impact on the TWUA's campaign at the J. P. Stevens mills in nearby Roanoke Rapids. In commenting on the unionization effort in its town, a Roanoke Rapids paper had emphasized the violence in Henderson and the defeat of those union locals.

As one pro-TWUA worker in Roanoke Rapids recalled saying shortly before the vote at Stevens, "If they had had an election before all hell broke
loose over in Henderson, they would have won. But now people are so
scared, there's no way they'll vote for the union." Indeed, the TWUA lost.[6]
Its continuing efforts in the region were also hampered because it had no
choice but to spend $1.5 million supporting the Henderson strikers rather
than devoting that money to organizing campaigns.

Yet the elimination of Locals 578 and 584 cannot be seen as the most
decisive moment for labor in the textile South. There had been too many
critical junctures in the past: immediately after World War I, the late
1920s, the General Strike of 1934, the late 1930s, World War II, and Operation Dixie, which began in 1946. Each of these periods saw regionwide
challenges to the status quo, albeit with meager resources, but unions
never gained more than a slender toehold. The defeat of Locals 578 and
584 can be seen, then, as the stomping out of an isolated ember from a
nearly extinguished regional brushfire. As rare and vulnerable as unionized textile mills were in the South, it is all the more amazing that Harriet
and Henderson workers accomplished as much as they did during the
1950s.

For southern mill managers, however, the Harriet and Henderson
strike only reinforced their already-strong conviction that when one was
confronting unions, extraordinary measures and unblinking intransigence
were worth the trouble. It seemed even more clear, however, that it was
better to take a strong stand in the beginning than to endure fifteen years
with a functioning union. To mill owners throughout the region, the experience of Harriet and Henderson officials with unionized workers vali-
dated the notion that no level of workplace democracy was worth the
hassles it created.

Were more money and more benefits the overriding concerns of union
members and union leaders in the postwar era? Did workers expect little
of their unions besides periodic wage increases and larger benefit packages? Did the grievance procedure stifle and constrain shop-floor activism? Harriet and Henderson workers certainly wanted more money, and
they enjoyed their Christmas bonus and their week of paid vacation. In
day-to-day union operations, however, issues such as wages and hours
were rarely raised, and when they were, the disagreements usually involved the establishment of work assignments. On any meaningful scale,
the grievance procedure empowered mill workers, who were able for
the first time to assert themselves without fear of arbitrary retribution.

Harriet and Henderson workers experienced unionization as a form of emancipation. Why else would they have struggled so long for their arbitration clause? Conventional wisdom, which emphasizes how much rank-and-file union members lost in the postwar years, clearly does not mesh well with the evidence from Henderson.

It has also been suggested that the triumph of bureaucratic grievance procedures contributed to the alienation of women from participation in unions and shifted union attention away from issues of primary importance to women.[7] If the experience of women union members in Henderson is any indication, this argument contains more than a kernel of truth if unions are defined narrowly as their top-ranking leadership at the local level and their regional and international officers and representatives, almost all of whom were men. In daily life at work, however, women union members in Henderson relied heavily on the grievance procedure to assert their rights and to elect women shop stewards to represent them in the initial stage of the grievance process. Women workers consistently received the full support of the male leadership in their union locals, and in 1958, they defended their arbitration clause steadfastly.

Of course, one small, southern textile community cannot pretend to be representative of all American workers. Nevertheless, this research is suggestive in many respects. First, this study explores workers' aspirations from the workers' perspective. While the specific content of workers' grievances has received little scholarly attention, this study demonstrates that local concerns, whether settled through direct action or the grievance procedure, were of enormous importance to workers seeking any sort of justice in the workplace. Harriet and Henderson union members raised concerns that were to some extent industry-specific, such as how many hanks of a certain type of yarn would be necessary to make a peg point. Yet it seems likely that issues like the right to choose when to work and when to rest, and the right to influence the pace and content of their jobs, might have been universal concerns among American workers. Further research at the local level might reveal a common range of aspirations, including, but not limited to, a desire for more money. Local research might also reveal a wide spectrum in the effectiveness of local unions in different industries, and even within the same international union.

Historians, however, have generally been so certain that workers were concerned only with wages and benefits and were alienated by grievance procedures that research tends to focus on the lack of a unified American labor movement that was propelled by a militant rank and file and asserted itself on the shop floor and in the political arena. It is true that the entrenched promanagement legal philosophy in the United States has long been the bane of insurgent workers; and the inability or unwillingness of the union movement to alter the political balance of power is certainly an important topic, as is the fate of direct action in the workplace. There are dangers, however, when the scholarly agenda shifts from an examination of what happened to explanations for why something did not occur: for example, the actual concerns of the people involved can be overlooked. Also, contradictory evidence may be absorbed unreflectively into existing categories. Members of Locals 578 and 584 obviously did not concern themselves only with issues of "bread-and-butter" unionism, or business unionism, as they are commonly understood today, unless business unionism means aspiring to control workloads and the course of technological change as well as struggling for the right to earn *less* money by taking a day or two off each week. By no means, however, were union members in Henderson the self-conscious agents of a national working class. Nor did they achieve, by any reasonable standard, industrial democracy. But if anything short of revolution or militant direct action is defined as "business unionism," the term loses any concrete meaning and has little interpretive value.

From the perspective of workers in Henderson, the fifteen years of unionization were neither utopia nor a tragically limited pursuit of material gain. Grievance procedures were often slow, bureaucratic, and offered no certainty of victory, as their critics have pointed out. Yet despite the flaws inherent in the system, members of Locals 578 and 584 used the grievance procedure, often successfully, to struggle for what *they* perceived to be a more humane existence. Managers and union representatives estimated that 75 percent of all disputes, including those over workloads, were settled before grievances were formally written.[8] On a day-to-day basis, then, workers in Henderson could reasonably have perceived the grievance procedure to be a quick, effective dispenser of justice. This is not to return to the argument that grievance procedures represented the fulfillment of workers' dreams, especially since the combination of grievance procedures and increasing wages in places like Henderson by no means brought an end to serious labor conflict. Still, faced with the choice of continuing with a grievance procedure or trying their luck without the constraints of the formal process, Harriet and Henderson union members voted overwhelmingly for the status quo.

Despite the mill workers' tenacity, however, management was able to turn back the clock in Henderson, which supports the theme of defeat and failure for the postwar labor movement. The fact of decline, in terms of organized labor's inability to withstand such management offensives, to prevent capital flight, and to inspire a serious national debate over workers' rights, cannot be denied. However, there is a tendency to place a disproportionate share of the blame on union officials and union members for their postwar predicament. If only union officials and members across the country had discarded bread-and-butter principles for a more militant class consciousness, and had thereby linked significant local insurgencies into a strong political challenge to entrenched powers, a challenge that took place outside the Democratic Party, workers would have gained greater control over their destinies.[9] This argument has a certain appeal. The limits of local insurgencies are obvious. Strong labor influence in government circles and on the shaping of legal theory would have made an enormous difference, for example, in the outcome of the Henderson strike.

But a central premise of this argument requires further examination. The argument assumes that a proven strategy for working-class liberation exists and could have been followed successfully, despite all constraints, if union members and leaders had only made better decisions. This assumption is usually based on another, not always stated, axiom—that adequately class-conscious labor movements evolved in other industrialized nations, like Great Britain, France, and Germany. By succumbing to business unionism and by failing to create an independent socialist political party, this line of reasoning goes, American workers have paled in comparison with their western European counterparts, who recognized that open-ended bargaining, shop-floor control, and political clout at the national level were a more certain route to liberation.

This is an ironic assumption, because historians of the labor movements in Great Britain, France, and Germany have not found what historians of American labor have generally understood to be there. A recent comparative study of shop-floor bargaining in the postwar era, for example, argued that "the contrast between workplace industrial relations" in the United States and Great Britain "is overdrawn and misleading."[10] Another researcher who has studied workers on both sides of the Atlantic after World War II "challenges assumptions about the greater passivity of the American labor movement and suggests fewer divergences between the American and British workplace experience than has usually been assumed."[11]

At the same time that historians of American labor seemed most certain of British superiority, scholars of British labor were debating how workers there became so thoroughly accepting of the capitalist status quo. Some critics of British labor have pointed to France as the country that serves as a model of working-class development in the industrialized world. Yet historians of French labor have complained about the relative disunity, lack of leadership, and low rates of union membership among workers in that country. Likewise, historians of German labor have offered sharp criticisms of the performance of the German working class, emphasizing, according to a recent overview, their failure "to achieve effective organization outside the skilled sectors or to prevent even their members from falling in with the jingoistic patriotism and militarism promoted by the empire and the ruling elite."[12] Historians have pointed every direction in search of a class-conscious proletariat—what American workers in the postwar era clearly were not—and have found nothing but exceptions.[13] The point is not that international comparisons are useless but, rather, that unless they are grounded in concrete evidence, they have little explanatory value.

This research contributes a building block in the quest for a more meaningful conceptualization. By scratching beneath the surface of grievance procedures and wage issues in the textile industry, one finds poignant stories of workers struggling, occasionally successfully, for more decent lives. Before disparaging labor conflicts as mere bread-and-butter disputes, it is vital to figure out exactly what they meant, especially to the participants. Although it appears that this approach could liberate researchers, and workers, from the current interpretive straitjacket, it is not at all certain what framework will take its place. To be sure, a new scholarly attitude will not suddenly produce workplace democracy either in the past or in the future. Nevertheless, it is important to rethink the conceptualization that separates "wages" and "working conditions" from the realm of serious, life-transforming concerns. From the standpoint of workers' rights, the end result of unionization in Henderson is certainly depressing. It would be a judgment detached from historical context, however, to dismiss their concerns as superficial or to blame the Henderson workers' defeat on an allegedly improper ideology. Although the Henderson experience offers workers no prescription for success, it underscores the vulnerability of even modest strides, important as they were, toward democracy.

APPENDIX A

Population and Racial Composition of Henderson Town

Year	Whites (%)	Blacks (%)	Total
1890	1,514 (36.1)	2,677 (63.9)	4,191
1900	1,552 (41.4)	2,194 (58.6)	3,746
1910	2,019 (44.8)	2,484 (55.2)	4,503
1920	3,163 (60.2)	2,056 (39.4)	*5,222
1930	3,502 (55.2)	2,843 (44.8)	6,345
1940	3,795 (49.6)	3,852 (50.4)	7,647
1950	6,004 (54.6)	4,989 (45.4)	*10,996
1960	7,427 (58.3)	5,313 (41.7)	12,740

*Each of these totals includes three persons classified as "other."
Source: U.S. Census data.

APPENDIX B

Population and Racial Composition of Vance County

Year	Whites (%)	Blacks (%)	Total
1890	6,434 (36.6)	11,143 (63.4)	*17,581
1900	6,929 (41.5)	9,755 (58.5)	16,684
1910	9,421 (48.5)	10,004 (51.5)	19,425
1920	12,625 (55.4)	10,171 (44.6)	*22,799
1930	15,285 (56.0)	12,009 (44.0)	27,294
1940	15,996 (53.4)	13,958 (46.6)	*29,961
1950	17,488 (54.5)	14,602 (45.5)	*32,101
1960	17,973 (56.2)	14,017 (43.8)	*32,002

*Asterisks denote that the following number of people were classified as "other": 1890, 4; 1920, 3; 1940, 7; 1950, 11; 1960, 12.
Source: U.S. Census data.

APPENDIX C

Record of Sales, Taxes, Income, and Dividends for Harriet and Henderson Cotton Mills, 1944–1958

Year	Net Sales	Gross Income	Income Taxes	Net Income	Dividends
1944	4,040,875	456,683	337,593	119,089	15,153
1945	4,033,336	360,158	261,498	98,660	20,204
1946	5,248,272	658,086	273,514	384,572	75,765
1947	6,610,592	1,151,962	481,364	670,597	202,040
1948	6,137,654	959,972	399,618	560,353	202,040
1949	4,586,350	403,296	167,445	235,850	151,530
1950	5,883,099	649,610	290,573	359,036	181,836
1951	6,481,486	1,028,163	569,730	458,433	181,836
1952	6,404,406	518,000	278,778	239,221	121,224
1953	6,440,720	539,271	290,452	248,819	85,867
1954	5,338,443	73,406	34,717	38,689	35,357
1955	6,919,875	239,579	125,980	113,598	0
1956	7,565,022	697,661	379,774	317,886	60,612
1957	7,446,528	433,112	233,142	199,970	60,612
1958	6,594,146	213,702	111,955	101,747	40,408
Total	89,730,812	8,382,668	4,236,141	4,146,526	1,434,484

Source: Copied verbatim from "Report to Stockholders of Harriet and Henderson Cotton Mills," 3 January 1959, as verified by A. M. Pullen & Company, Certified Public Accounts, in LHH.

NOTES

Abbreviations

CR	Minutes from Stockholders' and Board of Directors' Meetings of the Harriet and Henderson Cotton Mills
Harriet/578	Transcripts of biweekly union-management meetings between Harriet Mill management and TWUA Local 578
HDD	*Henderson Daily Dispatch*
Henderson/584	Transcripts of biweekly union-management meetings between Henderson Mill management and TWUA Local 584
LHH	Luther H. Hodges Papers, North Carolina State Archives, Raleigh, North Carolina
N&O	*Raleigh News & Observer*
NCTMA	North Carolina Textile Manufacturers Association Papers, Raleigh, North Carolina
SLA	Amalgamated Clothing and Textile Workers' Union Central North Carolina Joint Board Collection, Southern Labor Archives, Georgia State University, Atlanta, Georgia
SRDO	Textile Workers Union of America Southern Regional Director's Office Papers, Manuscript Department, Duke University Library, Durham, North Carolina

Introduction

1. See, for example, Zieger, "History of the CIO," 485, and, more recently, Brody, "Workplace Contractualism," 181, 204.

2. Among those who have made similar observations are Zieger, "History of the CIO," 516; Kazin, "Struggling with Class Struggle," 507; and Brody, "Workplace Contractualism," 202.

3. See, for example, Harris, *The Right to Manage*, 156, 203; Lichtenstein, *Labor's War at Home*, 243, 244; Schatz, *The Electrical Workers*, 137, 155; Kazin, "Struggling with Class Struggle," 510; and Fraser, "The 'Labor Question,'" in Fraser and Gerstle, *Rise and Fall of the New Deal Order*, 57.

4. See, for example, Tomlins, *The State and the Unions*, 318–26; Griffith, *Crisis of American Labor*, 176; Fraser, "The 'Labor Question,'" 77; Lichtenstein, "From Corporatism to Collective Bargaining," 133, 122; and Gabin, *Feminism in the Labor Movement*, 173.

5. Brody, "Workplace Contractualism," 176.

6. Lichtenstein, *Labor's War at Home*, 179–80. Lichtenstein elaborates on this thesis in "Great Expectations," 113–41.

7. Tomlins, *The State and the Unions*, 322. For another statement of this thesis, see Fraser, "The 'Labor Question,'" 76.

8. Davis, *Prisoners of the American Dream*, 102.

9. See Faue, *Women, Men, and the Labor Movement*, and "Paths of Unionization," 296–319, quotes on 296.

10. Bernstein, *Turbulent Years*, 788.

11. David Brody makes this point in "The CIO after 50 Years," 470–71, and "Workplace Contractualism," 202.

12. See David Brody's 1975 essay "Radical Labor History and Rank-and-File Militancy," reprinted in his *Workers in Industrial America*, 146–58; Brody's 1976 essay "Working-Class History in the Great Depression," in ibid., 158–66; Lichtenstein, *Labor's War at Home*, 5, 8–25; and Kazin, "Struggling with Class Struggle," 502–4.

13. See Lichtenstein, *Labor's War at Home*, 15; Tolliday and Zeitlin, "Shop Floor Bargaining, Contract Unionism, and Job Control," 230.

14. Schatz, *The Electrical Workers*, 117.

15. Jefferys, *Management and Managed*, 114.

16. See also Tolliday and Zeitlin, "Shop Floor Bargaining, Contract Unionism, and Job Control," 235.

17. Davis, *Prisoners of the American Dream*, 122.

18. Brody, "Workplace Contractualism," 203–5, quote on 203.

19. Stein, "Southern Workers in National Unions," 208–9; Halpern, "Interracial Unionism in the Southwest," 158–82.

20. Gabin, *Feminism in the Labor Movement*, 4.

21. Cobble, *Dishing It Out*, 9. Among those chipping away at familiar representations of the AFL have been Tomlins, "AFL Unions in the 1930s"; Kazin, *Barons of Labor*; and Montgomery, *The Fall of the House of Labor*.

22. Zieger, *Organized Labor in the Twentieth-Century South*, 4.

23. Ibid., 3.

24. Griffith, *Crisis of American Labor*.

25. Flamming, *Creating the Modern South*, 285.

26. See Baron, *Work Engendered*, and *Labor History* 34 (Spring–Summer 1993), edited by Elizabeth Faue, which is devoted entirely to "Gender and the Reconstruction of Labor History."

27. This is in apparent contrast with the automobile industry, in which women had access to only about 12 percent of a shrinking number of jobs, prompting some to demand greater access to positions traditionally reserved for men. See Gabin, *Feminism in the Labor Movement*, 172.

28. Douglas Flamming ran into the same roadblock at the Crown Mills, which employed no African Americans at all. See *Creating the Modern South*, xxix–xxx. Hall et al., *Like a Family*, also pays little attention to race. I. A. Newby's competing overview, *Plain Folk in the New South*, contains the strongest discussion in the cotton-mill literature of the origins and consequences of racially exclusive labor policies. See especially chapter 16, "Race," 462–92.

29. See Stein, "Southern Workers in National Unions," and Halpern, "Interracial Unionism in the Southwest."

Chapter 1

1. Tilley, *Bright-Tobacco*, viii.

2. Ibid., 206, 211; Escott, *Many Excellent People*, 175.

3. Tilley, *Bright-Tobacco*, 167.

4. Daniel, *Breaking the Land*, 32–35; Escott, *Many Excellent People*, 171–95; Tilley, *Bright-Tobacco*, 288; Goodwyn, *Democratic Promise*.

5. Tilley, *Bright-Tobacco*, 409.

6. Crow, "Cracking the Solid South," 333–54; Daniel, *Breaking the Land*, 34–35; Tilley, *Bright-Tobacco*, 414.

7. Tilley, *Bright-Tobacco*, 261–65, 416, 638.

8. Woodward, *Origins of the New South*, 131–35, 305–6; Escott, *Many Excellent People*, 213.

9. Letter from B. N. Duke to John D. Cooper, 16 June 1893, quoted in Durden, *Dukes of Durham*, 132.

10. CR, 1, 8 August 1895; *Henderson Gold Leaf*, 6 June, 11 July 1895.

11. *Henderson Gold Leaf*, 15 April 1897. Approximate production averages are listed in CR, 25 April 1899; 8 January 1900; and 16 January 1901, which noted a profit of $82,774.67 in 1900 on investment capital of $250,000.

12. Cooper interview; CR, 1 July 1901. Incorporated separately, the Henderson and Harriet mills had the same stockholders and directors.

13. Harriet #2 opened in 1909, #3 in 1913. The category of "yarn mill" excluded huge mills like Cannon and Dan River, which produced cloth mainly from their own yarn. See *N&O*, 15 August 1927.

14. Hall et al., *Like a Family*, 3–43; Newby, *Plain Folk*, 1–2, 23–56; Durden, *Dukes of Durham*, 125–27; Escott, *Many Excellent People*, 175–78, 220; McHugh, *Mill Family*, 3.

15. U.S. Censuses, 1900 and 1910, household data for Vance County.

16. For discussions of race and the segregation of mill work, see Hall et al., *Like a Family*, 66; Newby, *Plain Folk*, 71–75, 462–92.

17. CR, 9 December 1896, 12 April 1897; U.S. Household Census, 1900.

18. Hall et al., *Like a Family*, 67–77; Newby, *Plain Folk*, 124.

19. Roberson, Jackson, Adams, and Nipper interviews.

20. Figures for 1910 can be found in Frankel, "Women, Paternalism, and Protest," 48. Male/female ratios in Henderson during these years are similar to regional estimates by Newby in *Plain Folk*, 123.

21. *Henderson Gold Leaf*, 9 January 1896; Newby, *Plain Folk*, 87.

22. CR, 23 April 1907.

23. See Hall et al., *Like a Family*, 105–11; McHugh, *Mill Family*, 7–8.

24. Wright, *Old South, New South*, 142; Newby, *Plain Folk*, 568.

25. CR, 19 July 1916.

26. Wilkins, Littleton, and Roberson interviews.

27. Adams and Jackson interviews.

28. CR, 15 July 1925; Hoffmann, "Henderson or Hell." See also Newby, *Plain Folk*, 340–44.

29. Emma Harris, Abbott, and Ralph Harris interviews.

30. Braswell interview (1984); Roberson, Emma Harris, Ralph Harris, and Adams interviews. See also Pope, *Millhands and Preachers*, 49–69, and Hall et al., *Like a Family*, 222–23.

31. Henderson Chamber of Commerce, "Facts about Henderson and Vance County."

32. Blackburn, *Heritage of Vance County*, 18–19, 160–61; CR, 19, 25 January 1921; Tilley, *Bright-Tobacco*, 638–39; Wester interview.

33. McHugh, *Mill Family*, 25.

34. Hall et al., *Like a Family*, 158; Newby, *Plain Folk*, 66.

35. CR, 27 April 1920.

36. CR, 21 January 1914.

37. Roberson interview. See also Newby, *Plain Folk*, 128, 198, and Hall et al., *Like a Family*, 93–98.

38. Hall et al., *Like a Family*, 94–98. I. A. Newby argues further that sexual exploitation by foremen was relatively rare, probably for fear of retribution by neighbors. See *Plain Folk*, 329–30. Sexual harassment was apparently widespread at Fulton Bag and Cotton Mills in Atlanta, however, during a strike in 1914 and 1915. See Fink, "Efficiency and Control," 25.

39. Collins and James Ellis interviews. For evidence of worker-supervisor collusion at Fulton Bag and Cotton Mills, see Fink, "Efficiency and Control," 26–27.

40. CR, 27 April 1920, 25 January, 26 April 1921.

41. CR, 26 April 1921. The commissaries were discontinued in November 1922 when the bleakest of conditions had passed. The fair prices were confirmed by former Harriet Mill worker Esther Roberson, who was not one to give the company undue credit. For discussions of company stores, see McHugh, *Mill Family*, 20, and Newby, *Plain Folk*, 220.

42. Hall et al., *Like a Family*, 185–95.

43. CR, 15 July 1908.

44. CR, 9 August, 14 December 1898, 12 December 1900, 7 January 1901, 3 March 1902, 28 April 1903, 18 October 1905, 8 January 1906, 23 April 1907, 11 December 1912, 21 July 1915, 17 January 1917, 15 January 1919, 21 January 1920; Abbott interview.

45. CR, 21 January 1920.

46. See, for example, Broadus Mitchell, *The Rise of Cotton Mills in the South*, and Cooper interview.

47. CR, 14 December 1910. See Woodward, *Origins of the New South*, 133; Pope, *Millhands and Preachers*, 20; Hall et al., *Like a Family*, 29; Escott, *Many Excellent People*, 213.

48. CR, 18 April 1910.

49. CR, 14 January, 15 April 1914. Welfare programs were far more extensive at the Crown Mills in Dalton, Georgia. By 1920 Crown Mill workers enjoyed a company-sponsored kindergarten, grade school, band, baseball team, life insurance program, savings program, and hospital. See Flamming, *Creating the Modern South*, 129.

50. See Henderson Chamber of Commerce, "Facts about Henderson and Vance County."

51. Pope, *Millhands and Preachers*, 218.

52. CR, 18 January, 23 October 1922; *HDD*, 7 September 1927.

53. CR, 25 February, 22 April, 1 July 1924.

54. CR, 25 February, 15 July 1924; *HDD*, 11 September 1924. There is no evidence that Henderson Mill hands joined the strike.

55. *HDD*, 12 September 1924.

56. CR, 15 October 1924; *HDD*, 5 August 1927.

57. Hall et al., *Like a Family*, 212; Pope, *Millhands and Preachers*, 207. For a more extensive discussion of the strikes of 1924 and 1927, see Clark, "The TWUA in a Southern Mill Town," 31–56.

58. Statement by "The South Henderson Harriet Cotton Mill Employees," delivered by Tom Duke and W. J. Journegan, *HDD*, 5 August 1927.

59. *N&O*, 12, 30 August 1927.

60. CR, 12 August 1927.

61. *HDD*, 12 August 1927.

62. *N&O*, 12 August 1927.

63. *N&O*, 13 August 1927.

64. CR, 20 January 1932; Wilkins interview.

65. *HDD*, 17 August 1927; *N&O*, 17, 20 August 1927. See the profile of Alfred Hoffmann in Hall et al., *Like a Family*, 340–41.

66. Johnson interview.

67. *N&O*, 30 August 1927.

68. *N&O*, 1 September 1927.

69. *HDD*, 5, 7 September 1927.

70. CR, 19 October 1927. Few mills had personnel departments before the 1920s. See Newby, *Plain Folk*, 128.

71. *HDD*, 12 September 1927. See Pope, *Millhands and Preachers*, 307, for evidence of similar conciliatory gestures made to defeated workers in Gastonia after the 1929 strike.

72. See Hall et al., *Like a Family*, 328–40 (quote on 340). For detailed treatment of events in 1934, see Irons, "Testing the New Deal."

73. For lesser-known conflicts, see John L. Bell Jr., *Hard Times*, 31–40, and Selby, "'Better to Starve in the Shade.'"

74. *HDD*, 11 September 1934.

75. *HDD*, 6, 7 September 1934.

76. *HDD*, 17 September 1934.

77. CR, 23 October 1934.

78. Hall et al., *Like a Family*, 349–50; Irons, "Testing the New Deal."

79. *N&O*, 24 June 1928; CR, 18 July 1928.

80. CR, 20 April 1932; John L. Bell Jr., *Hard Times*, 21–30.

81. CR, 18 October 1933; Hall et al., *Like a Family*, 289–91, 302–3; James A. Hodges explains the 1933 boom in *New Deal Labor Policy*, 55–57.

82. CR, 16 January 1935.

83. Wilkins, Nipper, Ralph Harris, Collins, Clayborne Blue, Harvey Harris, Lila Mae Ellis, Melvin Renn, and Forsythe interviews.

Chapter 2

1. "Harriet-Henderson Cotton Mills—and Modernization," 24. In this context, the term "modernization" refers to a systematic strategy for reducing production costs.

2. CR, 15 April, 15 July, 21 October 1936; 20 January, 27 April, 21 July, 20 October 1937.

3. CR, 20 April 1938.

4. See Blicksilver, *Cotton Manufacturing*, 162.

5. Cooper interview.

6. CR, 14 February, 25 April 1939. There are no comparable figures for the Henderson Mill.

7. Walker, "Comparison of the 1911 Cotton Yarn Mill," 160.

8. Ibid.

9. *Textile Bulletin* 57 (15 November 1939): 30. Clayborne Blue interview.

10. CR, 17 January 1940.

11. *N&O*, 4 July, 12 August 1939; 28 September 1940; 6 February 1942.

12. By 1943, 75 percent of the cotton mills produced exclusively for the war effort. See U.S. Department of Labor, *Union Agreements*, 1; CR, 16 October 1940, 15 July, 21 October 1942, 22 October, 21 July 1943; Blicksilver, *Cotton Manufacturing*, 151–56.

13. "Harriet-Henderson Cotton Mills—and Modernization," 29; Roberson interview. The stretch-out was the main focus for millhands' complaints throughout the 1930s. See Hodges, *New Deal Labor Policy*, and Irons, "Testing the New Deal."

14. Roberson and Faulkner interviews.

15. Johnson, Nipper, and Roberson interviews.

16. Braswell (1984), Wilkins, and Adams interviews.

17. Johnson interview.

18. Ibid.

19. Wilkins interview. J. Harry Bunn's obituary is in *HDD*, 14 July 1937.

20. Jackson interview.

21. Richards, "History of the TWUA," 64–67, 136–38; Hodges, *New Deal Labor Policy*, 170; Marshall, *Labor in the South*, 169–71.

22. *Textile Bulletin* 57, no. 7 (1 December 1939): 26.

23. See Richards, "History of the TWUA," 91–122 (quote on 104), and Hodges, *New Deal Labor Policy*, 157–79. Also see the testimony of Solomon Barkin in U.S. Senate Committee on Labor and Public Welfare, *Labor-Management Relations in the Southern Textile Manufacturing Industry, Part 2*, 22.

24. Gross, *The Reshaping of the National Labor Relations Board*, 107.

25. Richards, "History of the TWUA," 91–122, especially 112–13, 117.

26. Ibid., 152–54; Lichtenstein, *Labor's War at Home*, 73; Marshall, *Labor in the South*, 225; U.S. Department of Labor, *Union Agreements*, 1.

27. Witney, *Wartime Experiences*, 25, 119, 121, 126, 128, 132, quote on 144.

28. Lichtenstein, *Labor's War at Home*, 51.

29. Ibid., 79–80; Richards, "History of the TWUA," 158.

30. For an example in the northern textile industry, see Gerstle, *Working-Class Americanism*, 207–13.

31. Richards, "History of the TWUA," 150, 161, 167, 173.

32. U.S. Department of Labor, *Union Agreements*, 1.

33. Richards, "History of the TWUA," 162, 170.

34. Ibid., 165, 176.

35. Ibid., 163, 166–73; Smith, *Mill on the Dan*, 491–98.

36. Lichtenstein, *Labor's War at Home*, 120.

37. Transcript of speech, 14 August 1944, in Governor R. Gregg Cherry Papers.

38. Richards, "History of the TWUA," 152; Frankel, "Women, Paternalism, and Protest," 204; Abbott interview.

39. Fry interview; Richards, "History of the TWUA," 92.

40. Johnson, Nipper, and Jones interviews.

41. Jones and Johnson interviews.

42. Clayborne Blue interview.

43. Johnson, Nipper, and Faulkner interviews; *HDD*, 24 March 1943.

44. Johnson, Faulkner, Nipper, and Harvey Harris interviews; Frankel, "Women, Paternalism, and Protest," 141.

45. Jones and Faulkner interviews.

46. Johnson interview.

47. Cooper interview.

48. In a memo dated 19 March 1959, LHH, North Carolina governor Luther Hodges reported that John D. Cooper Jr., Marshall Y. Cooper, and Bennett H. Perry together controlled a majority interest in the Harriet and Henderson Cotton Mills.

49. Lichtenstein, *Labor's War at Home*, 53, 78–79.

50. *HDD*, 23 May 1950.

51. Management's frustration with less capable employees hired during the war is discussed in Harriet/578, 17 November 1948.

52. CR, 22 October 1943.

53. Richards, "History of the TWUA," 99, 104, 164.

54. Ibid., 168–70; Smith, *Mill on the Dan*, 491–98.

55. Richards, "History of the TWUA," 166.

56. Transcript of speech by a member of the Fourth Regional WLB, given 14 August 1944, in Governor R. Gregg Cherry Papers.

57. *Heritage of Vance County*, 11; Wester interview.

58. *HDD*, 24 March 1943.

59. Cooper interview; CR, 16 October 1940, 22 January 1941, 21 January 1942.

60. Johnson interview.

61. *HDD*, 24 March 1943.

62. Faulkner interview.

63. Eula McGill, quoted in Griffith, *Crisis of American Labor*, 115.

64. *HDD*, 24 March 1943. There were 530 votes cast out of 601 eligible voters.

One ballot was ruled invalid. These numbers can be found in the "Report on Consent Election" for the Harriet Cotton Mills, NLRB Case File 5-R-1210, National Archives, Washington, D.C.

65. Johnson interview.

66. Jackson interview. Election results are in the *HDD*, 29 June 1943, and in the "Report on Consent Election" for the Henderson Cotton Mills, NLRB Case File 5-R-1290, National Archives, Washington, D.C. There were three voided ballots and eighty-five nonvoters.

67. Johnson and Adams interviews.

68. Typescript copies of each first contract can be found in SRDO. Specific contract provisions will be discussed in detail in subsequent chapters.

69. U.S. Department of Labor, *Union Agreements*, 35–39.

70. Ibid., 5, 12, 16.

71. There is a copy of the stipulation in SRDO. See also the letter dated 15 July 1945 from L. L. Shepard, TWUA, to R. R. Lawrence, TWUA, copy to J. D. Cooper Jr. in Arbitration #8 folder; Arbitration #7 transcript, 30 May 1945; and Marshall, *Labor in the South*, 228–29. In February 1945, the NWLB ordered twenty-three major southern cotton mills, including the Harriet and Henderson Mills, to establish a fifty-five-cent minimum wage for pieceworkers. Of the twenty-three mills, Harriet and Henderson were the only ones that already had a minimum wage.

72. Jackson and Adams interviews. There had actually been 124 "no" votes.

73. Jackson interview. The continued high percentage of union membership in Henderson over the following fifteen years is confirmed in a private memorandum by Governor Luther H. Hodges, dated 17 April 1959, in LHH.

74. CR, 22 October 1943.

75. CR, 19 April 1944.

76. Fry interview. Fry was a regional TWUA representative in the 1940s and 1950s.

Chapter 3

1. See the list of early grievances in the Harriet Mill Records, hereafter cited as "Harriet Mill Grievances." Reid's case is labeled "NONE(J), 1943."

2. U.S. Senate Committee on Labor and Public Welfare, *Labor-Management Relations in the Southern Textile Manufacturing Industry*, 221.

3. Harriet Mill Grievances, #8, 16 July 1943.

4. Harriet Mill Grievances, #114, 24 September 1943.

5. Harriet Mill Grievances, #115, 24 September 1943.

6. Harriet Mill Grievances, #8, 16 July 1943.

7. Ibid.

8. Harriet Mill Grievances, #5, 2 July 1943.

9. Ibid.

10. Harriet Mill Grievances, #137, 15 February 1944, 6 March 1944.

11. Harriet Mill Grievances, NONE(F), 1943.

12. The superintendent ordered the supervisors to make sure that workers

kept all of their frames running. Harriet Mill Grievances, #133, 12 February 1944.

13. Harriet Mill Grievances, #6, 7 July 1943.

14. Harriet Mill Grievances, NONE(N), 7 July 1943.

15. Arbitration #2 transcript, 17 November 1943, 4.

16. Arbitration #2 transcript, 17 November 1943.

17. Ibid., 17.

18. Decision by Arbitrator Frazier Hood for hearing held 17 November 1943, Arbitration #2 folder.

19. Braswell (1984), Adams, and Wilkins interviews. Also see Gersuny and Kaufman, "Seniority and the Moral Economy of U.S. Automobile Workers."

20. Harriet Mill Grievances, #125, 15 January 1944.

21. Harriet Mill Grievances, #109, 3 October 1943. Copies of the contract can be found in SRDO.

22. 1943 Contract, Section 7(f); Lila Mae Ellis interview.

23. 1943 Contract, Sections 7(d) and 7(e).

24. Harrict Mill Grievances, #9, 10 July 1943.

25. Harriet Mill Grievances, #138, 15 February 1944.

26. For a discussion of how other union members viewed seniority principles as fair, if not perfect, see Schatz, *The Electrical Workers*, 113–19.

27. Arbitration #2 transcript, 17 November 1943, 20–21.

28. Harriet Mill Grievances, #126, 27 January 1944.

29. Henderson/584, 10 August 1949.

30. Henderson/584, 18 May 1948.

31. Local 584 Master Grievance List, #89.

32. Harriet/578, 15 February 1956.

33. The fate of Gupton's grievance is listed on the Local 578 Master Grievance List, #302.

34. Harriet/578, 16 August 1956.

35. There is evidence, however, that Roberson submitted a note from her doctor shortly after her layoff. The note can be found in the Arbitration #32 folder, and it is referred to in Barrett, "Arbitrator's Decision," 526.

36. Harriet/578, 30 August 1956.

37. Harriet/578, 16 August 1956.

38. Document dated 3 December 1956 in Arbitration #32 folder. Evidence of expenditures for machinery can be found in Chapter 5.

39. Roberson interview.

40. Fry interview; *HDD*, 31 March 1951. In 1951, Locals 578 and 584 asked the company to allow retirement privileges for "technologically displaced workers" if the affected hands were at least fifty-five years old and had worked there for fifteen years. The company rejected the proposal.

41. Arbitration #10 transcript, 5 September 1946.

Chapter 4

1. Hall et al., *Like a Family*, 299.

2. Arbitration #19 transcript, 27 February 1950, 32.

3. Arbitration #13 transcript, 14 September 1947, 39.

4. Harriet/578, 12 October 1954.

5. Arbitration #19 transcript, 27 February 1950, 33.

6. Harriet/578, 12 October 1954.

7. Harriet/578, 18 April 1956.

8. Wilkins interview.

9. Harriet/578, 18 April 1956.

10. See especially Arbitration #3 transcript, 19 January 1944, 10–11, and Arbitration #28 transcript, 21–22 September 1955, 10–20. See also Chapters 5–7.

11. Henderson/584, 24 August 1950.

12. Henderson/584, 13 November 1957; Roberson and Adams interviews.

13. Harriet/578, 12 October 1954.

14. See Richards, "History of the TWUA," 183–212.

15. 1943 Contract, Section 7(g).

16. Harriet/578, 11 January 1950.

17. Harriet/578, 15 September 1954.

18. Henderson/584, 24 August 1950.

19. Arbitration #19 transcript, 27 February 1950, 31–32.

20. Henderson/584, 27 October 1948.

21. 1943 Contract, Section 14(b).

22. Harriet/578, 12 October 1954, 19 October 1949.

23. Harriet/578, 12 October 1954.

24. Harriet/578, 15 March 1949.

25. Henderson/584, 13 October 1948.

26. Henderson/584, 27 October 1948.

27. Ibid.

28. Henderson/584, 20 January 1949.

29. Arbitration #19 transcript, 27 February 1950, 32–33.

30. Henderson/584, 11 January 1950. The second shift began at 3:00 P.M.

31. Henderson/584, 6 January 1950.

32. Arbitration #19 transcript, 27 February 1950, 31, 33.

33. Ibid., 33.

34. Henderson/584, 26 April 1950.

35. Henderson/584, 24 August 1950.

36. Local 584 Master Grievance List, #127 and #128.

37. Henderson/584, 10 October 1951.

38. Henderson/584, 26 September 1951, 10 October 1951.

39. Henderson/584, 10 October 1951.

40. Testimony by TWUA representative Toby Mendes, Arbitration #8 transcript, 9 November 1945, 39; "Harriet Mill Grievances," #144, 11 April 1944.

41. Frankel, "Women, Paternalism, and Protest," 111.

42. Henderson/584, 27 October 1948; Hall et al., *Like a Family*, 282.

43. Jones and Adams interviews.

44. Henderson/584, 13 November 1957; Harriet/578 transcripts, 26 January 1955.

45. Arbitration #4 transcript, 20 March 1944, 69–70.

46. "Harriet Mill Grievances," #8, 16 July 1943.

47. Arbitration #8 transcript, 9 November 1945, 39, 40, 42.

48. Ibid., 42. Bartholomew lost his job.

49. Harriet/578, 17 November 1948. On the day that this case was to be arbitrated, the company agreed to reinstate Betts with full seniority but with no back pay for the nearly four months she had been without work.

50. Henderson/584, 8 November 1950.

51. Ibid.

52. CR, 17 March 1954.

53. Harriet/578, 26 January 1955.

54. Harriet/578, 15 September 1954.

55. Harriet/578, 2 August 1956. At this time the company offered no health insurance to its production workers.

56. Harriet/578, 15 September 1954.

57. A few workers who received warnings in this wave did not file grievances. "Maybe they felt theirs was justifiable," explained TWUA representative Julius Fry. See Harriet/578, 12 October 1954.

58. Harriet/578, 12 October 1954.

59. Ibid.

60. CR, 21 July 1954.

61. Harriet/578, 8 September 1955.

62. Ibid.

63. Harriet/578, 20 June 1956.

64. Ibid.

65. Ibid. This warning was upheld by Proctor but was later removed by John D. Cooper.

66. Ibid.

67. Harriet/578, 20 November 1957.

68. Robert Wettach, "Arbitrator's Award," 21 April 1958; memo from J. D. Cooper to Farmer and Proctor, 2 May 1958. Both documents are in the Arbitration 34 folder.

Chapter 5

1. At least 220 formal grievances relating to workloads were filed during the union years. See the Master List of Grievances for both Locals 578 and 584 in CR. The three-fourths estimate can be found in the Arbitration #25 transcript, 11–12 February 1954, 54.

2. CR, 21 July 1943.

3. Arbitration #14 transcript, 15 June 1948, 10; Cooper interview; Blicksilver, *Cotton Manufacturing*, 151–56. See also Lichtenstein, *Labor's War at Home*, 111.

4. The quote is from Blicksilver, *Cotton Manufacturing*, 156. The statistics are from the testimony of Solomon Barkin, director of research, TWUA-CIO, in U.S. Senate Committee on Labor and Public Welfare, *Labor-Management Relations in the Southern Textile Manufacturing Industry, Part 2*, 85.

5. Harriet/578, 15 March 1949.

6. CR, 21 March, 18 April 1945.

7. CR, 21 March, 18 April 1945, 20 March, 17 April, 18 December 1946; Blicksilver, *Cotton Manufacturing*, 162.

8. *N&O*, 17 August 1949; Blicksilver, *Cotton Manufacturing*, 156.

9. CR, 19 January 1949; memo dated 2 September 1949 in the Arbitration #17 folder.

10. *N&O*, 24 August 1947.

11. *N&O*, 19 June 1949.

12. Blicksilver, *Cotton Manufacturing*, 158–60; "Address of Hearne Swink," 5; "Address of Halbert M. Jones," Third Annual Meeting of Cotton Buyers and Classers, Asheville, N.C., 31 May 1957, NCTMA; testimony of Solomon Barkin, director of research, TWUA-CIO, in U.S. Senate Committee on Labor and Public Welfare, *Causes of Unemployment*, 375–76.

13. Blicksilver, *Cotton Manufacturing*, 158–60; testimony of Solomon Barkin in U.S. Senate Committee on Labor and Public Welfare, *Causes of Unemployment*, 378, 401–2; "Address of Halbert M. Jones," NCTMA.

14. Tire cords and bags accounted for 1 million of the 1.3 million drop in bales of cotton used by industries after 1947. See Blicksilver, *Cotton Manufacturing*, 158–59.

15. Harriet/578, 15 March 1949.

16. Henderson/584, 26 May 1949.

17. Arbitration #17 folder. The union's strategy in this case will be discussed in Chapter 7.

18. CR, 21 March, 17 October, 21 December 1951, 16 January, 19 March, 16 July 1952; Blicksilver, *Cotton Manufacturing*, 166.

19. CR, 17 January, 21 March, 18 July, 17 October 1951; 19 March, 16 July, 15 October 1952.

20. *N&O*, 2, 19 July 1950. See also Gilman, *Human Relations in the Industrial Southeast*, 100, and Blicksilver, *Cotton Manufacturing*, 156.

21. Henderson/584, 11 March 1953; Blicksilver, *Cotton Manufacturing*, 160–61. Harriet and Henderson eliminated cloth production several years later.

22. Henderson/584, 11 March 1953.

23. John Abersold, "Arbitration #26 Award," 22 August 1954; memo regarding payment, 3 September 1954, in Arbitration #26 folder.

24. CR, 15 April 1953.

25. On rare occasions, awards were significantly larger. In the Henderson Mill case described above, the company won seven of the eleven workload grievances, but one group of hands won their case and split $28,000 in retroactive pay, which was by far the largest settlement in this company's arbitration history. That payment, however, completed an investment of over $2 million in renovations. See Arbitration #25 folder and Jackson interview.

26. CR, 21 October, 15 December 1953, 20 January, 17 March, 21 July 1954, 16 March 1955. See also Blicksilver, *Cotton Manufacturing*, 159.

27. Blicksilver, *Cotton Manufacturing*, 161–62. See also "Address of Halbert M. Jones," NCTMA.

28. Gilman, *Human Relations in the Industrial Southeast*, 95, 98, 100; "Ad-

dress of Hearne Swink," 6. Gilman concluded that the textile industry was "the only major employer of industrial labor that continues to sell its product in what can be regarded as a freely competitive market" (94).

29. Quote is from Gilman, *Human Relations in the Industrial Southeast*, 100; Blicksilver, *Cotton Manufacturing*, 156–57; testimony of Boyd Payton, southern director, TWUA, in U.S. Senate Committee on Interstate and Foreign Commerce, *Problems of the Domestic Textile Industry*, 1065.

30. See testimony of Julius Fry (misspelled as "Frye") in U.S. Senate Committee on Interstate and Foreign Commerce, *Problems of the Domestic Textile Industry*, 1099. For mill earnings see Appendix C.

31. "Address of Hearne Swink," 4, NCTMA; "Address of Halbert M. Jones," NCTMA; Blicksilver, *Cotton Manufacturing*, 148. The quote is by Jones, who continued: "Good cotton buying, classing, and receiving cannot guarantee textile mill profitability, but it can greatly assist. Poor buying can bankrupt a textile firm and offset all other advantages which that firm may have."

32. These were "voluntary" limits set by Japan in 1956 under threat of restrictive legislation.

33. See Gilman, *Human Relations in the Industrial Southeast*, 94.

34. Attorney Bennett Perry, Harriet/578, 27 September 1951; see also Gilman, *Human Relations in the Industrial Southeast*, 100.

35. CR, 17 March 1954.

36. CR, 21 March, 20 January 1954, 16 March 1955.

37. CR, 20 October 1954.

38. The specific proposals and the strike will be discussed in Chapter 7.

39. CR, 16 March 1955.

40. Troy, "Growth of Union Membership in the South," 412. North Carolina ranked dead last among southern states in its percentage of unionized nonagricultural employees—8.3 percent in 1953. In 1953 the TWUA-CIO had 7,300 members in North Carolina, compared to the TWUA-AFL's 5,600.

41. Solomon Barkin testimony, U.S. Senate Committee on Labor and Public Welfare, *Labor-Management Relations in the Southern Textile Manufacturing Industry, Part 2*, 86–87; Table 3, appendix to testimony by Boyd Payton, southern director, TWUA, AFL-CIO, in U.S. Senate Committee on Interstate and Foreign Commerce, *Problems of the Domestic Textile Industry*, 1073; Emil Rieve, general president, Textile Workers Union of American, CIO, testimony in U.S. Senate Committee on Labor and Public Welfare, *Labor-Management Relations in the Southern Textile Manufacturing Industry*, 356, 362. According to Rieve, from 1948 to 1950 the TWUA-CIO lost 30,000 southern members. Also see Griffith, *Crisis of American Labor*, for an analysis of the CIO's postwar failure to organize the southern cotton industry. The forty-two largest southern cotton-mill corporations each employed more than 3,000 people, which excluded the Harriet and Henderson Mills from this group. With the exception of the Dan River Mill and its 12,500 employees, however, the Harriet and Henderson Mills were each about the same size as the average individual plant belonging to any of the conglomerates.

42. Arbitration #28 folder; Arbitration #29 transcript, 20 October 1955, 40–41.

43. The awards were made on 20 and 21 December 1955.

44. See Appendix C for profitability; CR, 17 October 1956, 16 January 1957.

45. See Blicksilver, *Cotton Manufacturing*, 157. Mill activity dropped 4.2 percent in 1956 and 7.2 percent in 1957; "Address of Halbert M. Jones," NCTMA; testimony of Boyd Payton, U.S. Senate Committee on Interstate and Foreign Commerce, *Problems of the Domestic Textile Industry*, 1064–65, 1077; testimony of Solomon Barkin, U.S. Senate Committee on Labor and Public Welfare, *Causes of Unemployment*, 363, 366.

46. CR, 18 July, 17 September 1956. The Harriet and Henderson Mills appear to have had more modern equipment than many of their competitors. In 1958, 59 percent of textile machinery in the United States was over thirteen years old. See "Harriet-Henderson Cotton Mills—and Modernization," 23–35; and Blicksilver, *Cotton Manufacturing*, 163–64.

47. CR, 17 October 1956.

48. CR, 16, 19 March 1958.

49. "Address of Halbert M. Jones," NCTMA.

50. The quote is from Blicksilver, *Cotton Manufacturing*, 157–58. Boyd Payton testimony in U.S. Senate Committee on Interstate and Foreign Commerce, *Problems of the Domestic Textile Industry*, 1071; "Cotton Textile Industry Enters Tight Squeeze," *HDD*, 1 January 1958.

51. CR, 17 September 1956; for income and profit statistics, see Appendix C.

52. CR, 19 March 1958.

53. Arbitration #13 transcript, 14 August 1947, 22; Julius Fry testimony and Boyd Payton testimony in U.S. Senate Committee on Interstate and Foreign Commerce, *Problems of the Domestic Textile Industry*, 1099, 1064–65. Average textile wages in the South were slightly less, roughly $1.40 per hour. Wages in all cotton mills still lagged far behind the national manufacturing average, which had risen to $2.06 per hour. During 1950–58, while average textile wages increased $26\frac{1}{2}$ cents per hour, the average wage for employees at General Motors increased 89.6 cents per hour; for those at United States Steel, $1.054 per hour; and for those at General Electric, 86.3 cents per hour.

54. Harriet/578, 27 September 1951.

55. For an expanded discussion of these points, see Clark, "The TWUA in a Southern Mill Town," 206–21.

56. Wilkins interview.

57. See Braverman, *Labor and Monopoly Capital*, 107; Daniel Bell, *The End of Ideology*, 270; and Lichtenstein, *Labor's War at Home*, 137.

58. Bennett Perry, Arbitration #12 transcript, 21 January 1947, 18.

59. Ibid., 15. The company had defended sub-peg-point hourly wage for some spinners as long as the average for all spinners equaled the peg point.

60. Henderson/584, 5 November 1953.

61. See, for example, Harriet/578, 18 August 1948.

62. Henderson/584, 14 August 1957.

63. See Appendix C.

Chapter 6

1. Arbitration #2 transcript, 17 November 1943, 21; Arbitration #4 transcript, 20 March 1944, 7.

2. From Arbitration #4 transcript, 20 March 1944: Fuller, 37; Pulley, 5; Vann, 8. Bobbins of roving came from the card room to be spun into yarn. The last bit of roving on an empty bobbin had to be ripped, or "wrung off," before a full bobbin of roving could be installed.

3. Arbitration #6 transcript, 1 November 1944, 19, 23–24, 38, 40, 41.

4. Local 584 Master Grievance List, #102; Henderson/584, 15 March, 26 May 1949.

5. Arbitration #25 transcript, 11–12 February 1954, 15. Different sizes of roving were delivered to the appropriate spinning frames, depending on the coarseness of the yarn to be produced.

6. Ibid., 19.

7. Harriet/578, 20 January 1954.

8. Arbitration #26 transcript, 14 May 1954, 50.

9. Harriet/578, 10 June 1954.

10. Harriet/578, 8 November 1954, 19 January 1955.

11. Lissie Harris, Arbitration #3 transcript, 19 January 1944, 11; Pulley, Arbitration #4 transcript, 20 March 1944, 2–4; South, Arbitration #25 transcript, 11–12 February 1954, 15; Harriet/578, 20 January 1954; Arbitration #26 transcript, 14 May 1954, 45.

12. Arbitration #4 transcript, 20 March 1944, 23, 19.

13. Camp interview. At Harriet and Henderson, Camp officially worked under Carl Page, who did not have comparable training.

14. Cooper interview.

15. Arbitration #9 transcript, 22 May 1946, 51; Camp interview.

16. Samuel Yulke, Arbitration #20 transcript, 19 July 1950, 42.

17. Camp interview. The sixty-eight-unit standard was first mentioned in Arbitration #13 transcript, 14 August 1947, 64, 84.

18. Arbitration #2 transcript, 17 November 1943, 22.

19. Arbitration #3 transcript, 19 January 1944, 1–2.

20. Ibid., 14.

21. Arbitration #4 transcript, 20 March 1944, 14, 21.

22. Arbitration #13 transcript, 14 August 1947, 13.

23. Ibid., 64.

24. Braswell (1984) interview.

25. Arbitration #4, transcript of second hearing, 22 March 1944.

26. Ibid.

27. Arbitration #26 transcript, 14 May 1954, 77–78.

28. Carson, "Rating Time Studies," 57.

29. Henderson/584, 11 March 1953.

30. Union Brief, Arbitration #26, May 1954, 16.

31. CR, 17 March 1954.

32. "Address of Halbert M. Jones," Third Annual Meeting of Cotton Buyers and

Classers, Asheville, N.C., 31 May 1957, NCTMA; News Release from North Carolina Cotton Quality Improvement Committee, 1 October 1954, NCTMA; Blicksilver, *Cotton Manufacturing*, 157.

33. Arbitration #6 transcript, 1 November 1944, 11.

34. Arbitration #13 transcript, 14 August 1947, 51, 58.

35. Harriet/578, 7 August 1957.

36. Arbitration #26 transcript, 14 May 1954, 36–38, 43, 47–49; Arbitration #25 transcript, 11–12 February 1954, 28–29.

37. Arbitration #3 transcript, 19 January 1944, 8, 15.

38. Arbitration #3 transcript, 19 January 1944, 8; Henderson/584, 28 August 1957.

39. Arbitration #26 transcript, 14 May 1954, 140–41.

40. Ibid., 46.

41. Arbitration #6 transcript, 1 November 1944, 28.

42. Arbitration #9 transcript, 22 May 1946, 52.

43. Ibid., 53.

44. See Arbitration #2 transcript, 17 November 1943, 20.

45. Arbitration #7 transcript, 30 May 1945, 23.

46. Henderson/584, 26 August, 29 September 1948.

47. Arbitration #14 transcript, 15 June 1948, 5.

48. Arbitration #4 transcript, 20 March 1944, 34.

49. Henderson/584, 26 April 1950.

50. Arbitration #13 transcript, 14 August 1947, 27.

51. Arbitration #23 transcript, 6 May 1952, 7.

52. Richard Lester, Arbitration #4 Award, 7 July 1944.

53. Arbitration #20 transcript, 19 July 1950, 6.

54. Arbitration #26 transcript, 14 May 1954, 78.

55. Arbitration #23 transcript, 6 May 1952, 3; Arbitration #26 transcript, 14 May 1954, 78.

56. See Carson, "Rating Time Studies," 57.

57. Harriet/578, 20 January 1954.

58. Harriet/578, 18 April 1956.

Chapter 7

1. See the section entitled "Education and Training of Arbitrators," and survey results, in McKelvey, *The Profession of Labor Arbitration*, 170–75, 178–79. In 1952 most arbitrators received a standard rate of $100 per day; see also Larkin, "Introduction," ix.

2. Copelof, *Management-Union Arbitration*, xiii; see also Arbitration #13 file, 14 September 1947.

3. See Larkin, "Introduction," viii–xiii; see also Alexander, "Evaluation of Arbitrators," 97.

4. Alexander, "Evaluation of Arbitrators," 96–98; McKelvey, *Management Rights and the Arbitration Process*, Appendix E, 231–32; Braden, "Policy and Practice of American Arbitration Association," 92.

5. Alexander, "Evaluation of Arbitrators," 95–99.

6. Arbitration #3 Award, 19 February 1944.

7. Arbitration #6 Award. The hearing was on 1 November 1944.

8. Arbitration #9 Award, 17 June 1946.

9. Letter from Cole, of Cole, Merrill and Nadell, Att., Paterson, N.J., to Harriet and Henderson management, 5 November 1948, in Arbitration #14 folder. Cole later published his perspectives on labor arbitration, *The Quest for Industrial Peace*, which included a plea for fair play and commitment to the process by both sides.

10. See the Master Lists of Arbitration Cases for Harriet and Henderson Mills in CR.

11. Arbitration #4, transcript of second hearing, 22 March 1944.

12. Solomon Barkin testimony, in U.S. Senate Committee on Labor and Public Welfare, *Labor-Management Relations in the Southern Textile Manufacturing Industry, Part 2*, 40–41. The *Whitin Review* article, "Harriet-Henderson Cotton Mills—and Modernization," was inserted, unattributed, by Barkin in U.S. Senate Committee on Labor and Public Welfare, *Causes of Unemployment*.

13. Arbitration #4 transcript, 20 March 1944, 25.

14. After 1944 the company no longer allowed TWUA engineers inside the mills to study jobs. See Arbitration #14 transcript, 15 June 1948, 14.

15. Arbitration #4 transcript, 20 March 1944.

16. Arbitration #14 transcript, 15 June 1948, 3, 13; Union Brief, Arbitration #14, 15 June 1948.

17. Letter from David Cole to both the TWUA and the company, 7 January 1949, in Arbitration #14 folder.

18. List of demands, Arbitration #17, 12 September 1949.

19. Stipulation, dated 12 September 1949, in Arbitration #17 folder.

20. Harriet/578, 23 March 1950; Arbitration #20 transcript, 19 July 1950, 1.

21. Barkin, *Textile Workers' Job Primer*, 11.

22. Ibid., 44.

23. Arbitration #25 transcript, 11–12 February 1954, 24; Union Brief, Arbitration #25, 3.

24. Company Brief, Arbitration #25, 25.

25. Adam Abruzzi, Arbitration #25 Award, 21 April 1954.

26. Ibid.; Jackson interview.

27. John Abersold, Arbitration #26 Award, 22 August 1954, 11, 20.

28. Harriet/578, 8 November 1954.

29. Henderson/584, 12 May 1954.

30. Arbitration #28 transcript, 21–22 September 1955, 5.

31. Arbitration #25 transcript, 11–12 February 1954, 50; *HDD*, 15 November 1954.

32. *HDD*, 17 November, 3, 23 December 1954.

33. CR, 19 January 1955; *HDD*, 31 December 1954; "Agreement Between Henderson Cotton Mills and Textile Workers Union of America (C.I.O.)," 3 January 1955, CR.

34. The quote is in CR, 19 January 1955; Harriet/578, 19 January 1955.

35. Harriet/578, 4 May 1955; Henderson/584, 12, 27 January 1955; Arbitration #28 transcript, 21–22 September 1955, 164–65.

36. Harriet/578, 4 May 1955.

37. Harriet/578, 3 August 1955.

38. Harriet/578, 4 May, 8 June 1955; CR, 16 March 1955.

39. Letter from Constangy to Carl Page, 27 July 1949; memo from Page to John D. Cooper Jr., 4 August 1947; and letter from Page to Constangy, 30 August 1949, in Arbitration #17 folder; Fry and Jackson interviews.

40. Testimony of William Shiflett and Emil Rieve, U.S. Senate Committee on Labor and Public Welfare, *Labor-Management Relations in the Southern Textile Manufacturing Industry*, 221, 359–60.

41. Arbitration #28 transcript, 21–22 September 1955, 35, 96, 38; memo from Page to company attorneys, 15 August 1955, Arbitration #28 folder.

42. Arbitration #28 transcript, 21–22 September 1955, 10, 12–13, 17.

43. Ibid., 17; Henderson/584, 13 April 1955.

44. Arbitration #28 transcript, 21–22 September 1955, 50.

45. Harriet/578, 19 January 1955, 8 November 1954.

46. Harriet/578, 8 November 1954.

47. Arbitration #28 transcript, 21–22 September 1955, 19, 23.

48. Ibid., 20.

49. Ibid., 24.

50. Henderson/584, 13, 27 April 1955; Arbitration #28 transcript, 21–22 September 1955, 32, 46.

51. Arbitration #28 transcript, 21–22 September 1955, 44.

52. Henderson/584, 13 April 1955.

53. Ibid.

54. Arbitration #28 transcript, 21–22 September 1955, 93.

55. Ibid., 67, 82, 78, 79.

56. Company Brief, Arbitration #28, 1–2, 13.

57. CR, 19 March 1958; Cooper interview.

58. Adam Abruzzi, Arbitration #28 Award, 14. Considering that Abruzzi had recently decided a major grievance in favor of the union, as discussed above, it may seem surprising that Harriet and Henderson officials allowed him to hear this case. They could have rejected him, but they recalled that in that earlier arbitration, Abruzzi had decided seven of eleven individual grievances against the union. Even Frank Constangy, the noted antilabor attorney who advised company officials, described the company's previous experience with Abruzzi as "much more favorable than would appear at first glance." See letter from Constangy to Carl Page, 5 May 1954, in Arbitration #25 folder.

59. See letter from Constangy to Carl Page, 3 January 1956, in Arbitration #28 folder. Constangy also emphasized, positively, Abruzzi's decision on the issue of roving carts.

60. See Abruzzi's *Work Measurement* and *Work, Workers, and Work Measurement*, quote on 57; and Daniel Bell's *The End of Ideology*, chap. 11, "Work and Its Discontents," especially 241–42.

61. See Seitz, "How Arbitrators Decide Cases: A Study in Black Magic," in Kahn, *Collective Bargaining and the Arbitrator's Role*, 159–64.

62. In most parts of the United States in the mid-1950s, arbitration awards were not legally binding, although several federal courts had begun to enforce them under Section 301 of the 1947 Taft-Hartley Act. See Braden, "Policy and Practice of American Arbitration Association," 90.

63. Harriet/578, 21 March 1956, 16 July 1958; Henderson/584, 28 August 1957.

64. Transcript of private management meeting, Harriet/578, 3 September 1957.

65. Harriet/578, 7 August 1957; transcript of private management meeting, Harriet/578, 3 September 1957.

66. Memo by John D. Cooper Jr., 2 May 1958, in Arbitration #34 folder.

67. Harriet/578, 4 March 1958.

68. Section 5(b), in contract signed 3 January 1955.

69. See letter from Constangy to Carl Page, 5 May 1954, in Arbitration #25 folder.

70. Harriet/578, 20 April 1956.

71. Memo from John D. Cooper to J. C. Proctor, 11 August 1958, in Harriet/578; Harriet/578, 13 August 1958.

72. Harriet/578, 3 September 1958.

73. CR, 15 October 1958.

74. Text of letter from Luther Jackson and Local 578 president Charlie Ranes to Henderson mayor Carroll Singleton, reprinted in *HDD*, 8 November 1958; letter from Julius Fry to John D. Cooper Jr., 20 October 1958, SLA.

75. *HDD*, 8 November 1958.

76. "Union Statement and Proposal to the Company at Beginning of Bargaining Session on Wednesday, November 12, 1958," SLA.

77. See Harriet/578, 3 September 1958. Nelson Lichtenstein identifies this divisive potential in *Labor's War at Home*, 15.

78. Braswell (1984) interview; *HDD*, 30 November 1958.

79. "Union Statement and Proposal to the Company at Beginning of Bargaining Session on Wednesday, November 12, 1958," SLA; and reply from Cooper to union negotiators, 13 November 1958, SLA.

Chapter 8

1. Testimony of Emil Rieve, U.S. Senate Committee on Labor and Public Welfare, *Labor-Management Relations in the Southern Textile Manufacturing Industry*, 359–60. See also the testimony of TWUA attorney Robert Strange Cahoon, in ibid., 321–23; and Griffith, *Crisis of American Labor*, especially 88–105.

2. Correspondence from Keir Jorgensen, research director, Amalgamated Clothing and Textile Workers Union, New York, to Daniel Clark, 16 July 1991; Troy, "Growth of Union Membership in the South," 50.

3. Table No. 6, in "Appendix to Testimony of Boyd Payton," U.S. Senate Committee on Interstate and Foreign Commerce, *Problems of the Domestic Textile*

Industry, 1077; correspondence from Keir Jorgensen to Daniel Clark, 16 July 1991. During the same period, twenty-six nonunion mills closed.

4. Testimony of Emil Rieve, U.S. Senate Committee on Labor and Public Welfare, *Labor-Management Relations in the Southern Textile Manufacturing Industry*, 356.

5. NCTMA, particularly Boxes 3 and 13.

6. Wilkins interview.

7. Roberson, Jackson, and Adams interviews.

8. Bass and DeVries, *Transformation of Southern Politics*, 228–29.

9. Cooper, Jackson, and Wester interviews.

10. Jackson and Adams interviews. See *HDD*, 31 March 1951 through 7 May 1951, and *N&O*, 31 March 1951 through 9 May 1951, for coverage of the TWUA's largely unsuccessful strike.

11. Jackson, Braswell (1991), Roberson, and Adams interviews.

12. Braswell (1991) interview; *Henderson City Directory, 1959–60*, 348–49. In 1958, Henderson's twelve thousand residents were served by eighty-nine grocery stores, most of which were still small, family-owned operations. The number of grocery stores in Henderson had peaked at one hundred in 1951.

13. Jackson, Littleton, and Braswell (1991) interviews.

14. All vote totals can be found in the clerk of the court's office, Henderson, North Carolina. Until 1950, residents of North Henderson, which included the Henderson Mill village, were part of the "East Henderson" voting district. Residents of South Henderson, which included the Harriet Mill village, were part of the "South Henderson #1" district. Mill workers and their voting-age family members were the dominant majority in these two districts, but because not all voters in these districts were mill workers, vote totals do not give an exact indication of union members' preferences.

15. Because Vance County, like most of the South at this time, was virtually a one-party state, voter turnout for primaries gives the most accurate indication of participation. As of 1950, in Vance County there were 7,990 registered Democrats, 65 Republicans, 2 Independents, and 9 who listed no affiliation. Except for general elections that featured presidential races, very few voters bothered to go to the polls after the primaries.

16. East Henderson (Henderson Mill) totaled 406 for Hoey, 120 for others; South Henderson #1 (Harriet Mill) showed 144 for Hoey, 83 for others; relatively wealthy West Henderson had 446 votes for Hoey, 98 for others. See Vance County Voting Records.

17. Ibid.

18. Ibid.

19. See Bass and DeVries, *Transformation of Southern Politics*, 218–21; Ashby, *Frank Porter Graham*, 224–25, 257–58, 264; and Pleasants and Burns, *Frank Porter Graham*.

20. In wealthy West Henderson, voter participation jumped from 751 in 1948 to 1,185 in 1950. A plurality of 547 backed Smith; there were 502 votes for Graham and 131 for Reynolds. This was the first time since unionization that the mill vil-

lagers and the town's elite differed in a U.S. Senate primary. The 1950 race saw the largest voter turnout in North Carolina history. See Ashby, *Frank Porter Graham*, 263.

21. *HDD*, 25 May 1950. In Henderson's wealthiest district, Smith dominated Graham in the second primary, 592–380.

22. *HDD*, 1, 18 May 1950.

23. Bass and DeVries, *Transformation of Southern Politics*, 219; Ashby, *Frank Porter Graham*, 258; Pleasants and Burns, *Frank Porter Graham*, 92, 268.

24. Littleton interview; Vance County Voting Records. South Henderson voters gave Hight only a modest majority, 284–261.

25. Wright, *Old South, New South*, 239–57; Cobb, *Selling of the South*, 115–19; Daniel, *Breaking the Land*, 260–66.

26. *HDD*, 20 October 1958.

27. *HDD*, 28 August 1958.

28. *HDD*, 12 February, 12 July, 16 August, 23 September 1958; Daniel, *Breaking the Land*, 262.

29. Blicksilver, *Cotton Manufacturing*, 157; *HDD*, 14 October 1950, 1 January, 29 July, 16 August 1958.

30. *HDD*, 2 January, 1, 11 February, 11, 29 March, 8 April, 1 May, 1 October 1958.

31. *HDD*, 6 November 1950, 2 January 1953, 31 January 1955.

32. Blackburn, *Heritage of Vance County*, 56–57; *HDD*, 20 October 1955; Wester interview. By the 1980s, Rose's was Henderson's largest employer.

33. Blackburn, *Heritage of Vance County*, 57; *HDD*, 1, 25 July, 22 August, 30 September 1958.

34. Blackburn, *Heritage of Vance County*, 48–49, 62; Wester interview; *HDD*, 2 January 1958. Carolina Bagging, founded in 1908, was once the world's largest producer of jute bagging for cotton bales. In 1956 it became part of Textron and shifted to the production of synthetics.

35. Braswell (1991) and Jackson interviews; *HDD*, 13 November 1958.

36. There is no formal study of race relations or the civil rights movement in Henderson. Michael Myerson discusses black student protests in Henderson in 1970, led by Ben Chavis, in *Nothing Could Be Finer*, 57–60. Ruth Anita Hawkins Hughes's *Contributions of Vance County People of Color* contains numerous personality profiles and anecdotes and serves its purpose as a corrective to the domination of white personalities in Blackburn, *Heritage of Vance County*.

37. *HDD*, 1, 18 May 1950.

38. *HDD*, 28 April 1955.

39. *HDD*, 4 May 1955. In city elections, aldermen for each ward were elected by voters throughout the entire city; and given that whites comprised over 54 percent of the city's population, there was little chance for blacks to run successful campaigns even in wards with high concentrations of African Americans. Although mill villagers were ineligible to vote in city elections, it would clearly have been in their interest to support candidates who supported the rights of workers, but there is no evidence that this happened.

40. *HDD*, 11, 14 August 1958.

41. See Draper, *Conflict of Interests*, for an examination of racism among white southern union members.

42. *HDD*, 20 January 1959.

43. *HDD*, 19 April 1951, 19, 26 December 1958.

44. U.S. Census data; *HDD*, 27 April 1955, 10 March 1958.

45. Most construction in Henderson during the 1950s was for new homes. See *HDD*, 1 April 1950, 1 April 1955, 3 January, 3 February, 3 April, 1 May 1958.

46. Wester interview; *HDD*, 2 May 1955; Blackburn, *Heritage of Vance County*, 12–13.

47. State Employment Security Commission of North Carolina, Bureau of Research and Statistics, August 1948. According to the ESC, only 164 blacks were employed in the service sector in 1948.

48. See *Henderson City Directory* volumes for 1950–59, Vance County Public Library.

49. *HDD*, 19, 24 March, 30 May 1955; Blackburn, *Heritage of Vance County*, 48. Other significant new businesses begun during the 1950s included an oil company (1952), a dairy (1952), a farm equipment dealer (1953), and a tire recapping service (1956).

50. Braswell (1991), Jackson, Roberson, and Adams interviews.

51. *HDD*, 10 January 1955.

52. *HDD*, 21 November 1958.

53. *HDD*, 2 May 1950, 10 May 1950 (quote).

54. Wester interview; *HDD*, 10 May, 16 November (quote), 27 November 1950.

55. *HDD*, 7 May 1951.

56. Cobb, *Selling of the South*, 50–54, 81; Luther Hodges, *Businessman in the Statehouse*, 57; *HDD*, 31 January 1955; Wester interview.

57. *Textile Bulletin* 64, no. 4 (15 April 1947): 47.

58. Luther Hodges, *Businessman in the Statehouse*, 57–62, 77; Cobb, *Selling of the South*, 73.

59. *HDD*, 21 July 1958.

60. *HDD*, 31 January 1955.

61. *HDD*, 13, 14 January, 24, 25 October 1955; Wester interview; Blackburn, *Heritage of Vance County*, 152. As of January 1955, Tillery's Commercial and Industrial Bank claimed resources of $1,104,317 versus Citizen's Bank's $15,003,242.

62. Wester interview.

63. Ibid.; *HDD*, 13 January 1955, 12 February 1958; Blackburn, *Heritage of Vance County*, 158, 166, 216–17, 261, 264, 271–72, 279, 285–86, 329, 384. In addition to Cooper, three Citizen's Bank directors were also directors at the Harriet and Henderson Cotton Mills.

64. Wester interview.

65. Cobb, *Selling of the South*, 85–87.

66. Wester interview; Braswell (1991) interview; *HDD*, 6 January, 20, 22 March 1955. North Henderson (Henderson Mill) opposed annexation by a vote of 276–268. South Henderson (Harriet Mill) voted against, 248–172.

67. *HDD*, 5 February 1955.

68. *HDD*, 20 March, 29 April, 4, 19 May 1955. Most mill workers, of course, lived outside the city limits and were ineligible to vote in this election.

69. *HDD*, 22 June 1955.

70. Wester interview; *HDD*, 16 June (quote), 21, 22 June 1955; CR, 28 June 1955, 3 March 1956.

71. *HDD*, 1 January, 12 February, 8, 15 March 1958.

72. *HDD*, 6, 9 November 1950, 2 January 1953, 31 January 1955, 9 September 1958; Blackburn, *Heritage of Vance County*, 163.

73. Wester interview; Cobb, *Selling of the South*, 85, 91, 98, 120. Also see U.S. Senate Committee on Labor and Public Welfare, *Labor-Management Relations in the Southern Textile Manufacturing Industry, Part 2*, 5.

74. *HDD*, 8, 10, 12, 14 March 1958; Wester interview. The investors would receive no share of the new company and would not be eligible for any type of dividend. Their return would be the enhanced prosperity of the community.

75. *HDD*, 15, 20, 24, 25, 26, 31 March 1958.

76. *HDD*, 29, 31 March, 1, 18, 22 July 1958; Wester interview. The largest single contribution was for $6,000.

77. *HDD*, 23 July 1958.

78. *HDD*, 11 September, 2 October 1958.

79. *HDD*, 30 October 1958.

80. *HDD*, 1, 27 October 1958.

81. *HDD*, 6 November 1958.

82. *HDD*, 29 March, 21 July, 18 November 1958; Wester interview.

Chapter 9

1. Roberson, Jackson, and Wilkins interviews.

2. Forsythe interview.

3. Adams interview.

4. "Union Statement and Proposal to the Company at Beginning of Bargaining Session on Wednesday, November 12, 1958," SLA; and Reply from Cooper to Union Negotiators, 13 November 1958, SLA.

5. Memo from William Pollock to TWUA secretary-treasurer John Chupka, 5 November 1958, SLA.

6. Wilkins, Roberson, Jackson, Carter, Adams, and Braswell (1984) interviews.

7. *HDD*, 2, 12 December 1958; Fry interview.

8. Jackson, Adams, Braswell (1984), and Roberson interviews. Weekly allocations from the international TWUA can be found in SLA.

9. *HDD*, 17 November 1958.

10. *HDD*, 18, 22 November, 10, 11 December 1958.

11. *HDD*, 6 November, 9 December 1958.

12. *HDD*, 11 December 1958.

13. *HDD*, 26, 30 December 1958, 10, 21 January 1959.

14. CR, 21 January 1959.

15. *HDD*, 20 January 1959.

16. Wilkins interview.

17. Braswell (1984), Jackson, and Carter interviews; *HDD*, 9 February 1959; *N&O*, 10 February 1959.

18. Copies of the temporary restraining order, dated 13 February 1959, can be found in LHH. Judge Bickett made the order permanent on 5 March 1959.

19. *HDD*, 12 February 1959.

20. Telegram from C. C. Harris and E. A. Cottrell to Luther Hodges, 14 February 1959, LHH; *HDD*, 16 February 1959; *N&O*, 16 February 1959.

21. *HDD*, 16 February 1959.

22. *N&O*, 17 February 1959.

23. Millis and Brown, *From the Wagner Act to Taft-Hartley*, 201–2.

24. Montgomery, *Workers' Control in America*, 158–60; Lichtenstein, *Labor's War at Home*, 238–41; Forbath, *Law and the Shaping of the American Labor Movement*, 193–98.

25. U.S. Senate Committee on Labor and Public Welfare, *Labor-Management Relations in the Southern Textile Manufacturing Industry*, 325–26.

26. Fry interview.

27. *N&O*, 23 March 1959. More biographical data can be found in SLA.

28. *N&O*, 17 February 1959.

29. Braswell (1984) interview.

30. Wilkins interview; *HDD*, 16 February 1959.

31. *HDD*, 16, 17 February 1959.

32. Ibid.

33. See petition dated 23 April 1959, LHH; and letter from Earline Collins, Florence Huffman, Mary E. Powell and Edith B. South to Governor Hodges, 22 April 1959, LHH.

34. Carter interview.

35. *HDD*, 20 February 1959; Roberson interview.

36. *HDD*, 23 February 1959; *N&O*, 24 February 1959.

37. *HDD*, 18 February 1959; *N&O*, 19 February 1959.

38. *HDD*, 20 February 1959.

39. *HDD*, 24 February 1959.

40. Memo from John D. Cooper, 20 February 1959, "To All Employees of the Harriet and Henderson Cotton Mills Who Have Not Yet Returned to Work," LHH.

41. Letter from Harriet and Henderson Cotton Mills to the Union Locals, 12 March 1959, SLA. The statement was issued on 25 February 1959.

42. *HDD*, 24 February 1959.

43. Telegram, Payton to Hodges, 5 March 1959, LHH.

44. Telegram, Scheidt to Payton, 5 March 1959, LHH.

45. Telegram, Payton to Hodges, 6 March 1959, LHH.

46. *N&O*, 10 March 1959.

47. Letter from William F. Womble to Hodges, 7 March 1959, LHH. Womble's salutation was "Dear Gov."

48. Memo, Giles to Hodges, 3 March 1959, LHH.

49. Ibid.

50. *HDD*, 27 February 1959; *N&O*, 1 March 1959. A memo entitled "Summary of Violence in the Strike-Bound Mill Area of Henderson-Vance, 16 February 1959 through 8 May 1959," produced by the State Highway Patrol, 18 May 1959, LHH, details the severity of the blasts.

51. Confidential Memo from Agent C. M. Horton to Director, Special Investigation, Harriet-Henderson Mill Strike, Henderson, N.C., 19 March 1959, LHH.

52. Letter, Hodges to R. Graham Dozier, Executive Vice President, Rocky Mount, N.C., Chamber of Commerce, 13 April 1959, LHH. Between five and fifteen SBI agents were in Henderson at any time during the strike.

53. Roberson and Jackson interviews.

54. "Summary of Violence."

55. Letter, Mrs. Odell Cottrell to Governor Hodges, 23 March 1959, LHH.

56. Letter, Jeannette Bachman to Hodges, 21 March 1959, LHH.

57. *N&O*, 24 February 1959.

58. *HDD*, 19 February 1959.

59. *HDD*, 17 December 1958, 30 January, 27 February 1959 (quote).

60. Letter, Agnes Barnett to Hodges, 3 March 1959, LHH.

61. Memo, Robert E. Giles to Hodges, 3 March 1959, LHH.

62. *HDD*, 25 February 1959; *N&O*, 26 February 1959.

63. Lieutenant Robert Chadwick's "Daily Reports" from the picket lines, 3 March 1959, LHH.

64. "Statement by Governor Luther H. Hodges," 21 March 1959, LHH; *N&O*, 3 March 1959; Chadwick's "Daily Reports," 2, 3 March 1959.

65. Chadwick's "Daily Reports," 11, 13 March 1959.

66. *N&O*, 3 March 1959.

67. Braswell (1984) and Jackson interviews.

68. "A Statement of Henderson Mill Strikers," 6 March 1959, LHH.

69. Chadwick's "Daily Reports," 4, 5 March 1959.

70. Ibid., 17 March 1959.

71. Ibid., 4, 5, 19 March, 9, 10 April 1959; "Summary of Violence"; Earline Collins Blue interview.

72. Jackson interview. Jackson mixes testaments, but his message is clear; Chadwick's "Daily Reports," 23 March 1959.

73. Chadwick's "Daily Reports," 12 March, 16 April 1959; *N&O*, 15 April 1959; Jackson and Braswell (1984) interviews. The police department had twenty-three regular officers—twenty-two men and one woman—seventeen of whom were regularly available for strike duty. They also hired ten special policemen, none of whom was in uniform. The sheriff's department consisted of Cottrell and three regular deputies, with ten special deputies hired for strike duty. See Chadwick's "Daily Reports," 10 April 1959. At least one police officer, Desk Sgt. P. L. (Buck) Ellis Jr., was satisfied with the use of state power to restrain strikers. See the letter from Ellis to Hodges, written sometime after 20 April, LHH.

74. Memo, SBI Director Malcolm Seawell to Hodges, 4 June 1959, LHH.

75. Chadwick's "Daily Reports," 17 March 1959; private memo, Luther Hodges, 15 April 1959, LHH.

76. Roberson interview.

77. Memo, Robert Giles to Hodges, 3 March 1959, LHH.

78. Transcript of telephone call, Hodges to John D. Cooper Jr., 12 March 1959, LHH.

79. *HDD*, 11 March 1959; *N&O*, 10 March 1959; Millis and Brown, *From the Wagner Act to Taft-Hartley*, 201–2.

80. For a discussion of the ineffectiveness of filing unfair labor charges with the NLRB, see James A. Hodges, *New Deal Labor Policy*, 191–98.

81. Transcript of telephone call, Hodges to Perry, 20 March 1959, LHH.

82. Memo, dated 19 March 1959, either by Robert Giles or Ed Rankin, summarizing a 12 March 1959 meeting with Hodges, LHH.

83. Ibid.

84. *HDD*, 3 March 1959.

85. Memo, dated 19 March 1959, summarizing a 16 March 1959 meeting with the governor, LHH.

86. Transcript of phone conversation between Luther Hodges and Carroll Singleton, 18 March 1959, LHH; Memo by Hodges, 20 March 1959, LHH.

87. *HDD*, 24 March 1959.

88. Fry interview.

89. Adams interview; "A Statement of Henderson Mill Strikers," 6 March 1959, LHH.

90. *N&O*, 4 March 1959.

91. Chadwick's "Daily Reports," 10 March 1959.

92. *N&O*, 16 March 1959; Jackson interview.

93. Chadwick's "Daily Reports," 16 March 1959.

94. Private memos by Hodges, 20, 23 March 1959, LHH.

95. *N&O*, 22 March 1959; Chadwick's "Daily Reports," 23 March 1959.

96. *N&O*, 21 March 1959; Luther Hodges, *Businessman in the Statehouse*, 228.

97. Private memos by Luther Hodges, 31 March, 2 April 1959, LHH.

98. *N&O*, 21 March 1959; transcript of Boyd Payton's radio address on WHVH, Henderson, 25 March 1959, LHH; Fry interview.

99. Letter from Whiteford Blakeney, of Blakeney and Alexander, Attorneys at Law, to Hodges, 22 March 1959, LHH. Enclosed in this correspondence was the proposed speech entitled "A Statement by the Governor of North Carolina with Respect to the Strike Situation at Henderson, North Carolina."

100. These identical phrases, and many other identical sentences, can be found in both Blakeney's suggested "Statement," dated 22 March 1959, and in a press release, dated 2 April 1959, from the governor's office, LHH.

101. Letter, Hodges to Dowd, 17 March 1959; letter, Hodges to Love, 14 May 1959; letter, Hodges to Dillard, of Dillard Paper Co., Greensboro, N.C., 23 April 1959; all in LHH.

102. See letters to Hodges from Ruffin, 16 March 1959; Cannon, 29 April 1959; Cone, 12 March 1959; Love, 11 May 1959; and Hanes, 11 March 1959, all in LHH.

103. Letter, Foil to Hodges, 22 March 1959, LHH. Also see the letter from Robert Tate to Hodges, 19 March 1959, LHH.

104. For example, see the letter from Stark Dillard to Hodges, 27 April 1959, LHH.

105. Letter, Hodges to Gilmore, 6 March 1959, LHH.

106. Letter, Rankin to Hodges, 14 August 1959, and letter, William Rorie Jr. to Hodges, 26 May 1959, both in LHH.

107. Letter, Giles to Hall, 28 May 1959, LHH. See also memo, 14 June 1959, Giles to Hodges, and letter, Robert Pace, editor of the *Durham Labor Journal*, to Hodges, 5 June 1959, both in LHH.

108. Personal memo by Hodges, 17 April 1959, LHH.

109. Memo, Rankin to Hodges, 6 March 1959, LHH. Morgan is profiled in Blackburn, *Heritage of Vance County*, 299.

110. Memo, Rankin to Hodges, 10 April 1959, LHH. Voit Gilmore is identified in Luther Hodges, *Businessman in the Statehouse*, 63.

111. Letter, Griffith of R. H. Griffith Yarns, Chattanooga, Tenn., to Hodges, 24 March 1959, LHH.

112. See CR, 22 July 1959.

113. *N&O*, 11 April 1959.

114. Chadwick's "Daily Reports," 10 April 1959.

115. *HDD*, 2, 6, 7 April 1959.

116. *HDD*, 4 April 1959; *N&O*, 4 April 1959.

117. *HDD*, 9 April 1959.

118. *HDD*, 3 April 1959.

119. *N&O*, 3 April 1959.

120. *N&O*, 16 April 1959; Chadwick's "Daily Reports," 5:30 P.M. Supplement Report, 15 April 1959; and Chadwick's "Daily Reports," 16 April 1959.

121. *N&O*, 17 April 1959.

122. Letter, Hodges to Cooper, 16 April 1959, LHH.

123. Transcript of phone call, Hodges to Payton, 16 April 1959, LHH.

124. Hodges, "Memorandum for the File," 17 April 1959, LHH.

125. Private memo, Luther Hodges, 16 April 1959, LHH.

126. Private memo by Hodges regarding meeting on 13 April 1959, written on 17 April 1959, LHH.

127. Memo entitled "Lack of Police Action on Part of Henderson Police, 15 April 1959, 16 April 1959," in Chadwick's "Daily Reports."

128. Private memo, Luther Hodges, 20 April 1959, LHH.

129. Ibid.

130. *HDD*, 18 April 1959; *N&O*, 18, 19 April 1959.

131. Private memo, Luther Hodges, 20 April 1959, LHH.

132. *HDD*, 18 April 1959; *N&O*, 18 April 1959; "Company's Counter-Proposal for Paragraph (r) under Section 8," 17 April 1959, LHH.

133. Wilkins, Adams, and Braswell (1984) interviews; *HDD*, 18 April 1959.

134. Wilkins interview.

135. The vote was 575–25, as reported in *N&O*, 20 April 1959.

136. Transcript of phone call, Hodges to Payton, 20 April 1959, LHH.

137. Telegram, John D. Cooper Jr. to Hodges, 23 April 1959, and private memo, Luther Hodges, 23 April 1959, both in LHH.

138. Fry interview. Fry hinted, without elaboration, that his relationship with Payton had been strained.

139. Memo by Hodges, 23 April 1959, LHH.

140. "Special Report," by Sergeant T. E. Cook, Highway Patrol, 20 April 1959, LHH.

141. Letter, S. T. Peace to Hodges, 20 April 1959, LHH.

142. Chadwick's "Daily Reports," 22, 23 April 1959; *N&O*, 21 April 1959; letter regarding flares, Carroll Singleton to Major General Robert Sink, 24 April 1959, LHH.

143. *N&O*, 26 April 1959.

144. "Statement by Governor Luther H. Hodges in Connection with the Henderson Strike Situation," 22 April 1959, LHH.

145. Telegrams, Cooper to Hodges, 23 April 1959, and Hodges to Cooper, 23 April 1959, both in LHH.

146. Telegram, Hodges to Payton, 22 April 1959, LHH.

147. Letter, Singleton to Cooper, 24 April 1959, LHH.

148. Letter, W. Y. Bryan to Hodges, 2 April 1959, LHH.

149. Letter, Finch to Hodges, 24 April 1959, LHH. Mrs. Finch was an accomplished musician, taught Sunday school for forty-two years at the First Methodist Church, and raised three children. Her husband owned Vance Coal and Lumber Company and in 1961 succeeded Carroll Singleton as mayor of Henderson. See Blackburn, *Heritage of Vance County*, 195.

150. Multipage petition, dated 25 April 1959, LHH.

151. By checking every legible name that was accompanied by a legible address, I could make seventy positive identifications.

152. Letter, C. F. King to Hodges, 24 April 1959, LHH.

153. *Freedom Fighter*, 9 August 1960 (a fairly complete collection of *Freedom Fighter* issues can be found in the Donald E. Roy Collection, Duke University Archives, Durham, N.C); Braswell (1991) interview.

154. Undated letter to Hodges, LHH.

155. Adams interview; letter, Bercaw to Hodges, 18 March 1959, LHH.

156. Letter, Snodderly to Hodges, 3 March 1959, LHH; *HDD*, 3 March 1959. Both of the mill village Pentecostal Holiness pastors, Curtis Stowe and Carlton Eades, openly supported the union, as did the Reverend Charles Robbins.

157. Letter, Guthrie to Hodges, 19 March 1959, LHH.

158. Letter, W. Y. Bryan to Hodges, 2 April 1959, LHH.

159. Letter, Oakley to Hodges, 22 April 1959, LHH.

160. Roberson interview.

161. See copy of Associated Press story, from Raleigh, dated 25 April 1959, attached to letter from Stark Dillard to Hodges, 27 April 1959, LHH. Also see *HDD*, 10 April 1959.

162. "Statement by Governor Luther H. Hodges," 8 May 1959, LHH; *N&O*, 13 May 1959. This was the first deployment of the National Guard in a North Carolina labor conflict since the wave of cotton-mill strikes in 1934.

163. Adams and Braswell (1984) interviews.

164. Report by David George, 17 May 1959, SLA.

165. The formal charges and verdicts for the sixty-two defendants on trial during the special session can be found in LHH, attached to a copy of Judge William

Bickett's 5 March 1959 order making permanent his restraining order of 13 February 1959.

166. Memo, N.C. Attorney General Malcolm Seawell to Hodges, 4 June 1959, LHH.

167. See the complete list of cases and sentences during the special session, in LHH.

168. Statement by Judge Mallard, 15 May 1959, LHH.

169. Carter and Jackson interviews.

170. *N&O*, 15 through 25 July 1959; Luther Hodges, *Businessman in the State-house*, 241–45; and Payton, *Scapegoat*, 52–90.

171. *N&O*, 25 July 1959.

172. TWUA Resolution, 25 May 1961, Box 1441, SLA.

Chapter 10

1. CR, 16 January, 1957.

2. CR, 16 March 1960.

3. Report by David George, SLA.

4. *Freedom Fighter*, 26 April 1960; Roberson, Adams, Wilkins, and Braswell (1984) interviews; memos and relief check receipts from TWUA secretary-treasurer John Chupka to Locals 578 and 584, SLA.

5. As of 1980, there were still some four thousand southern textile firms, approximately three-fourths of which were family-owned, like Harriet and Henderson. See Chip Hughes, "A New Twist for Textiles," 339.

6. F. K. Taylor, quoted in Conway, *Rise, Gonna Rise*, 4.

7. See Faue, *Women, Men, and the Labor Movement*, xiv; Faue, "Paths of Unionization," 296–97; and Frederickson, "Heroines and Girl Strikers," 84–112.

8. Arbitration #25 transcript, 11–12 February 1954, 54.

9. Kazin, "Struggling with Class Struggle," 507.

10. Tolliday and Zeitlin, "Shop Floor Bargaining, Contract Unionism, and Job Control," 219–44, quote on 222.

11. Jefferys, *Management and Managed*, 219–24, quote on xii.

12. See Reddy, *Money and Liberty in Modern Europe*, especially the section entitled "The Nonexistent Norm," 213–19, quote on 215. For an introduction to debates in British working-class historiography, see Nield, "A Symptomatic Dispute?" See also Wilentz, "Against Exceptionalism."

13. For a recent overview of this problem, see Leonard Berlanstein's "Introduction" to his edited volume, *Rethinking Labor History*, 1–14.

SELECTED BIBLIOGRAPHY

Manuscripts and Archives

Amalgamated Clothing and Textile Workers' Union Central North Carolina Joint Board Collection. Southern Labor Archives, Georgia State University, Atlanta, Georgia.

R. Gregg Cherry Papers. North Carolina Division of Archives and History, Raleigh, North Carolina.

Company Records, Harriet and Henderson Cotton Mills, Henderson, North Carolina. Private collection, currently in author's possession.

Luther H. Hodges Papers. North Carolina Division of Archives and History, Raleigh, North Carolina.

North Carolina Textile Manufacturers Association Papers. Raleigh, North Carolina.

"Report on Consent Election" for the Harriet Cotton Mill. NLRB Case File 5-R-1210, National Archives, Washington, D.C.

"Report on Consent Election" for the Henderson Cotton Mill. NLRB Case File 5-R-1290, National Archives, Washington, D.C.

Donald Roy Collection. Duke University Archives, Durham, North Carolina.

Textile Workers Union of America Southern Regional Director's Office Papers. Manuscript Department, Duke University Library, Durham, North Carolina.

Newspapers and Journals

The Freedom Fighter (published by Locals 578 and 584)
Henderson Daily Dispatch
Henderson Gold Leaf
Raleigh News & Observer
Textile Bulletin (1943–59)

Interviews by Author

Note: All tapes and transcripts are in author's possession.

Abbott, Mary. Henderson, N.C., 7 November 1987.
Adams, Edith. Henderson, N.C., 22 February 1984.
Blue, Clayborne. Henderson, N.C., 4 November 1987.
Blue, Earline Collins. Henderson, N.C., 4 November 1987.
Braswell, Joseph. Henderson, N.C., 22 February 1984, 15 February 1991.
Camp, William. Henderson, N.C., 6 May 1986.
Carter, Clifton E., Jr. Henderson, N.C., 30 January 1984.
Collins, Lucy. Henderson, N.C., 3 November 1987.
Cooper, Marshall Y., Sr. Henderson, N.C., 23 April 1986.
Crocker, Grover. Henderson, N.C., 5 November 1987.
Ellis, James. Henderson, N.C., 7 November 1987.
Ellis, Lila Mae. Henderson, N.C., 7 November 1987.

Faulkner, Roy. Henderson, N.C., 3 November 1987.
Forsythe, Eleanor. Henderson, N.C., 2 November 1987.
Fry, Julius. Greensboro, N.C., 2 April 1984.
Harris, Emma. Henderson, N.C., 5 November 1987.
Harris, Harvey. Henderson, N.C., 6 November 1987.
Harris, Ralph. Henderson, N.C., 5 November 1987.
Jackson, Luther. Macon, N.C., 19 February 1984.
Johnson, Woodrow. Henderson, N.C., 4 November 1987.
Jones, Rachel. Henderson, N.C., 2 November 1987.
Littleton, Sam. Henderson, N.C., 4 November 1987.
Newton, Johnnie E. Henderson, N.C., 3 February 1984.
Nipper, George. Henderson, N.C., 2 November 1987.
Renn, Edith. Henderson, N.C., 5 November 1987.
Renn, Melvin. Henderson, N.C., 6 November 1987.
Roberson, Esther. Henderson, N.C., 17 February 1984.
Wester, W. D. Henderson, N.C., 11 February 1991.
Wilkins, Lloyd. Henderson, N.C., 3 February 1984.

Labor Pamphlets, Government Documents, and Reports

Alexander, Gabriel. "Evaluation of Arbitrators: An Arbitrator's Point of View."
In *The Arbitrator and the Parties: Proceedings of the Eleventh Annual
Meeting of the National Academy of Arbitrators*, ed. Jean T. McKelvey.
Washington: Bureau of National Affairs, 1958.

Barrett, Gerald A. "Arbitrator's Decision" (Arbitration #32, Harriet Cotton
Mills). *Labor Arbitration Reports* 27 (1957): 523–28.

Braden, J. Noble. "Policy and Practice of American Arbitration Association." In
*Management Rights and the Arbitration Process: Proceedings of the Ninth
Annual Meeting, National Academy of Arbitrators*, ed. Jean T. McKelvey.
Washington: Bureau of National Affairs, 1956.

Henderson Chamber of Commerce. "Facts about Henderson and Vance County:
Slogan: A Cow, a Sow, and 50 Chickens on Every Farm." North Carolina
Collection, Wilson Library, University of North Carolina at Chapel Hill.

"The Henderson Story." Special collection of articles from *America's Textile
Reporter*. No publication date (ca. 1960).

Hoffmann, Alfred. "Henderson or Hell." Pamphlet published by the American
Federation of Full Fashioned Hosiery Workers, United Textile Workers,
American Federation of Labor. Philadelphia, 1927.

Kahn, Mark L., ed. *Collective Bargaining and the Arbitrator's Role: Proceedings
of the Fifteenth Annual Meeting, National Academy of Arbitrators*.
Washington: Bureau of National Affairs, 1962.

Larkin, John D. "Introduction: The First Decade." *Management Rights and the
Arbitration Process: Proceedings of the Ninth Annual Meeting, National
Academy of Arbitrators*, ed. Jean T. McKelvey. Washington: Bureau of
National Affairs, 1956.

McKelvey, Jean T., ed. *The Arbitrator and the Parties: Proceedings of the*

Eleventh Annual Meeting of the National Academy of Arbitrators. Washington: Bureau of National Affairs, 1958.

——. *Critical Issues in Labor Arbitration: Proceedings of the Tenth Annual Meeting, National Academy of Arbitrators.* Washington: Bureau of National Affairs, 1957.

——. *Management Rights and the Arbitration Process: Proceedings of the Ninth Annual Meeting, National Academy of Arbitrators.* Washington: Bureau of National Affairs, 1956.

——. *The Profession of Labor Arbitration: Selected Papers from the First Seven Annual Meetings of the National Academy of Arbitrators, 1948-1954.* Washington: Bureau of National Affairs, 1957.

Maggs, Douglas. "Decision of Arbitrator" (Arbitration #30, Harriet Cotton Mills). *Labor Arbitration Reports* 26 (1956): 390–93.

Seitz, Peter. "How Arbitrators Decide Cases: A Study in Black Magic." In *Collective Bargaining and the Arbitrator's Role: Proceedings of the Fifteenth Annual Meeting, National Academy of Arbitrators,* ed. Mark L. Kahn. Washington: Bureau of National Affairs, 1962.

U.S. Department of Labor, Bureau of Labor Statistics. *Union Agreements in the Cotton Textile Industry* (Bulletin No. 885). Washington: GPO, 1946.

U.S. Senate Committee on Interstate and Foreign Commerce. *Problems of the Domestic Textile Industry.* Washington: GPO, 1958.

U.S. Senate Committee on Labor and Public Welfare. *Causes of Unemployment in the Coal and Other Domestic Industries.* Washington: GPO, 1955.

——. *Labor-Management Relations in the Southern Textile Manufacturing Industry.* Washington: GPO, 1950.

——. *Labor-Management Relations in the Southern Textile Manufacturing Industry, Part 2.* Washington: GPO, 1951.

Books, Articles, Dissertations, and Theses

Abruzzi, Adam. *Work Measurement: New Principles and Procedures.* New York: Columbia University Press, 1952.

——. *Work, Workers, and Work Measurement.* New York: Columbia University Press, 1956.

Anderson, Eric. *Race and Politics in North Carolina, 1872-1901: The Black Second.* Baton Rouge: Louisiana State University Press, 1981.

Ashby, Warren. *Frank Porter Graham, a Southern Liberal.* Winston-Salem, N.C.: John F. Blair, 1980.

Backman, Jules, and M. R. Gainsbrugh. *Economics of the Cotton Textile Industry.* New York: National Industrial Conference Board, 1946.

Barkin, Solomon. *Textile Workers' Job Primer, Volume 1.* New York: Textile Workers Union of America, 1953.

Baron, Ava, ed. *Work Engendered: Toward a New History of American Labor.* Ithaca: Cornell University Press, 1991.

Bass, Jack, and Walter Devries. *The Transformation of Southern Politics: Social Change and Political Consequence since 1945.* New York: Basic Books, 1976.

Bell, Daniel. *The End of Ideology.* New York: Collier Books, 1961.

Bell, John L., Jr. *Hard Times: Beginnings of the Great Depression in North Carolina, 1929–1933.* Raleigh: North Carolina Department of Cultural Resources, Division of Archives and History, 1982.

Bernstein, Irving. *The Lean Years: A History of the American Worker, 1920–1933.* 1960. Reprint, Boston: Houghton Mifflin, Sentry, 1972.

―――. *Turbulent Years: A History of the American Worker, 1933–1941.* Boston: Houghton Mifflin, 1970.

Blackburn, George T. II, General Chairman, Vance County Historical Society. *The Heritage of Vance County, North Carolina, Volume 1.* Winston-Salem, N.C.: Hunter Publishing Company, 1984.

Blicksilver, Jack. *Cotton Manufacturing in the Southeast: An Historical Analysis.* Atlanta: Bureau of Business and Economic Research, School of Business Administration, Georgia State College of Business Administration, 1959.

Braverman, Harry. *Labor and Monopoly Capital: The Degradation of Work in the Twentieth Century.* New York: Monthly Review Press, 1974.

Brody, David. "The CIO after 50 Years: A Historical Reckoning." *Dissent* (Fall 1985): 457–72.

―――. *Workers in Industrial America: Essays on the Twentieth-Century Struggle.* New York: Oxford University Press, 1980.

―――. "Working-Class History in the Great Depression." In *Workers in Industrial America: Essays on the Twentieth-Century Struggle.* New York: Oxford University Press, 1980.

―――. "Workplace Contractualism in Comparative Perspective." In *Industrial Democracy in America: The Ambiguous Promise*, ed. Nelson Lichtenstein and Howell John Harris. New York: Woodrow Wilson Center Press and Cambridge University Press, 1993.

Butler, Lindley S., and Alan D. Watson, eds. *The North Carolina Experience: An Interpretive and Documentary History.* Chapel Hill: University of North Carolina Press, 1984.

Byerly, Victoria. *Hard Times Cotton Mill Girls: Personal Histories of Womanhood and Poverty in the South.* Ithaca, N.Y.: ILR Press, 1986.

Carlton, David. *Mill and Town in South Carolina, 1880–1920.* Baton Rouge: Louisiana State University Press, 1982.

Carson, R. G. "Rating Time Studies." *Textile Bulletin* 80 (January 1954): 57–59.

Cash, Wilbur J. *The Mind of the South.* New York: Vintage Books, 1941.

Chafe, William. *Civilities and Civil Rights: Greensboro, North Carolina, and the Black Struggle for Freedom.* New York: Oxford University Press, 1981.

Clay, James W., Douglas M. Orr Jr., and Alfred W. Stuart. *North Carolina Atlas: Portrait of a Changing Southern State.* Chapel Hill: University of North Carolina Press, 1975.

Cobb, James C. *The Selling of the South: The Southern Crusade for Industrial Development, 1936–1980.* Baton Rouge: Louisiana State University Press, 1982.

Cobble, Dorothy Sue. *Dishing It Out: Waitresses and Their Unions in the Twentieth Century*. Urbana: University of Illinois Press, 1991.

Cole, David. *The Quest for Industrial Peace*. New York: McGraw-Hill, 1963.

Conway, Mimi. *Rise, Gonna Rise: A Portrait of Southern Textile Workers*. Garden City, N.Y.: Anchor Press, 1979.

Copelof, Maxwell. *Management-Union Arbitration: A Record of Cases, Methods, and Decisions*. New York: Harper and Brothers, 1948.

Crow, Jeffrey J. "Cracking the Solid South: Populism and the Fusionist Interlude." In *The North Carolina Experience: An Interpretive and Documentary History*, ed. Lindley S. Butler and Alan D. Watson. Chapel Hill: University of North Carolina Press, 1984.

Daniel, Pete. *Breaking the Land: The Transformation of Cotton, Tobacco, and Rice Cultures since 1880*. Urbana: University of Illinois Press, 1985.

———. *Standing at the Crossroads: Southern Life since 1900*. New York: Hill and Wang, 1986.

Davis, Mike. *Prisoners of the American Dream: Politics and Economy in the History of the U.S. Working Class*. London: Verso, 1986.

Draper, Alan. *Conflict of Interests: Organized Labor and the Civil Rights Movement in the South, 1954–1968*. Ithaca, N.Y.: ILR Press, 1994.

Durden, Robert F. *The Dukes of Durham, 1865–1929*. Durham, N.C.: Duke University Press, 1975.

Escott, Paul. *Many Excellent People: Power and Privilege in North Carolina, 1850–1900*. Chapel Hill: University of North Carolina Press, 1985.

Faue, Elizabeth. "Paths of Unionization." In *Work Engendered: Toward a New History of American Labor*, ed. Ava Baron. Ithaca: Cornell University Press, 1991.

———. *Women, Men, and the Labor Movement in Minneapolis, 1915–1945*. Chapel Hill: University of North Carolina Press, 1991.

Fink, Gary M. "Efficiency and Control: Labor Espionage in Southern Textiles." In *Organized Labor in the Twentieth-Century South*, ed. Robert Zieger. Knoxville: University of Tennessee Press, 1991.

Fink, Gary M., and Merl E. Reed, eds. *Essays in Southern Labor History: Selected Papers, Southern Labor History Conference, 1976*. Westport, Conn.: Greenwood Publishing Corp., 1976.

Flamming, Douglas. *Creating the Modern South: Millhands and Managers in Dalton, Georgia, 1884–1984*. Chapel Hill: University of North Carolina Press, 1992.

Forbath, William. *Law and the Shaping of the American Labor Movement*. Cambridge: Harvard University Press, 1991.

Frankel, Linda Jean. "Women, Paternalism, and Protest in a Southern Textile Community: Henderson, North Carolina, 1900–1960." Ph.D. diss., Harvard University, 1986.

Fraser, Steve. "The 'Labor Question.'" In *The Rise and Fall of the New Deal Order, 1930–1980*, ed. Steve Fraser and Gary Gerstle. Princeton: Princeton University Press, 1989.

Fraser, Steve, and Gary Gerstle. *The Rise and Fall of the New Deal Order,*
1930–1980. Princeton: Princeton University Press, 1989.

Frederickson, Mary. "Four Decades of Change: Black Workers in Southern
Textiles, 1941–1981." *Radical America* 16 (November–December 1982): 27–44.

———. "Heroines and Girl Strikers: Gender Issues and Organized Labor in the
Twentieth-Century South." In *Organized Labor in the Twentieth-Century*
South, ed. Robert Zieger. Knoxville: University of Tennessee Press, 1991.

Freeman, Joshua B. *In Transit: The Transport Workers Union in New York*
City, 1933–1966. New York: Oxford University Press, 1989.

Friedlander, Peter. *The Emergence of a UAW Local, 1936–1939: A Study in*
Class and Culture. Pittsburgh: University of Pittsburgh Press, 1975.

Gabin, Nancy. *Feminism in the Labor Movement: Women and the United Auto*
Workers, 1935–1975. Ithaca: Cornell University Press, 1990.

Gerstle, Gary. *Working-Class Americanism: The Politics of Labor in a Textile*
City, 1914–1960. New York: Cambridge University Press, 1989.

Gersuny, Carl, and Gladis Kaufman. "Seniority and the Moral Economy of U.S.
Automobile Workers, 1934–1946." *Journal of Social History* (Spring 1985):
463–75.

Gilman, Glenn. *Human Relations in the Industrial Southeast: A Study of the*
Textile Industry. Chapel Hill: University of North Carolina Press, 1956.

Goodwyn, Lawrence. *Democratic Promise: The Populist Moment in America.*
New York: Oxford University Press, 1976.

Green, James. *The World of the Worker: Labor in Twentieth-Century America.*
New York: Hill and Wang, 1980.

Griffith, Barbara S. *The Crisis of American Labor: Operation Dixie and the*
Defeat of the CIO. Philadelphia: Temple University Press, 1988.

Gross, James A. *The Reshaping of the National Labor Relations Board:*
National Labor Policy in Transition, 1937–1947. Albany: State University of
New York Press, 1981.

Hall, Jacquelyn Dowd. "Disorderly Women: Gender and Labor Militancy in the
Appalachian South." *Journal of American History* 73 (September 1986):
354–82.

Hall, Jacquelyn Dowd, Robert Korstad, and James Leloudis. "Cotton Mill
People: Work, Community, and Protest in the Textile South, 1880–1940."
American Historical Review 91 (April 1986): 245–86.

Hall, Jacquelyn Dowd, James Leloudis, Robert Korstad, Mary Murphy, Lu Ann
Jones, and Christopher B. Daly. *Like a Family: The Making of a Southern*
Cotton Mill World. Chapel Hill: University of North Carolina Press, 1987.

Halpern, Rick. "Interracial Unionism in the Southwest: Fort Worth's
Packinghouse Workers, 1937–1954." In *Organized Labor in the Twentieth-*
Century South, ed. Robert Zieger. Knoxville: University of Tennessee Press,
1991.

"Harriet-Henderson Cotton Mills—And Modernization." *Whitin Review* 21
(September–October 1954): 23–35.

Harris, Howell. *The Right to Manage: Industrial Relations Policies of*

American Business in the 1940s. Madison: University of Wisconsin Press, 1982.

Haynie, Duke. "The Henderson Strike." M.A. thesis, University of North Carolina, 1962.

Hearden, Patrick. *Independence and Empire: The New South's Cotton Mill Campaign, 1865–1901*. DeKalb: Northern Illinois University Press, 1982.

Henderson City Directory, 1959-60. Asheville, N.C.: Southern Directory Co., 1960.

Hodges, James A. *New Deal Labor Policy and the Southern Cotton Textile Industry, 1933–1941*. Knoxville: University of Tennessee Press, 1986.

Hodges, Luther H. *Businessman in the Statehouse: Six Years as Governor of North Carolina*. Chapel Hill: University of North Carolina Press, 1962.

———. *The Business Conscience*. Englewood Cliffs, N.J.: Prentice-Hall, 1963.

Hughes, Chip. "A New Twist for Textiles." In *Working Lives: The "Southern Exposure" History of Labor in the South*, ed. Marc Miller. New York: Pantheon Books, 1980.

Hughes, Ruth Anita Hawkins. *Contributions of Vance County People of Color*. Raleigh, N.C.: Sparks Press, 1988.

Irons, Janet. "Testing the New Deal: The General Textile Strike of 1934." Ph.D. diss., Duke University, 1988.

Janiewski, Dolores E. "From Field to Factory: Race, Class, Sex, and the Woman Worker in Durham, 1880–1940." Ph.D. diss., Duke University, 1979.

———. *Sisterhood Denied: Race, Gender, and Class in a New South Community*. Philadelphia: Temple University Press, 1985.

Jefferys, Steve. *Management and Managed: Fifty Years of Crisis at Chrysler*. New York: Cambridge University Press, 1986.

Kazin, Michael. *Barons of Labor: The San Francisco Building Trades and Union Power in the Progressive Era*. Urbana: University of Illinois Press, 1987.

———. "Struggling with Class Struggle: Marxism and the Search for a Synthesis of U.S. Labor History." *Labor History* 28 (1987): 497–514.

Key, V. O., Jr. *Southern Politics in State and Nation*. New York: Knopf, 1949.

Klare, Karl. "Judicial Deradicalization of the Wagner Act and the Origins of Modern Legal Consciousness, 1937–1941." *Minnesota Law Review* 62 (1977–78): 265–339.

Korstad, Robert, and Nelson Lichtenstein. "Opportunities Found and Lost: Labor, Radicals, and the Early Civil Rights Movement." *Journal of American History* 75 (December 1988): 786–811.

Kousser, J. Morgan. *The Shaping of Southern Politics, Suffrage Restriction and the Establishment of the One-Party South: 1880–1910*. New Haven: Yale University Press, 1974.

Leiter, Jeffrey, Michael D. Schulman, and Rhonda Zingraff, eds. *Hanging by a Thread: Social Change in Southern Textiles*. Ithaca, N.Y.: ILR Press, 1991.

Lichtenstein, Nelson. "From Corporatism to Collective Bargaining." In *The Rise and Fall of the New Deal Order, 1930–1980*, ed. Steve Fraser and Gary Gerstle. Princeton: Princeton University Press, 1989.

————. "Great Expectations: The Promise of Industrial Jurisprudence and Its Demise, 1930–1960." In *Industrial Democracy in America: The Ambiguous Promise*, ed. Nelson Lichtenstein and Howell John Harris. New York: Woodrow Wilson Center Press and Cambridge University Press, 1993.

————. *Labor's War at Home: The CIO in World War II*. New York: Cambridge University Press, 1982.

Lichtenstein, Nelson, and Howell John Harris, eds. *Industrial Democracy in America: The Ambiguous Promise*. New York: Woodrow Wilson Center Press and Cambridge University Press, 1993.

Lichtenstein, Nelson, and Stephen Meyer. *On the Line: Essays in the History of Auto Work*. Urbana: University of Illinois Press, 1989.

McDonald, Joseph A. "Textile Workers and Unionization: A Community Study." Ph.D. diss., University of Tennessee, 1981.

McHugh, Cathy L. *Mill Family: The Labor System in the Southern Cotton Textile Industry, 1880–1915*. New York: Oxford University Press, 1988.

McKinney, John C., and Edgar T. Thompson. *The South in Continuity and Change*. Durham: Duke University Press, 1965.

McLaurin, Melton A. *Paternalism and Protest: Southern Cotton Mill Workers and Organized Labor, 1875–1905*. Westport, Conn.: Greenwood Publishing Corp., 1971.

Marshall, F. Ray. *Labor in the South*. Cambridge: Harvard University Press, 1967.

————. *The Negro and Organized Labor*. New York: John Wiley & Sons, 1965.

Miller, Marc, ed. *Working Lives: The "Southern Exposure" History of Labor in the South*. New York: Pantheon Books, 1980.

Millis, Harry A., and Emily Clark Brown. *From the Wagner Act to Taft-Hartley*. Chicago: University of Chicago Press, 1950.

Mitchell, Broadus. *The Rise of Cotton Mills in the South*. Baltimore: Johns Hopkins University Press, 1921.

Mitchell, George Sinclair. *Textile Unionism and the South*. Chapel Hill: University of North Carolina Press, 1931.

Montgomery, David. *The Fall of the House of Labor: The Workplace, the State, and American Labor Activism, 1865–1925*. New York: Cambridge University Press, 1987.

————. *Workers' Control in America: Studies in the History of Work, Technology, and Labor Struggles*. New York: Cambridge University Press, 1979.

Moody, J. Carroll, and Alice Kessler-Harris. *Perspectives on American Labor History: The Problems of Synthesis*. DeKalb: Northern Illinois University Press, 1989.

Morland, John Kenneth. *Millways of Kent*. Chapel Hill: University of North Carolina Press, 1958.

Myerson, Michael. *Nothing Could Be Finer*. New York: International Publishers, 1978.

Newby, I. A. *Plain Folk in the New South: Social Change and Cultural Persistence, 1880–1915*. Baton Rouge: Louisiana State University Press, 1989.

Nield, Keith. "A Symptomatic Dispute?: Notes on the Relation between Marxian Theory and Historical Practice in Britain." *Social Research* 47 (1980): 479–506.

Payton, Boyd E. *Scapegoat: Prejudice/Politics/Prison*. Philadelphia: Whitmore Publishing Company, 1970.

Peace, Samuel Thomas. *"Zeb's Black Baby": Vance County, North Carolina*. Durham: Seeman Printery, 1955.

Perlman, Selig. *A Theory of the Labor Movement*. New York: Macmillan, 1928.

Pleasants, Julian, and Augustus Burns. *Frank Porter Graham and the 1950 Senate Race in North Carolina*. Chapel Hill: University of North Carolina Press, 1990.

Pope, Liston. *Millhands and Preachers: A Study of Gastonia*. New Haven: Yale University Press, 1942.

Powell, William S. *North Carolina through Four Centuries*. Chapel Hill: University of North Carolina Press, 1989.

Reddy, William M. *Money and Liberty in Modern Europe: A Critique of Historical Understanding*. New York: Cambridge University Press, 1987.

Richards, Paul David. "The History of the Textile Workers Union of America, CIO, in the South, 1937 to 1945." Ph.D. diss., University of Wisconsin, 1978.

Schatz, Ronald. *The Electrical Workers: A History of Labor at General Electric and Westinghouse, 1923-60*. Urbana: University of Illinois Press, 1983.

Selby, John G. " 'Better to Starve in the Shade Than in the Factory': Labor Protest in High Point, North Carolina, in the Early 1930s." *North Carolina Historical Review* 65 (January 1987): 43–64.

————. "Industrial Growth and Worker Protest in a New South City: High Point, North Carolina, 1859–1959." Ph.D. diss., Duke University, 1984.

Smith, Robert Sidney. *Mill on the Dan: A History of Dan River Mills, 1888-1950*. Durham, N.C.: Duke University Press, 1960.

"Smoother Operation Results from Long-Range Modernization Program." *America's Textile Reporter* 71 (19 December 1957): 51.

Stein, Judith. "Southern Workers in National Unions: Birmingham Steelworkers, 1936-1951." In *Organized Labor in the Twentieth-Century South*, ed. Robert Zieger. Knoxville: University of Tennessee Press, 1991.

Tilley, Nannie May. *The Bright-Tobacco Industry, 1860-1929*. Chapel Hill: University of North Carolina Press, 1948.

Tindall, George B. *The Emergence of the New South, 1913-1945*. Baton Rouge: Louisiana State University Press, 1967.

Tippett, Tom. *When Southern Labor Stirs*. New York: Jonathan Cape and Harrison Smith, 1931.

Tolliday, Steven, and Jonathan Zeitlin. "Shop Floor Bargaining, Contract Unionism, and Job Control: An Anglo-American Comparison." In *On the Line: Essays in the History of Auto Work*, ed. Nelson Lichtenstein and Stephen Meyer. Urbana: University of Illinois Press, 1989.

Tomlins, Christopher. "AFL Unions in the 1930s: Their Performance in Historical Perspective." *Journal of American History* 4 (March 1979): 1021–42.

———. *The State and the Unions: Labor Relations, Law, and the Organized Labor Movement, 1880–1960.* New York: Cambridge University Press, 1985.

Troy, Leo. "The Growth of Union Membership in the South, 1939–1953." *Southern Economic Journal* (April 1958): 407–20.

Tullos, Allen. *Habits of Industry: White Culture and the Transformation of the Carolina Piedmont.* Chapel Hill: University of North Carolina Press, 1989.

Walker, R. Z. "A Comparison of the 1911 Cotton Yarn Mill with That of Today." *Textile Bulletin* 77 (March 1951): 150–60.

Waynick, Capus, John C. Brooks, and Elsie W. Pitts. *North Carolina and the Negro.* Raleigh: North Carolina Mayors' Co-operating Committee, 1964.

Wilentz, Sean. "Against Exceptionalism: Class Consciousness and the American Labor Movement, 1790–1920." *International Labor and Working-Class History* 26 (Fall 1984): 1–24.

Witney, Fred. *Wartime Experiences of the National Labor Relations Board, 1941–1945.* Urbana: University of Illinois Press, 1949.

Woodward, C. Vann. *Origins of the New South, 1877–1913.* A History of the South, vol. 9. Baton Rouge: Louisiana State University Press, 1951.

Wright, Gavin. *Old South, New South: Revolutions in the Southern Economy since the Civil War.* New York: Basic Books, 1986.

Young, James R. *Textile Leaders of the South.* Columbia, S.C.: R. L. Bryan Company, 1963.

Zieger, Robert. *American Workers, American Unions, 1920–1985.* Baltimore: Johns Hopkins University Press, 1986.

———. "Toward the History of the CIO: A Bibliographical Report." *Labor History* 26 (Fall 1985): 485–516.

———, ed. *Organized Labor in the Twentieth-Century South.* Knoxville: University of Tennessee Press, 1991.

INDEX

Morgan, Thomas, 187
Mt. Pleasant, N.C., 185
Multon, Helen, 138
Murphy, Elmore, 108

National Academy of Arbitrators
   (NAA), 125, 126, 142
National Defense Mediation Board, 39,
   40
National Industrial Recovery Act, 23,
   24
National Labor Relations Act, 1935,
   32
National Labor Relations Board
   (NLRB), 33, 40, 42, 43, 172, 181
National War Labor Board (NWLB),
   33–34, 35–36, 40, 45, 47, 101, 125
Nelson, Eugene, 69, 71, 77
Nelson, Linville, 76
New Bern, N.C., 186
Nipper, George, 37, 38
Norris, Roger, 38
North Carolina: political climate, 153–
   54, 161, 165–66, 175, 185–87, 196–
   98. *See also* Hodges, Luther H.
North Carolina General Assembly, 10
North Carolina State Bureau of Inves-
   tigation (SBI), 176, 198
North Carolina State Employment
   Security Commission, 156, 169
North Carolina State School of Tex-
   tiles, 15, 27, 28, 29
North Carolina Textile Manufacturers
   Association, 95–96, 98, 150

Oakley, Betty Jo, 196
Operation Dixie, 7, 203
Overseers. *See* Foremen: and labor
   relations
Owen, George, 73–74

Page, Carl, 101, 103, 113, 119, 131, 135,
   136, 139–40, 142, 143, 144
Pakistan, 92
Panic of 1893, 10, 12
Parrish, Roy, 53

Paternalism, 17–18, 22–23, 24–25, 31
Payton, Boyd, 173, 174, 175, 183–84,
   188, 189–90, 192, 193, 197–98
Peace, S. T., 193
Peck, Tommy, 84
Pendergrass, Madorline, 58
Peoples, Ed, 77
Peoples, Myrtle, 84
Perfect Packed Pickle Company,
   164–66
Perry, Bennett, 39, 47, 66, 73, 74,
   79–80, 101, 122, 181
Pollock, William, 169
Powell, Henry T., 163
Proctor, James, 29, 30, 31, 37, 50, 52,
   54, 56, 58, 60–61, 66, 67, 71, 72, 80,
   81, 82, 83, 84, 85, 115, 120, 122, 123,
   144
Pulley, David, 56–57
Pulley, Hattie, 109

Race. *See* African Americans
Raleigh News and Observer, 21–22, 92,
   172, 174, 175, 177, 189, 193, 198
Ranes, Charlie, 84, 142, 143, 169
Rankin, Ed, 187
Rankin, Grady, 186
Redding, B. D., 49
Redding, B. H., 85
Reid, Jessie, 49
Religion, 18, 191, 195–96
Renn, Mae, 66–67, 114, 116, 122
Renn, Melvin, 137
Reynolds, Robert, 154
Richmond, Va., 10
Rieve, Emil, 135, 149
Riverside Mills, 35, 40
Roanoke Rapids, N.C., 163, 198, 202–3
Roberson, B. H., 107, 111, 143
Roberson, Esther, 13, 14, 16, 30, 38,
   61–62, 116, 150, 168, 180, 196
Roberson, J. L., 182
Roberts, Aliene, 67, 71, 82
Rockfish Mills, 29
Rose, Charlie, 171
Rose, C. R., 55

time studies, 110–23; and speed ratings, 112–14; factors influencing, 114–23, 140, 142–43; and 1943–50 arbitrations, 127–28; union challenges time studies, 128–33; and 1954 strike, 133–34; conflicts in 1955–58, 134–45, 170

Work rules, 49–50, 71–72
World War I, 13, 16, 17
World War II, 29, 33, 40–41, 88, 125
Wynn, Raymond, 60, 121

Zollicoffer, A. A., 181–82, 188